HARLEY-DAVIDSON
BOLT-ON PERFORMANCE
Maximum Performance for Big Twins and Sportsters

JERRY SMITH

CarTech ®
Auto Books & Manuals

Edited By: Travis Thompson

Layout By: Bruce Leckie

ISBN 1-884089-87-9

Order No. SA88

Printed in China

CarTech®, Inc.,
39966 Grand Avenue
North Branch, MN 55056
Telephone (651) 277-1200 • (800) 551-4754 • Fax: (651) 277-1203
www.cartechbooks.com

OVERSEAS DISTRIBUTION BY:

Brooklands Books Ltd.
P.O. Box 146, Cobham, Surrey, KT11 1LG, England
Telephone 01932 865051 • Fax 01932 868803
www.brooklands-books.com

Brooklands Books Aus.
3/37-39 Green Street, Banksmeadow, NSW 2109, Australia
Telephone 2 9695 7055 • Fax 2 9695 7355

Front Cover: **Have fun!** (Dain Gingerelli)

Front Cover, Left Inset: **Under the dense thicket of plumbing you can see the headers connecting to the turbocharger. Unlike a naturally aspirated bike, a turbo bike doesn't need a specially designed exhaust system, just a pipe long enough to vent the hot exhaust gas.** (Buzz Buzzelli/*American Rider* magazine)

Front Cover, Right Inset: **The type and quality of tools used on a bike show up in the end result. Use only the best for your high-performance project. Second-rate tools belong in your kitchen drawer.** (John Hyder)

Back Cover, Upper Left: **Any time you increase the horsepower and torque of an engine, you need to beef up the primary drive — especially the clutch. Replace the old primary chain while you're at it.** (John Hyder)

Back Cover, Upper Right: **The braided stainless-steel brake line on this custom front brake not only looks better than rubber, it works better, too. It resists swelling, and the Teflon hose offers less resistance to the flow of brake fluid, so more of your effort goes toward stopping the bike.** (Jerry Smith)

Back Cover, Lower: **ProCharger's supercharger for Harley-Davidsons uses a conservative 7 psi of boost and produces a claimed 55-percent power gain on pump gas from a stock motor. It clears the rider's leg, and both EFI and carbureted versions are available.** (ProCharger)

TABLE OF CONTENTS

ACKNOWLEDGEMENTS

There are several people who need to be thanked for their help with this book. The first and foremost is Dain Gingerelli, editor of *IronWorks,* who years ago helped me get started as a freelance writer, and who most recently suggested me to CarTech to write this book. Dain supplied some of the photos in the book (you can tell which ones are his — they're the really good ones), and pretty much went out of his way to lend a hand whenever I needed it. I'm in his debt, and not for the first — or, I'm sure, the last — time.

Buzz Buzzelli, editor of *American Rider,* and Mark Tuttle Jr., editor of *Rider,* supplied photos, advice, and the occasional motorcycle industry hotshot's unlisted phone number, as well as pulling a well-placed string for me now and then.

Ron Goodger went to Laughlin and took a lot of photos for me during a time when I was too busy writing this book to leave the house for a cup of coffee, never mind spending a week riding to Arizona and back.

Larry Works shot photos, and patiently listened to me whine about the rough patches in the book's progress. For that alone he deserves sainthood, or at the very least a Twin Cam Road King to replace his Evo, Elvis.

Don Emde, editor of *Parts Magazine,* which I've written for since its first issue, gave me a furlough during the writing of this book, and provided photos and valuable industry contacts.

Steve Hendrickson, editor-in-chief of CarTech, played the role of editor, counselor, shrink, and drill sergeant as the occasion demanded. How he deals with 30 guys like me at a time without going around the bend is beyond comprehension.

And finally, a lot of people in the aftermarket took time away from much more important things to answer my questions, often very slowly and in small words so I wouldn't get confused, and to send me product art. There were too many of them to thank individually, but you'll see many of their names in the chapters that follow. My thanks to all of them.

—JERRY SMITH

ABOUT THE AUTHOR

Jerry Smith started riding motorcycles in 1968. Since then he has drag raced, held a professional road-racing license, and demonstrated an uncanny ability to repeatedly dive headfirst from speeding dirt bikes without doing himself permanent harm. He served on the staff of *Rider, Cycle Guide,* and *Motorcyclist* magazines, and currently freelances for several monthlies, including *Rider, American Rider,* and *IronWorks.* He is the author of two motorcycle mysteries, and is a member of the Iron Butt Association. A native of California, he now lives on the Oregon coast with a pair of golden retrievers who would really rather not be around motorcycles of any kind, thank you very much.

INTRODUCTION

Ever since Harley started making bikes, Harley riders have been making them perform better. There are as many ways to do it as there are riders doing it. (Dain Gingerelli)

PERFORMANCE—MORE THAN JUST HORSEPOWER

Thanks to advertising, the term "high performance" is thrown around pretty freely these days. For some reason known only to the people in the company ad department, my computer's printer is the high-performance model. Each morning I brush my teeth with — no kidding — a high-performance toothbrush. To my mind neither one of these products does much in the

Performance is, to a large extent, whatever you want it to be, whether that's straight-line acceleration, top speed, or the ability to ride all day in comfort and get where you're going without feeling beat up. (Dain Gingerelli)

As the smallest and therefore lightest Harleys, Sportsters are popular starting points for high-performance projects. They've taught many a Big Twin rider not to call them "chick bikes." (Dain Gingerelli)

kind you'll need if you're heading to the drag strip or the canyons next weekend, to the kind you'll want on that cross-country ride you have planned for your next vacation. And we're keeping this a friendly game — with very few exceptions, every part you'll see is a bolt-on that can be installed, at least in theory, by a competent home mechanic equipped with some good hand tools, a shop manual, and common sense. A very small number of the products shown require a trip to a machinist, but they're worth the trouble.

Some of the bikes in the mini-features scattered throughout the book also required some more or less elaborate machining to accommodate larger cylinders, for example, or high-lift cams. Consider them for illustrative purposes only, and to give you something the shoot for when you're ready to really dig deep into a high-performance project.

way of performing — sometimes the printer doesn't perform at all. But that could just be because of my background, which includes fooling with motorcycles, some of them genuinely high-performance. Once you've seen the needle on a speedometer sweep past 160, it's hard to put brushing your teeth in the same category.

But even within the sport of motorcycling, the word performance means different things to different people. If you ride a Harley-Davidson Big Twin cruiser like a Softail or a Dyna, probably the first thing it brings to mind is horsepower. But if you ride a dresser — a Road King, or an Electra Glide — performance might mean a smoother ride, tires that last longer, or more torque at low RPM for passing.

And there's more overlap between the groups than a lot of people realize. Lots of Sportster riders who take advantage of their bikes' lower weight and sportier handling by scraping the end off the footpegs in the canyons want tires that not only stick well but last a long time. Lots of bagger riders want better handling. And not all Big Twin riders are speed-addled horsepower junkies, riding their big-inch

diggers from stoplight to stoplight. Plenty of them ride their bikes for fun, not for bragging rights, and yet still get off on the arm-stretching surge of a hopped-up Big Twin when the throttle is whacked open.

In this book we're going to look at many facets of performance, from the

STREETBIKE VS. RACEBIKE

Before we get going, though, let's talk about the kind of bike you think you want, as opposed to what you really want.

When shopping for performance, there's a natural tendency to buy as

If all roads were straight you could get away with a bike that only ran good in a straight line. In the real world handling in corners is important, too. (Dain Gingerelli)

The key to fast riding is balancing speed with restraint. That's the key to building a satisfying high-performance bike, too, one that will be fun to ride every day, not just once in a while. (Dain Gingerelli)

much of it as you can afford. It's the American way — if enough is good, then too much is even better. But when it comes to modifying motorcycles, especially Harleys, it's all too easy to ride right up to the point of diminishing returns and zoom on past it without stopping. Buy too much performance, and you can end up with a bike that's hard to start, idles poorly, and doesn't have enough power to pull the slack out of a dirty shirt until it's spinning near redline. Buy just enough performance, though, and your bike will start easily, idle more or less smoothly, and produce good power over a broad RPM spread. The choice is yours, but be sure you're aware of the consequences before you commit.

This isn't to say we're only going to be looking at mild-mannered modifications. In the following pages you're going to see some things — blowers and turbos and nitrous, oh my! — that might make you wish you could buy another Harley just to try them out. If you're a dedicated drag racer who doesn't care about anything but bringing home the brass at the end of the day, or a Bonneville salt rat who lives to get your own page in the record book, you can, and probably will, disregard everything I just said about not going over-

board. But if your idea of a big weekend is riding around with your buddies, all I ask is that you keep a glass of cold water handy to throw on yourself in case you get carried away and start imagining that a blown, nitrous-injected 130-incher with straight pipes is going to be a lot of fun on the next poker run.

DYNAMOMETERS—TRUTH OR DARE

No matter what route you take to your desired level of performance, remember that while talk is cheap, high-performance parts aren't. Some aftermarket companies promise you the moon to get you to buy their products, and when you call them up and ask for proof of their claims, the line goes dead. Even if the product has a good reputation, it might not always affect your bike's performance the way you think it does. This is where dynamometers come in.

The dynamometer is to high-performance tuning what the lie detector is to law enforcement, except the dynamometer actually works. Before you buy any high-performance engine parts for your bike, run it on a dyno so you'll know what kind of horsepower

and torque it makes in stock trim. Dynos have become such common tuning tools that you won't have to go too far to find a shop that has one. Most will charge you a flat hourly rate to use it, and they'll supply the operator. After you bolt on your high-performance goodies, go back to the dyno — the same one, since the results you'll get from the same bike will often vary slightly from dyno to dyno — and run your bike again. Even if you don't like what you learn, you'll be in a better position to know what went wrong, and how to make it right.

A word of caution, though. Even some of those aftermarket companies who are happy to let you see dyno charts demonstrating how well their product work don't tell you everything, or if they do, they whisper it. If you look down at the bottom of the chart, with a magnifying glass, you'll see written there in microscopic type that in order to get its Bumpstik 500 cam to put out big horsepower, Billy Bob's Cam Company had to change a few other things besides the cam — like the carb, the manifold, the air cleaner, the ignition module, and the entire exhaust system.

One of the great things about Harleys is that you don't have to sacrifice style for performance. The aftermarket is full of products that look as good as they perform. (Dain Gingerelli)

The kind of riding you do will determine the kind of performance you look for. Dyno-busting horsepower won't help you pass a long semi as much as instant torque when you twist the throttle. (Dain Gingerelli)

Now in all fairness, Billy Bob himself will likely point out, and quite correctly, that few riders who modify their engines stop at just a single component like a camshaft, and that most add a carb, some pipes, and maybe an ignition module anyway. But the results from such an exercise are not a meaningful indicator of the worth of the cam alone, only of the combination of parts used to get the results.

LEGALITIES

I hate fine-print legalese as much as the next guy — assuming the next guy isn't a lawyer — so I'm going to say this as briefly and simply as possible. Some of the parts in this book are not legal for highway use anywhere, at any time, for any reason. Installing them may violate any number of sections of your state vehicle code, and may even annoy the Feds. More important to most riders is the fact that fitting aftermarket parts to a Harley has the immediate effect of making the factory warranty disappear in a puff of smoke.

Should you worry about either of these possibilities? That's up to you. Sure, Harleys are very reliable these days, in marked contrast to bygone times when something as simple as a change in humidity could stop them in their tracks. And sure, there are thousands of riders running around with loud pipes and illegal taillights and no turn signals, their engines belching foul gases into the atmosphere at an appalling rate, and no one bothers them.

Just don't say you weren't warned.

OBLIGATORY DISCLAIMER

I'm assuming, perhaps at my own peril, that you, the reader, are a reasonably intelligent human being with the ability to distinguish fact from advertising hype. In this book you'll find some of each.

I turned to manufacturers of aftermarket parts for a lot of the information in the following pages, and took their word for most of it. The companies whose representatives I interviewed have, by and large, been in business long enough to demonstrate that they're probably doing something right. Their inclusion in this book by no means constitutes an endorsement of these companies or their products by me, my publisher, or anyone else connected with this book. Nor should the exclusion of any company or its products be construed as anything but the inevitable consequence of trying to squeeze a project of this magnitude into a finite amount of time with a solid deadline at the far end. The Harley-Davidson aftermarket is huge and growing every day, and contacting every company that makes parts in a given category would have been impossible. If my publisher had allowed me the page count to interview a second, or third, or fourth company about every topic, the book you're reading would weigh about twelve pounds and cost a couple hundred bucks. And if I had the time and money to try out every single part myself, on a variety of different Harleys, I wouldn't have to write books for a living.

Finally — and I leave this for last because I want it to stick in your mind as you read on — I have made no attempt to tell you what specific parts to put on your bike to make it run better. I can't tell you that, and neither can any aftermarket company without knowing a lot more about you, your bike, and how you ride. And that's assuming you can get any two aftermarket companies to agree with each other. Instead, I've given you the raw material to make intelligent choices when you start your high-performance project. Some of that information is spelled out, and some of it lies between the lines of interviews with aftermarket people — but it's there. Call me old-fashioned, but I believe you learn as much, if not more, by thinking for yourself as you do from letting others do your thinking for you.

The temptation to tell your buddies about your latest high-performance acquisition will be irresistible. You might not want to tell Harley-Davidson, however, if your warranty means anything to you. (Dain Gingerelli)

CHAPTER 1

INDUCTION

Open velocity stacks look great, and work great if tuned properly, but they're impractical on the street for several reasons, not least of which is all the stuff that can get sucked into them, like your knee. (Ron Goodger)

AIR CLEANERS

Despite years of actual research with flow benches and dynos, many die-hard backyard tuners still think that air cleaners lie smack in the middle of the path to more horsepower like a piece of particularly revolting roadkill, and that the only solution is to do away with them altogether. They point to race bikes with long velocity stacks leading into open carb throats, forgetting that race bikes aren't ridden on the street, and are rebuilt more often than most riders check their tire pressure.

The primary function of an air cleaner is filtration. Keeping dirt and grit and small animals out of the engine not only adds to its life span, but also keeps it running better for longer. High-performance engines ridden on the street can also benefit from a well-designed air cleaner, which can boost power in situations where an open velocity stack can take it away. It's a sad fact, however, that some air cleaners are designed, built, and manufactured primarily as cosmetic items whose styling counts for more than their performance. If you're looking for true performance and not just good looks, you need to pay close attention to what's inside an air cleaner.

Doherty Machine

Air filters on high-performance streetbikes are a necessary evil, says Tim Doherty, owner of Doherty Machine. But they don't have to hold an engine back from producing good power, and if they're made right, they can even contribute to the cause. "The key thing is what happens to the air after it passes through the filter," says Doherty. "Our air cleaners don't work because of the filter, they work because of the venturi. The reason we sell the whole unit is people need filtered air."

The venturi Doherty is talking about is really a radiused entry that blends the backing plate to the carb or throttle body, and is an integral part of his PACC line of air cleaners. In essence, it's a short, built-in velocity stack that smoothes the airflow going into the carb throat. The venturi increases the length of the intake tract

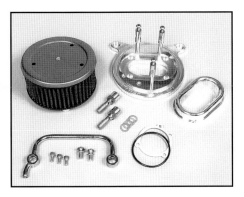

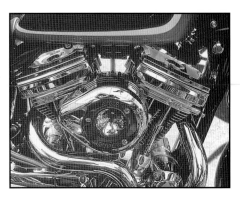

The Power PACC EFI air cleaner kit from Doherty Machine uses a one-piece billet backing plate and a snap-in venturi that leaves airflow unobstructed. A washable, high-volume air filter element is included. Two kits fit all fuel-injected touring models from 1995 to 2001. (Doherty Machine)

Carburetion can bring an engine to life, or stop it dead in its tracks. Few other engine systems offer you so many chances to screw up in so many different ways. (Ron Goodger)

Style's fine, but not if it compromises performance. Some radically styled air cleaners work no better than the stock Harley air cleaner, and some work even worse. In the battle between form and function, function kicks ass. (Ron Goodger)

Doherty Machine's PACC Air Cleaner kit for Sportsters use the same billet backing plate and reusable high-volume air filter as the EFI kit. It fits all popular carbs including Keihin CV, S&S (Super E or G), and Mikuni. (Doherty Machine)

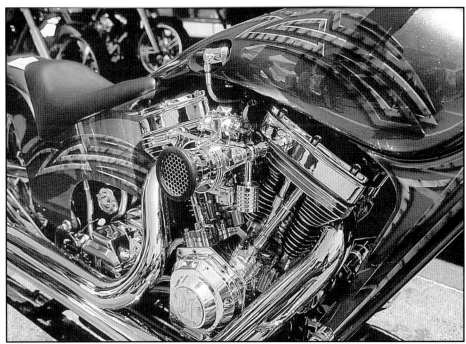

This is better than no air filter at all, although the holes are still too big to stop things that will kill an engine. At high engine speeds the mesh may impede airflow as much as a filter that actually filters, too. (Ron Goodger)

slightly and also increases the air's speed as it enters the carb or throttle body. "We took the elements of a high-performance air entry system, which would be a velocity stack, and incorporated an air filter with it that's practical to install," Doherty says. "It provides a 100 percent unobstructed airflow to the carb or throttle body, with virtually no restrictions. The shape of it is critical so

the air doesn't have any sharp corners to move around." There are six bolt holes in the backing plate, some combination of which will fit just about any model of Harley. The holes are covered by the velocity stack, so they're not exposed, and they won't affect airflow.

The trend toward big motors has prompted many riders to opt for huge air cleaners to go with the displacement.

But Doherty cautions that when it comes to air cleaners, bigger is not always better. "Our air cleaners are designed to provide optimum performance in a street application up to 125 cubic inches," he says of the relatively compact PACC unit. "It'll handle 125 cubic inches at 6500 rpm, and anything below that."

A critical part of any air cleaner is

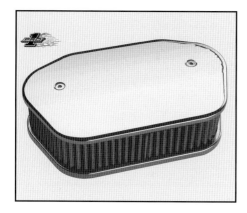

Pro-One's Stage 1 air cleaner features base and face plates CNC-machined from solid billet aluminum, in smooth or ball-milled styles. Available for 1993-and-later Evo motors, and S&S and Mikuni carbs, each unit comes complete with a washable and reusable air filter and all hardware for bolt-on installation. (Pro-One)

A good air cleaner is essential not only to performance, but to engine life, too. There's no point in pouring buckets of money into an engine only to run it unprotected from the elements. (Ron Goodger)

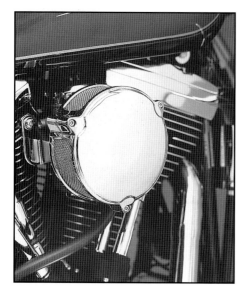

The Dragtron II air cleaner from Drag Specialties uses a dynamometer-designed radius-entry backing plate for maximum airflow. The 2-inch washable filter is encased in a heavy stainless-steel mesh. It's available for Big Twin CV carbs from 1990-2003 and Sportsters from 1988-2003. (Drag Specialties)

the filter element, not only for its filtration properties but also for its effect on airflow, and thus on performance. "The filter, in terms of size, needs to be able to move enough air through it," Doherty says. "Our filters are 2 3/4 inches tall. If we went to a 1-inch filter, it would kill everything, because the filter wouldn't have the ability to get the air through it, just like a stock element doesn't."

Stock Harley air filter elements are designed to meet EPA noise and emissions standards, but are hard pressed to live up to the requirements of a high-performance engine. Lots of riders replace the stock element with an after-market unit like a K&N, but Doherty says keeping the stock air cleaner offsets whatever gain in airflow you'd get with a freer-flowing element. "Why does our kit make so much more power than a stock Harley-Davidson backing plate with a K&N element? And it does, it's been tested by magazine after magazine. It does because of the ability of the venturi to control the air into the carb once it gets past the filter."

Things to beware of in any air cleaner assembly include a cover that's too close to the filter, which restricts the airflow. Any cover closer to the filter than about 1/4 inch probably isn't going to complement a high-performance engine. The design of the air filter element itself is important, too — the more surface area the better. The type of filter element doesn't seem to matter as much, according to Doherty. "We supply a high-quality, washable and reusable cotton-gauze filter element with our kit. A high-quality paper element rated at the same CFM would do essentially the same thing. I haven't tested foam filters against the style we're using, but I don't think the difference would be that much."

S&S

"There's more science than you think in an air cleaner," says Bruce Tessmer of S&S. "For example, if you look at our Super B air cleaner backing plate you'll notice there's a raised portion in the center around the bore. It has a radiused inlet that's kind of like a small air horn. On the cover itself there's a point that sticks in there that further directs the air into the carb without letting it tumble. If you look at the Super E, the backing plate is more complicated, but it still uses that radiused inlet. We sell a ton of these because they actually boost performance, way better than the stock air cleaner."

Tessmer explains why the radiused entry improves airflow to the carburetor: "Let's say you're sucking air into a pipe with a straight end. Air is going to

A classic in its field, the S&S teardrop air cleaner uses a back plate with an air-horn-style radiused entry. The cover has a directional cone inside, too. Together they give the air an easy, unobstructed path to the carb. They're available for just about every Harley made since 1966. (S&S)

approach it from all directions, and you're going to have turbulence, so you won't get as much air into it. Turbulence in your combustion chamber is a very good thing, but in your carb and manifold it sucks. If you put an air horn on it, air will follow the curve of the horn, and there'll be a lot less turbulence."

In racing, where winning is all that matters, you don't often see air cleaners on bikes. But Tessmer says a good air filter is a must, even for high-performance street engines, which is why S&S has spent so much time researching and developing better filter elements. "We came out with one last year that uses the same media that NHRA drag cars use. It's resin-impregnated and baked, and it looks like a brown paper bag. But it flows really well and it's tough. You can actually clean it off and reuse it. It does a better job of filtering than oiled foam."

Part of an air filter's job is to remove turbulence from incoming air before it gets to the carb mouth. Tessmer says long velocity stacks do the same thing, but not necessarily while the bike is in motion. "You can put a velocity stack on a bike on a dyno and it'll really kick ass. But you get it out there in the air with all kinds of turbulence, and the engine's coughing and wheezing and sputtering, and then all of a sudden it cleans up and goes. Maybe it's pushing air in, maybe it's sucking air out, it's tough to say." Either way, it's not what you're looking for in a high-performance engine. "If you look at Japanese motorcycles and almost all cars, they have airboxes. That's because you want still air available for intake so there are no side drafts or turbulence. The less turbulence you have the better off you are," continues Tessmer.

AIR FILTERS

There are times when it's easy to forget the idea is to ride Harleys, not just look at them. This battle between form and function often leads Harley riders to concentrate on secondary matters and ignore the really important stuff. For example, many more of them obsess about the style and manufacturer of their air cleaners than over the filter element inside. And that's a shame, because no matter how shiny a bike is, it won't go very far on a steady diet of dirty air. It's the air filter's job to keep that dirt out, and it only takes a few minutes every few thousand miles to help it do the best job it can.

Stock late-model Harley air filters use paper in a wire mesh as the filtering medium. But paper has some drawbacks that compromise its effectiveness compared to other filtering media we'll talk about later. In order to let engine air through, the paper element has holes in it. Not all the holes are the same size — some are bigger than others, and can pass dirt particles that a smaller hole would stop. And because each hole only gets one chance to be a hero, paper elements need a lot of them — that's why the material is pleated. The more pleats, the more surface area, and the more holes.

Another of paper's drawbacks is that it doesn't like moisture. On rainy rides, or in foggy or humid conditions, moisture in the air can cause the paper to swell up, decreasing airflow to the

A well-made and properly designed air filter can be tidy and unobtrusive like this one and still boost an engine's performance. It might be all most practical street-ridden bikes need. A much bigger filter might flow more air than the motor needs or can handle. (Ron Goodger)

The K&N air filter (left) has more pleats than the stock filter, and is washable and reusable. Its flow characteristics are designed to be a little better than the stocker's. (Jerry Smith)

engine. If the filter is already dirty, engine vacuum can suck the dirt farther into the paper filtering medium, and when it dries out again, the filter will be clogged.

Unlike the paper filters on many other brands of bikes, you can clean Harley filters by soaking them in lukewarm water with a mild detergent. Wash it as gently as you can, and don't whack

Not everything that can get into your engine and mess it up is as easy to see as the salt at Bonneville. Very tiny particles can do plenty of damage over time if your filter doesn't keep them out. (Dain Gingerelli)

Exposed air filters might look cool, but they'll get dirty fast. For an all-out performance bike, or a custom, it doesn't make much difference — you probably won't ride the bike all that often — but on a streetbike, some kind of cover will increase the filter's life. (Ron Goodger)

This filter is way too small to let this Sportster engine breathe right. A larger filter element in a well-designed housing with a radiused entry at the carb mouth would wake this bike up. (Jerry Smith)

the filter on a hard surface to try to dislodge the dirt. Let the filter air-dry, or blow low-pressure compressed air through it from the inside. Check the filter's cleanliness by holding it up to a strong light. If the light shines uniform-

ly throughout the filtering element, you've done the job right. Put the dry filter back on the bike — don't put air filter oil on it — and pat yourself on the back for saving the cost of a new filter.

Sooner or later, though, the stock

air filter will wear out, and when it's time to replace it, most riders opt for an aftermarket air filter element. These filters are usually made either of foam or cotton gauze, and both use oil as an additional filtering medium.

Foam filters have very large holes compared to paper filters, and each one is three-dimensional, more like a winding tunnel in a cave than a hole in a wall. Any particle of dirt hitching a ride on incoming air will eventually come to a turn in the passage, where it will go straight instead of turning and stick to an oil-covered surface. The dirt then becomes oil-soaked, and snares the next particle. This process continues until the passage is completely clogged, and that typically takes a lot longer than it does with a paper filter, which loses an entire filtering hole with every particle of dirt it catches. At this point you clean the foam filter, re-oil it, and put it back in.

Cotton gauze filters work partly like a paper filter, and partly like an oiled foam filter. Like a paper filter, the holes aren't of uniform size, and the route through them is pretty much a straight shot, so they use several layers of overlapping filtering material. This random weave is only a little bit harder for dirt to get through than paper, though, so oil is used to perform the same function it does in oiled foam filters. Like foam filters, cotton gauze filters are washable and reusable.

Name-brand aftermarket oiled foam and cotton gauze filters meet or exceed all motorcycle manufacturers' specifications for filtration. Both types of oiled filters are largely unaffected by moisture, and any oil mist blown into the airbox by the crankcase breather hose only adds to their filtering efficiency. But while these filters all flow as much air as the stock filter, some flow more, and others a lot more. The difference in airflow can upset your bike's jetting, usually on the lean side. If that's the case, you should increase the amount of fuel your engine gulps with each intake stroke to match the increased airflow. That's why many shops recommend installing a carb kit with an aftermarket air filter, or will suggest you drill out the low-speed air-screw plug and richen the mixture slightly.

When it comes to replacement air filters designed to fit in the stock Harley air cleaner can, you're pretty sure to get a filter that flows close to stock, or just a little bit better. K&N, makers of the most often-used aftermarket air filters in the Harley scene or any other, goes to great lengths to make sure their filters won't affect jetting much, if at all. For each application, they get a stock air cleaner assembly, complete with a stock filter, and hook it up to a device that measures airflow. Once they have a baseline flow rate for the stock setup, they design their replacement filter to closely match it.

But all bets are off if you install one of K&N's clamp-on air filters directly to a carburetor. There's no stock baseline for this combination — K&N has no way of knowing what kind of carb you're running, or what state of tune your engine is in — so don't be surprised if you have to adjust the jetting to make the engine run right. And don't be surprised if that exposed filter gets real dirty real quick.

Harley recommends inspecting the stock air filter at regular intervals, but if your engine is suddenly hard to start, runs poorly, or starts getting bad gas mileage, it might be because your air filter is dirty. The less air the filter passes,

Storz Performance Dyna Lite

Anyone who's been around racing long enough knows there are lots of ways to get more performance out of a bike, but they can all be boiled down to two main methods — increasing horsepower, or decreasing weight. Steve Storz, owner of Storz Performance in Ventura, California, used both tactics to punch up this Dyna Glide Sport.

The 88-ci Twin Cam motor was left stock except for a 42-mm Mikuni flatslide carb and a set of Bub Bad Dog pipes. The combination resulted in a motor that barks but doesn't bite back. Next Storz turned his attention to reducing the weight of some of the heavier components on the Dyna, replacing them with parts that were not only lighter but worked better than stock, too.

A set of Works Performance billet shocks replaced the stock units, and up front he slid on a set of 55-mm Ceriani inverted forks. Next the stock wheels and brakes went up on the shelf, and in their place went a pair of no-longer-produced magnesium wheels shod with Avon AM-series tires. The stock front brake was replaced by a Performance Machine six-piston caliper and 13-inch rotor, with a four-piston PM caliper and 10-inch rotor in the rear. The weight savings gained by changing out the suspension and wheels came to 22 pounds.

The 13-pound Bub Bad Dogs helped Storz chop another nine pounds off the bike, and an aluminum swingarm, sold only in Europe, and assorted carbonfiber body parts, also one-offs, reduced weight even more. Goodridge brake lines, Barnett throttle cables, a Ness throttle, and Performance Machine controls all added either a touch of class, a boost in performance, or both.

When the final weigh-in was done, Storz had taken a whopping 70 pounds off his Dyna Glide Sport. Because it's lighter than a stocker, it's faster, and even though he could have achieved the same acceleration by pumping the motor past its mild state of tune, reliability and rideabilty might have suffered. But extra horsepower wouldn't have made the lighter bike handle as well as it does. There are some things you can't do with more horsepower that you can with less weight.

K&N air filters use an oiled cotton-gauze filtering medium that's washable and reusable. There's a part number for just about every application from stock to custom. K&N tests stock replacement filters so they can closely match their filters to the stock flow. (K&N)

Taking 70 pounds off just about any Harley makes it accelerate faster and handle better. Add the usual gofast stuff and you have a real flyer. (Dain Gingerelli)

Special problems — like how to add more or bigger carburetors — call for special solutions. There are easier and more practical ways to solve this particular problem than the route this builder took. He gets big points for creativity, though. At least it's narrow. (Ron Goodger)

About as far from "bolt-on" as you can get, this Feuling three-cylinder motor (can't really call it a Harley, can we?) nonetheless neatly solves the problem of how to get more carburetion. Just add another cylinder. The plumbing is complex and beautiful. Not coming soon to a Harley dealer near you. Ever. (Ron Goodger)

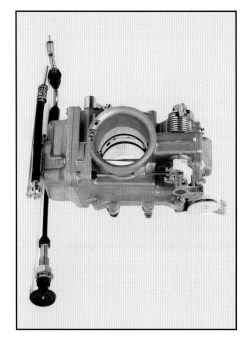

Mikuni's HSR48 smoothbore carb has an eight-roller-bearing flat slide that allows an unrestricted venturi at full throttle. The roller bearings provide smoother throttle control and allow the use of a lighter return spring. It comes with a rubber mounting flange, a choke cable, a remote idle adjuster, and extra jetting. (Mikuni)

the more gas your bike uses, and in extreme cases, the mixture can get rich enough to foul spark plugs. It only takes a minute to remove the air filter housing cover and inspect the element, and it's something you should do more often than Harley recommends if you often ride in the rain or in dusty conditions.

CARBURETORS

Harley-Davidsons, as delivered, start easily, run more or less smoothly, and get good gas mileage, thanks in large part to their constant-velocity carburetors. The 40-mm CV carb that comes on today's Harleys first appeared on the Sportster in 1989, followed by the Big Twins in 1990. It's a simple, rugged design that does everything it's asked to. But when you begin to ask more of it than its designers envisioned, the CV40 starts to show its limitations. That's why so many riders looking for more performance shelve their stock constant-velocity carburetors and go looking for a more versatile, performance-oriented carb.

Mikuni

Lee Chapin of Mikuni says the CV40 is "actually a pretty good design for what it's intended, which is motorcycles that are for the most part left as they're delivered from Harley-Davidson. It's very predictable because it's based on engine demand. When you open the throttle, that opens the butterfly valve in the carb body, allowing more air to pass underneath the slide and into the carb. That creates a negative pressure in a chamber above the slide, and that lifts the slide up."

Predictability is good in a carb, but high-performance carbs need adjustability, and here's where the CV40 starts to lag behind. Chapin explains, "You'll notice that stock carbs don't have provisions for removing the main jet easily, or for changing the low-speed fuel mixture screw, or the needle's position. These are all things that are required when you change things that affect the signal going into the engine, a more open air cleaner, or less restriction in the exhaust. These things all play havoc on the signal going to the carburetor."

Chapin explains how Mikuni HSR-series carburetors differ from the CV40 that comes on Harleys: "Rather than using a butterfly shaft we use a slide valve that moves up and down in the bore of the carb, sometimes called a guillotine-type or a flat slide. It's designed to let you control the throttle valve movement and the response of the engine. It differs from the round slide that many riders ran on their Harleys back in the 1970s and 1980s in that there's less turbulence and it gives better response time from the time the slide is in the closed position to when you open it. The distance between the leading edge of the slide and where the fuel is picked up — where the needle and needle jet are — is reduced considerably so the response time is improved."

Flat-slide, smoothbore carburetors have been used in all types of racing — dirt track, road racing, and motocross — for years because of their superior throttle control and response. "And this all relates to what happens at the rear tire," Chapin says. "This is how we ride motorcycles, by relating to what's going on at the rear tire through the engine, which is controlled by the carburetor."

While it sometimes seems as though the stock carb is specifically designed to make adjustments harder, Chapin says, Mikuni HSR carbs are designed for more, not less, accessibility. "For example, the main jets are easily accessed through the drain plug," he says. "The low speed is controlled primarily with the size of the pilot jet and the air-screw adjustment, which is an air adjustment screw rather than a fuel adjustment screw which gives you a broader range of effect. Midrange is controlled by the diameter of the needle and the clip position, and the main jet is the wide-open-throttle component. The needle has five clip positions and can be changed, and you can change the diameter of the needle, too. If you get an engine without a strong signal because of too big a carb, you can compensate for that by making the needle thinner, and you end up a little richer through the midrange. By moving the needle up and down you can effectively change fuel economy out on the highway, or the way the bike accelerates through the midrange."

Mikuni HSR flat-slide carbs have a cable-controlled enrichener circuit for cold starting, and an accelerator pump. When you whack the throttle open suddenly, air rushes into the carb before gasoline can be picked up from the float bowl, because air is lighter than gas. The resulting lean mixture can make your

Twin-carb set-ups like this one can increase power, but can also increase your tuning problems. You have to synchronize them, and they take up more space. Plenty of genuine 100-horsepower engines get by with a single, properly tuned carb. (Ron Goodger)

bike stumble right when you want it to accelerate. The accelerator pump compensates for this by giving the carb a squirt of gas every time you twist the throttle. The accelerator pump on a Mikuni is as tunable as the rest of the carb's metering circuits. "We can control the starting point, we can control the stroke, and we can control the size of the injector nozzle," Chapin says, "so the accelerator pump system can be tuned for engines with more or less demand. Dirt track racers who use this carb don't use the accelerator pump. They have plenty of signal, lots of RPM in the engine when they're racing. But a big heavy streetbike that's off the cam, not near peak torque, is going to want an accelerator pump."

A flat-slide carb has one more advantage over a constant-velocity in that the CV's butterfly reduces its effective throat diameter due to the restriction it places on the flow of air. "When you look at that horizontal butterfly shaft, a 40-mm CV carb has an effective flow area of about 37 mm. The butterfly is 40 mm, but if you take out the cross-section, you actually have less airflow."

How much of an improvement in

Carburetion used to be something between a science and an art. Now you can buy bolt-on, ready-to-run carbs on skin-pack cards, just like CD players and butane lighters. Progress is wonderful. (Mark Tuttle Jr.)

Since Harleys have two separate heads, why not use two separate carbs? There's plenty of room on the left for another one. It requires special heads, though, and a lot of other modifications to make it all work right. (Buzz Buzzelli/*American Rider* magazine)

performance can you expect from a carburetor? "We've often heard from riders that a carb is the best change or improvement they've made to their motorcycles," Chapin says. "It's a very easy, relatively inexpensive installation that allows the rider to realize the potential he's built into his engine The 42-mm Mikuni will work on a very stock engine making 60 or 70 horsepower, and we have a 48-mm version that's taking some motors up into the mid 160s. You can see from 60 to 160 horsepower using a simple bolt-on carburetor. When we take a stock model Harley, for example, and change out the carb and air filter and put on a set of pipes, it makes 8 more horsepower on an Evo and about 14 more on a Twin Cam."

Before you lay your money down for a high-performance aftermarket carb, Chapin says you need to decide exactly what you want out of your engine, and how much you're willing to spend to get it. "You have to be honest with yourself about how you're going to ride the motorcycle. If you're intending to ride it as delivered from Harley-Davidson, you can do that, but you're not going to have as much fun as you would if you added 10, 20, or even 30 horsepower to the engine, because no one likes to be the guy pulling up the tail end of a line of bikes. So everyone wants to mess with their engines. One of the things they do is change the air filter and exhaust. They can keep the stock carb and spend about $150 to recalibrate it, and maybe see some benefit or maybe not. The next step is to go with a true high-performance carburetor, which for around $400 can allow their engine to reach its full potential."

A lot of riders think bigger is better when it comes to carbs, but Chapin says that's not necessarily the case. "We're running a 48-mm carb on a stock Twin Cam," he says, "which you'd think would be far too much carburetor. But it's not, because it only becomes a 48-mm carb at wide-open throttle. Is it more carb than you need for a stock engine? Sure. A 42-mm carb would be a better choice. But it shows you how flexible and adaptable a carb the flatslide is. It's very forgiving."

There are situations, however, in which it's smarter to buy more carb than you need right now in case you need it later. "We have customers that'll call us and say they have an air filter and an exhaust system, and they need a carb. But they plan to do the Branch heads, an Andrews cam, and a 95-inch or a JIMS stroker motor eventually. In that case we'll recommend they go ahead and put a 45-mm Mikuni on it right off the bat. They're not going to give up anything — maybe it'll soften up the midrange torque a little bit — but it'll allow them to build up the engine and have the carb go with it," says Chapin.

If you're just bolting an air cleaner and a set of pipes on an otherwise stock bike, Chapin says a 42-mm carb would be a better choice. "Evo and Twin Cam motors use 40-mm ports with a shared common manifold. With the overlap of the camshafts and the sharing of a manifold we've actually found a 42 is the ideal size. It'll slip right into the stock intake manifold." A smaller carb will give the incoming charge more low-speed velocity for better low-RPM torque, so a big, heavy bike like a bagger ridden two-up will benefit more from a smaller carb in the rev range where the bike is ridden the most. Chapin continues, "If I thought I could sell them, I'd sell a 40-mm version for those bikes. But we don't sacrifice much with a 42. Again, remember it's only a 42 at wide-open throttle. Wherever your hand is, wherever the throttle is, that's the size of the carburetor."

A good high-performance carburetor can do a lot for your engine, but there are some things no carb, no matter how good it is, can do. Chapin explains, "We cannot change the physics of an engine. If a customer chooses a camshaft that makes peak torque at 4,100 rpm when he really rides his bike at 3,100 rpm, then we can't change the physical nature of that engine with just a carb." A carburetor can't do much to make up for a poor choice of exhaust systems, either. Chapin continues, "Harley engines need a certain physical dynamic to help the exhaust gases leave the cylinders. We can mask certain problems like straight pipes by making the carb too rich in certain areas by playing with the air-fuel ratio." Sometimes the carb gets the blame for things that aren't its fault. "Pre-ignition and detonation are things that people will blame the carb for. Harleys can get 40 to 50 miles per gallon with moderate compression, mild timing, and mild cams. When you put in a lot of compression, a lot of cam, and a lot of ignition timing, pre-ignition can occur due to poor gas, too much compression, or poor timing, and the carb gets blamed for it. Actually the carb has very little to do with pre-ignition."

If one carb is good, are two better? And what about manifolds that give each carb its own intake runner? Chapin answers, "Longer intake tracts can produce better fuel atomization. We've seen increased fuel mileage and improved torque figures. If it's a true dual carb — one on either side, or two side by side running down a split manifold — you can tune each cylinder slightly different. On an Evo motor, the rear cylinder runs a little bit on the lean side, so you can compensate for that. Is there a big advantage in horsepower? Hard to say, because the highest horsepower numbers that we've seen out there have been single-carb setups. The Japanese have run a single carb on each cylinder for many years, and they see a great deal of benefit from it, primarily because they're high-RPM engines. The closer you can get the carb to the intake valve, the more top-end power you get. But Harleys are typically low RPM motors, and you don't rev them that much. That common manifold, even though it has some issues, can make good power."

The air filter can and should be considered a tuning component of a carburetor, just like jets. Chapin explains, "Size is everything when it comes to an air filter, the bigger the better. The smaller a filter element, the more

restrictive it's going to be. But with issues like knee clearance, fitment, and style, we run into compromises. The filter we sell is 3 inches by 7 inches — a big round K&N filter. It won't fit behind the Twin Cam oval cover, there's just not enough room for it. We can jet for air cleaners or vice versa. If you're running too rich at wide-open throttle, you can remove the air filter and your air-fuel ratio will start to come around, and power will start to come up. On the other hand, if we have a guy dead-set on running a certain air cleaner, we can put it on the dyno, and even though we know it's restrictive and it's going to rob him of horsepower, we can jet it properly and get it as close as we can to whatever power that air filter will allow."

The design of the air cleaner housing and backing plate can improve performance, too, especially those with radiused inlets. "Any time you can straighten the air out, direct it, not make it do anything unusual, then it's more likely to end up in the cylinder," Chapin

says. "Any sharp, ragged edges create turbulence and slow the air down."

S&S

S&S Cycle has been in the carburetor business longer than a lot of today's aftermarket companies have been in business, period. "S&S pretty much made the original performance carburetors for Harley V-twins back in the 1960s," says Bruce Tessmer of S&S. "The very early ones were drag-race carbs. They were made to go fast and that was pretty much it. And of course guys were going to run them on the street. The high-performance motors back in those days would be pretty mild by today's standards, but they were fussy because of this carb that was really only made to go fast."

Time brought more street-friendly carbs to the S&S line. "When we introduced the Super B it was light-years ahead of all our other carbs. It had some drawbacks for the street, though. People didn't like the fact that it was

S&S Super E and G carbs have accelerator pumps, fully adjustable idle mixture screws, and changeable intermediate and main jets. They use a special enrichment device instead of a choke for starting. You can use your stock throttle cables on many models. (S&S)

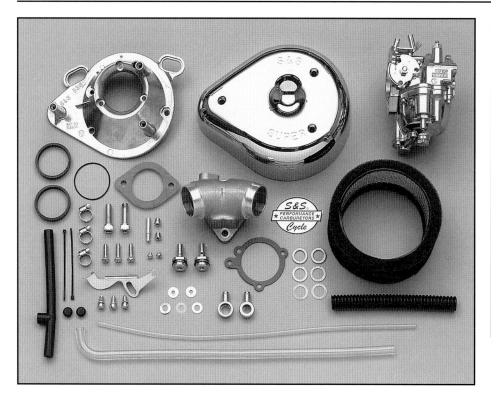

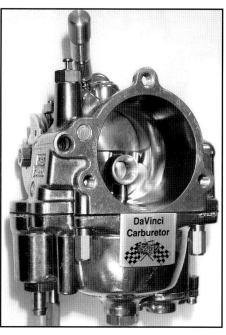

The DaVinci Performance Products Fire Power carb starts with an S&S carb, which is then blueprinted, calibrated, and modified for better performance. It comes with DaVinci's billet CNC Power Booster, a precision-machined 48-mm venturi, an easy-access jet plug, quick-access bowl screws, an idle screw extension, and a tumble-polished finish. (DaVinci Performance Products)

Since you can almost never get away with replacing just the carb, many companies sell complete kits. The S&S kit for Twin Cam motors comes with a Super E carb with a 47.6-mm bore recommended for stock and most modified applications. (S&S)

kind of long and pushed your leg out, and it didn't have an accelerator pump," explains Tessmer. Then in 1990 came the Super E. "It was short, the same length as stock, and it had an accelerator pump and an adjustable enrichment system. It was a lot easier to work with. Suddenly we had a long waiting list of people who wanted to buy one." The demand is still strong today, mainly, Tessmer says, because "they're very easy to tune and we can make very good power with them."

The 1 7/8-inch (47.6-mm) Super E and the 2 1/16-inch (52.3-mm) Super G remain the two hottest sellers in the S&S catalog, and are instantly recognizable on sight not only because of the classic S&S teardrop air cleaner that's usually bolted to them, but because of their simplicity of design. That simplicity, say Tessmer, is one of the butterfly carb's big advantages. "You've got a pivot point for the butterfly shaft, which is a lot easier to maintain clearance on. In a CV or a flat-slide carb, you have the slide going up and down. Those things can jam a lot easier than a throttle shaft can."

Tessmer admits the butterfly carb has some technical disadvantages when compared to a slide-type carb, but says they're not huge, or insurmountable. "A slide-type carb has a variable venturi. As the slide goes up and down the venturi around the jet gets bigger or smaller, so it tends to have pretty good throttle response. But with the accelerator pump that we have, we feel we can equal them."

What really appeals to high-performance enthusiasts, however, is how easy the S&S carb is to tune. "There are only two jets," Tessmer says. "Other carbs have a lot of jets and needles and all sorts of stuff you can fool around with. If you're not really good at it, you can really screw things up. You can design something really complicated, but if you can design something simple that does the job, you're way ahead of the game."

FUEL-INJECTION MODULES

Change comes slowly to Harley-Davidson, but when it does come it's almost always good. And yet there are always those who resist change. Fuel injection (FI) is a good example. A staple on cars since the 1980s, fuel injection has been available on selected Harley models since the late 1990s. Despite the dire predictions of some old-school die-hards — What if it breaks? How do you work on it? How do you make it work with a modified engine? — It's not only here to stay, but it's the wave of the future, as emissions regulations that spelled the end of carbureted cars eventually trickle down to the motorcycle industry.

The reliability of stock Harley-Davidson fuel injection is pretty well established, but when it comes to high-performance engines, it's not as easy to tune fuel injection to work with hop-up parts as it is a carburetor. The truth is, it's easier — if you install an aftermarket fuel-injection module like the Power Commander from Dynojet.

Gas Mileage

If you're getting lousy mileage, don't automatically blame the bike. The way you ride has a big effect on gas mileage. Where you ride makes a difference, too. (Dain Gingerelli)

For all the thousands of dollars Harley riders spend on non-functional chrome bits for their bikes, some can be remarkably tight-fisted when it comes to the price of a gallon of gasoline. A few trips too many to the gas pump, and they start blaming their carburetor. Lee Chapin of Mikuni has heard it all before, and says one of the things he wishes more riders were aware of is the effect of speed on fuel economy: "We get calls from people who ride to Sturgis from, say, Chicago. They're climbing, they're fighting a headwind, and they're riding really fast. Then they come up to us and say their gas mileage went to hell. Well, running into a 20 mph headwind at 60 mph, that's like riding at 80 mph." Chapin adds that the amount of horsepower required to power a bike increases by the cube of the increase in speed. As an example, it takes 85 percent more horsepower to increase a bike's speed from 110 to 135, even though the speed only increased 23 percent. Fuel mileage will suffer accordingly.

A few ambitious companies make their own complete fuel-injection systems, but most aftermarket companies that deal with fuel injection stick to making different throttle bodies and modules. (Dain Gingerelli)

Put in the simplest terms, fuel injection supplies gasoline to the engine through nozzles in the intake manifold. The nozzles are fed by a high-pressure fuel pump. Sensors on the bike monitor factors such as engine RPM, the throttle position, airbox inlet temperature, and barometric pressure, and based on these factors tell the computer how much fuel to inject on any given intake stroke.

There have been two types of fuel injection used on Harleys. The first fuel-injected Harleys used Magnetti-Marelli, and the later models — all the Softails and touring models from 2002 on up — use a system built by Delphi. The Magnetti-Marelli uses a twin-throat throttle body, and the Delphi uses a single-bore throttle body that looks a lot like a carburetor body.

The throttle body of a fuel-injection system is similar to a carburetor in one aspect that's critical to high-performance tuning — bore size. The Magnetti-Marelli system, for example, has some limitations in the throttle body size, so if you want to build a high-performance engine with Magnetti-Marelli injection, the intake restriction of the throttle body can be a limiting factor. There are, however, some companies that modify throttle bodies for high-performance applications by boring them out the same way you'd bore out a carburetor body. The later Delphi throttle bodies seem to have fewer restrictions. Some fuel-injected bikes are putting out in the neighborhood of 120 horsepower using stock Delphi throttle bodies.

The main problem with stock fuel injection is that the fuel curve — the formula, based primarily on throttle position and engine RPM, that the fuel-injection module uses to tell the injectors what to do — is pre-set from the factory. In one sense this is a good thing, because it allows the engine to maintain a consistent fuel-air ratio under a wide variety of conditions, such as high-altitude riding. Let's say you're cruising along at sea level on your fuel-injected bagger. The mixture will be slightly lean, which is how it was set at the factory, and how Harley wants the bike to run at that RPM and

Harley fuel injection made its debut in the FL touring family, and has trickled down to just about every other model except the Sportster. Fuel injection has proven itself tunable as well as easy to live with. In most cases replacing the stock fuel-injection module with an aftermarket one takes only a few minutes. You can go online any time to download new maps to suit different riding conditions, or check out new maps. (Dain Gingerelli)

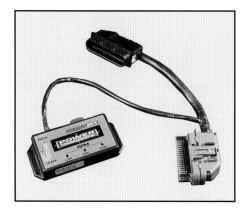

The Power Commander from Dynojet lets you make adjustments to the stock fuel-injection map for improvements in various parts of the powerband or to accommodate add-on performance parts. Maps are available from Dynojet's website, or you can custom-make your own. (Dynojet)

at that throttle position for emissions and fuel-economy reasons. If you suddenly decide to see what the Rocky Mountains look like, and find yourself tooling along at altitudes of, say, 5,000

to 10,000 feet, the fuel injection's pressure sensor will offset the air-fuel ratio to maintain the factory setting. On a carbureted bike, the higher up you go in elevation, the richer the air-fuel mixture will become as the air thins out. So while the carbureted bike is at the mercy of air density, the fuel-injected bike motors happily along, pretty much indifferent to it.

This gets to be more of a problem when you start bolting high-performance parts on your fuel-injected engine. The stock fuel injection has no way of determining and compensating for changes in airflow, only air density. So as you add different parts that change the amount of air flowing through the engine, you can run into situations where the stock curve, or map, is too lean in some areas or too rich in others.

In some cases an engine can wind up too rich at one point and too lean in another at the same time. For example, if you install an exhaust system with a bad reversion problem at a certain RPM, you could be too rich at the bottom of the rev range and too lean at the top. The stock map is no help — it's designed to maintain the stock air-fuel ratio no matter what you bolt on the engine — so you need a way to tell it to adjust the fuel richer and leaner in the right places. This is where fuel-injection modules like the Power Commander come in.

Stated very simply, a fuel injector has two wires running to it, one connected to 12-volt power and the other a ground wire. When the ground circuit is activated, a solenoid is triggered that opens the injector and squirts fuel into the intake manifold. When the ground connection is broken, the injector closes. So in essence, all the electronic wizardry of fuel injection comes down to the stock engine control unit making a decision based on air pressure, temperature, throttle position, and engine RPM, and then telling the injector when to switch on, and when to switch off.

What the Power Commander does is intercept the signal on its way to the injector and compare it to its own internal map. Based on what it finds, it decides to add or subtract fuel from the stock setting, then opens and closes the injector on its own. The whole process takes place in microseconds.

The beauty of the system, and a lot of the hard work that went into it, is in the individual maps, each tailored to work with a given bike, and written to accommodate a wide variety of high-performance accessories. For example, Dynojet has over 140 different maps just for Softails. And they're not just computer-modeled guesses, either. Each map is for a bike with a given combination of hop-up parts, and each one is the result of putting a bike with the exact combination of parts on a dyno and running it through the entire RPM/throttle-position range to see what the air-fuel ratio is, and what it needs to be.

It's not just equipment that the maps can be adjusted for, but different riding situations, as well. Because Harley riders tend to be concerned with fuel economy, Dynojet tries to strike a happy medium in the smaller throttle-position range at lower RPM where there's less load, such as at highway cruising speeds. They go after a slightly leaner mixture than they would at higher or wide-open throttle settings. It's richer than Harley sets it when the bike leave the factory, but slightly leaner than what could be called optimum, so fuel economy is improved. The difference in performance is so small that few if any riders would be able to notice it out on the road. For those few that can, it's possible to adjust the Power Commander using either the downloadable software or buttons on the unit itself to shift the fuel curve up or down for a smoother, cooler-running engine, or for slightly better fuel economy.

The Power Commander also offers ignition timing adjustability, which is vital on Harleys. Under certain circumstances most of them will detonate — if you're running in hot weather, for instance, or if the bike's been substantially modified. With a high-compression engine you definitely need to be able to adjust the timing to keep it from constantly detonating. Detonation can also be a problem for riders who travel two-up, or tow a trailer. The Power Commander's ignition map is part of its fuel map, so if Dynojet runs across a particular combination of factors — equipment or riding style — that has a significant detonation issue, they've already corrected for it.

Just as the fuel map has the capability of adding or subtracting fuel depending on the throttle position and engine RPM, the ignition timing adjustment is flexible over a wide range, too. Dynojet found that most of the time fuel-injected bikes will only detonate at very high throttle settings and very low RPM, such as in high-load situations where you're taking off from a stop and giving it a handful of throttle but the RPM is very low. They're able to retard the timing for that particular circumstance without having to retard the timing over the entire RPM-throttle position, only affecting the area that needs to be adjusted. On a carbureted bike the common fix is to move the ignition rotor, which might retard the timing 10 degrees everywhere, and then you'd lose throttle response and peak power. With the Power Commander, you can adjust the timing to retard at, say, 60 to 100 percent throttle but only

up to 2,500 rpm. Probably the only time you'd see that combination of throttle opening and engine RPM is under very high load, accelerating up a grade with a passenger and luggage. Once the revs come up, there's no longer any need to have the timing retarded so you get some ignition advance back to improve peak power.

You can load the Power Commander with the Dynojet-supplied maps, or program it yourself. If you don't feel like pitting yourself against your motorcycle in a battle of electronic wits, Dynojet will be more than happy to steer you to someone who'll do it for you. Because there's no way they can anticipate and map every possible combination of performance parts (their downloadable maps typically represent the most common setups) they have a number of shops across the U.S. that can make custom maps. With a piece of software you connect the Power Com-

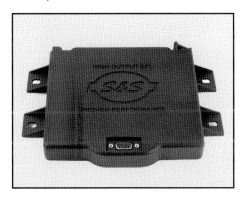

The Variable Fuel-Injection module from S&S is a direct replacement for the stock Harley-Davidson module, and works with the stock sensors and injectors. You can use existing S&S fuel-injection maps, or create custom ones. Software and a computer cable are included with the VFI Module. (S&S)

The Tuned Induction System from S&S fits 1995-2001 fuel-injected Evo and Twin Cam Big Twins. It comes with a two-barrel throttle body, a special fuel rail, high-flowing manifolds for front and rear cylinders, and dual tuned induction runner intake tracts. A single air cleaner is included. (S&S)

mander and the bike to a dyno, then tell the dyno what air-fuel ratio you're looking for at the given ranges of RPM and throttle position, and the dyno programs the bike. You can make a custom map this way in less than an hour.

SUPERCHARGERS AND TURBOCHARGERS

An internal combustion engine such as a Harley's is often likened to a pump. Its job is to suck in as much fuel and air as it can, convert it to energy, and push the burnt gas out as fast as possible. On the intake side of the engine, atmospheric pressure is what fills the cylinder. As the piston moves downward on the intake stroke it creates a partial vacuum in the cylinder, and when the intake valve opens air from outside at normal pressure rushes in to fill the void.

Superchargers (often called blowers) and turbochargers give nature a helping hand by increasing the pressure on the intake side of the engine and forcing in more air-fuel mixture than atmospheric pressure alone can. The

more fuel and air the cylinder takes in, the more energy it releases when it burns, and the more power the engine makes at a given RPM.

If there's a downside to forced induction, it's heat. The more power an engine puts out, the more heat it produces and has to get rid of. Air-cooled Harley motors are marginally cooled at best, especially the rear cylinder, and too much boost, either from a supercharger or a turbocharger, can cause severe overheating. That's why most companies that make blowers and turbos recommend leaving the engine almost completely stock.

Superchargers

Bill Bushling is the owner of Magna Charger, a manufacturer of bolt-on superchargers for Harley-Davidsons. His motto is, "If it isn't blown, it sucks," and he practices what he preaches. "I've done over 2500 vehicles with blowers," he says. "My Cessna 150 has a blower, and so does my lawn mower, and my fork lift. I even have a 143-mph blown 1947 Cushman."

Bushling says cylinder filling — how much of a cylinder's overall volume is filled on the intake stroke — is critical to performance, and that the way everyone has been going about getting it hasn't changed much in the last half-century. "If you pick up a 1950 hot rod magazine and see an article about how to build a Ford flathead, that's the same technology that's in place today for building a hot-rod Harley. Sure, the cylinder fill has gotten a little better, but for the most part you'll never see 95-percent cylinder filling on both cylinders of a Harley, except maybe in some drag-race application. On the street it's more of a dream than anything else."

Also critical is an understanding for the real-world difference between horsepower and torque. Bushling explains, "Horsepower is something you talk about in a bar. Torque, and how soon you can get to it, is what you're trying to improve. You put in wild cams, do some wild porting, and on and on, and when you're all done, the motor looks great on a dyno, but in reality when you're riding it at 3500

Tired of dropping little brass jets and trying to get the stink of gasoline off your hands in time for dinner? Make the quantum leap to forced induction and never worry about jets and needles again. (Buzz Buzzelli/*American Rider* magazine)

ProCharger's supercharger for Harley-Davidsons uses a conservative 7 psi of boost and produces a claimed 55-percent power gain on pump gas from a stock motor. It clears the rider's leg, and both EFI and carbureted versions are available. (ProCharger)

rpm it won't pull a gumdrop out of your mouth until you downshift."

Bushling says supercharging is not only better at making monster torque where you use it the most, but cheaper than traditional hop-up methods, too. "There are a lot of guys out there making phenomenal claims about what they do. The reality is a Twin Cam with all the stuff you can do to it will put out around 100-105 horsepower. Some people get more, most get less. Torque's going to be real close to that. We took a stock 88-inch Twin Cam, put a little bit better ignition on it to get the rev limiter up to 6500 rpm, and with the stock CV carb, just bolting the blower on, we got 108 horsepower and 108 foot-pounds of torque with 98 foot-pounds off idle. You're talking third-gear burnouts with a stock bike. It'll shred just about every out-of-the-box 113-incher because they're only about 95 horsepower, and will even take most 120-inchers, unless they're massaged."

A supercharger is driven by either a belt or by gears, and is designed to run at a slightly higher RPM than the engine. The "overdriven" blower is always running, but it doesn't really affect the engine until you open the throttle. And the effect, according to Bushling, is eye-opening. "The supercharger is at speed all the time, but normally it's running in a vacuum, so your motor is virtually a stock motor. We gear the supercharger for 140-percent cylinder fill. As soon as you turn the throttle wide-open at any RPM, you now have 140-percent cylinder fill. That takes your 88-inch bike and makes it 115 inches power wise, and it makes the power right now. With a stock, warmed-up Evo motor in a Softail frame, with a stock carb and slip-on mufflers, open the throttle all the way as fast as you can, and before you can physically hit the throttle stop the engine will have hit the rev limiter and bottomed out the rear suspension."

One way to get more power out of a naturally aspirated engine is to increase the compression ratio, and a supercharger increases the effective compression ratio of an engine. "Evos are 8.5:1 and Twin Cams are 8.9:1," says Bushling. "About 11:1 is as far as you want to go with premium pump gas. With the throttle wide open and a blower filling the cylinder at 140 percent, you're at 11:1 minus whatever the cam bleeds off." If you're thinking about putting a blower on an engine with high-compression pistons or milled heads, you should put it all back to stock first, because the added compression of the blower can quickly cause fatal detonation.

It's no surprise that Bushling prefers superchargers over turbochargers. "The problem with turbocharging is why did you buy a Harley in the first place?" he says. "If you're looking for performance and you don't care what it looks or sounds like, go buy a Suzuki Hayabusa, get it over with. I never could understand somebody buying a Harley and putting a turbo on it because now it sounds like a Honda or a Kawasaki. You've lost the exhaust note because you can't change the exhaust pipe, that's all part of the turbo."

Turbo lag — the time it takes for the turbocharger's impeller to spin up to boost-producing speed after you whack open the throttle — is another turn-off for Bushling. "Some turbo guys say there's no lag. Well, there's no lag, but there's no boost, either. You twist the

"Hey, mister, what's under the big lump on your motor?" "Power, son, and lots of it." Blowers don't have to be obvious. This one would slip right onto a clean bagger and almost disappear. Imagine being the first guy to tow your motor home to Daytona behind your bike. (Ron Goodger)

Here's how to be king of your particular jungle. Superchargers typically work better on Harley V-twins than turbochargers, because superchargers don't exhibit the lag that turbochargers do while waiting for the impeller to get up to speed. (Ron Goodger)

throttle, and the bike accelerates, but as a normally aspirated bike until the turbo comes on. If all you're looking for is a power gain at a certain RPM, then a turbo is a neat deal, because you don't care how long it takes you to get to the power, you just want it."

Turbochargers

Turbocharged motorcycles enjoyed a brief popularity in the mid 1980s when all four major Japanese motorcycle companies brought out turbo bikes. Despite initial hopes that turbocharging would bring big-bike performance to mid-size motorcycles, all were dropped after a few years. The reasons ranged from cost to complexity to crippling turbo lag.

Turbochargers use the engine's exhaust gas to spin an impeller. The impeller is connected by a shaft to a turbine wheel plumbed into to the intake side of the engine. The higher the engine revs, the more exhaust gas is produced, and the faster the impeller spins the turbine. The turbine in turn pumps enormous quantities of air into the engine, increasing horsepower and the volume of exhaust gas. The cycle feeds on itself, producing what some call "free horsepower."

There's a drawback to turbocharging, though, and that's the aforementioned turbo lag. When you open the throttle, it takes a finite amount of time for the exhaust gases to "spool up" the impeller and get it going fast enough to produce substantially more than atmospheric pressure on the intake side. Until

this happens, your engine feels — and produces power — like a stock engine. But when the boost hits, suddenly you're riding a bike with anywhere from half again to twice as much power as a stocker. That abrupt increase in power at the rear wheel isn't much of a problem if you're upright, but if the bike is leaned into a corner when the boost comes on, things could get ugly.

For this reason alone, most riders who equip their bikes with turbochargers do so for aesthetic reasons, or because they drag race or take part in dyno shootouts. Most riders who opt for forced induction for street riding go with superchargers, which have no lag. There is at least one turbocharger, however, that is claimed to be as popular among street riders as it is with racers. Aerocharger makes a motorcycle-specific turbocharger with variable-vane technology that it says practically eliminates turbo lag.

Aerocharger's Jim Czekala likens a regular turbocharger to a garden hose with no nozzle on the end. "The exhaust gases just whoosh on by and spin the impeller. What variable vanes do is act like your thumb when you put it over the end of the garden hose — it makes the water velocity higher." The vanes effectively change the volume of the turbocharger, depending on turbo RPM. "At low turbo speed, the vanes are close together, choking down the exhaust gas and increasing its velocity. Once the turbo spools up and starts making boost, the vanes open and slow the exhaust velocity. They're constantly modulating."

If you're willing to wait for your power, there's plenty on tap from a turbocharger. A good-running carbureted V-twin will eat your lunch in roll-ons from low RPM, but when the boost hits it's payback time. (Ron Goodger)

Under the dense thicket of plumbing you can see the headers connecting to the turbocharger. Unlike a naturally aspirated bike, a turbo bike doesn't need a specially designed exhaust system, just a pipe long enough to vent the hot exhaust gas. (Buzz Buzzelli/*American Rider* magazine)

Like most turbos, the Aerocharger doesn't affect off-boost performance. "The motor operates like a stock motor 95 percent of the time," says Czekala. "Only when you're at wide-open throttle does it change the way the engine works. When you're off the boost, you're basically riding a normally aspirated bike."

Most turbochargers need a lot of oil to keep cool and lubricated. Plumbing them into the engine's oil supply puts a lot of strain on the engine oil, as well as pumping a lot of heat into it. Aerocharger gets around this, and at the same time makes its kits true bolt-ons by giving the turbocharger its own independent oil supply. Czekala elaborates, "Our turbos don't require engine oil to cool them, so they don't heat the engine up at all. It has a reservoir built into it and a fiber wick that puts a fine mist of oil on the ceramic ball bearings. Oil consumption is really low, about 1 cc per thousand miles."

The turbocharger can be used with a stock or aftermarket carburetor. As with superchargers, the compression ratio should be kept reasonably low to avoid detonation problems when the engines is on the boost. Otherwise, turbochargers work fine on big-bore and modified engines. You'll have to shelve your trick exhaust system, though, because the exhaust system is an integral part of the turbo's plumbing. The Aerocharger exhaust system consists of a stainless-steel header pipe and a chrome-plated exhaust pipe.

Czekala admits the price of a turbocharger — anywhere from $3,000 to $4,000 for an Aerocharger kit — appears to be a drawback to many riders at first. "But the power output is way beyond what you can get with a normally aspirated motor," he says. "The upside is that when you sell your Harley you can take the kit off and you've got a stock bike, which is way more valuable than a modified bike. And you still have your turbo to put on your next bike."

It comes as a bit of a surprise to learn that most Aerocharger kits are sold not to racers or dyno junkies, but street riders. "The majority of kits we sell are for touring bikes. Fuel mileage is unaffected, unless you use the throttle a lot. At double the horsepower of a stock bike, you're using twice as much fuel. Of course, if you're using the power to pass a truck it'll take you half the time to do it," says Czekala.

NITROUS

Think back to the last time you went to the dentist and had some serious work done. You probably asked for nitrous oxide, otherwise known as laughing gas, to make the experience less unpleasant. The same gas that got you through your root canal can help hustle your bike through the quarter mile faster than a stock or lightly modified bike, or give you that extra boost you need to get by that slow-moving semi out on the highway.

"You need oxygen to burn gasoline, and if you have more oxygen you can burn more gas," says Dale Pulde, owner of HP Racing, which builds the nitrous kits that Edelbrock sells. Nitrous oxide is an oxidizer, which means it releases oxygen when it reacts with other chemicals. It consists of a three-part molecule made up of two atoms of nitrogen and one of oxygen. By itself it won't burn, but when exposed to the heat of combustion

inside an engine, the molecule breaks apart into oxygen and nitrogen. The extra oxygen increases horsepower, sometimes dramatically, depending on the amount of nitrous.

The nitrous is contained under pressure in a bottle ranging in size from small, one- or two-shot sizes to larger bottles that hold up to two pounds of the stuff. "For motorcycles, we make a 12 ounce and a two pound," says Pulde. "The 12-ounce is good for two, maybe three good hits, and it's pretty well shot. With the two-pounder you can get five to six, depending on how much you're shoving through it."

It sounds almost too good to be true, and there are in fact limitations to the use of nitrous on streetbikes. The bottle itself is the first problem — the larger it is, the harder it is to mount conveniently. "The bottle has to be mounted in the right position or it won't work very well," says Pulde. The pressure in a full bottle is so high — Pulde does all of his testing at 950 psi — that the gas becomes a liquid. "On the Edelbrock kit, we mount the bottle upside down so the liquid will be right at the base of the bottle. That way you don't need a siphon

tube that could fall off." Other mounting positions, such as those that position the bottle horizontally or at an extreme angle, require a siphon tube inside the bottle to make sure there's a steady supply of nitrous under acceleration when the liquid can slosh around inside the bottle. "Guys that mount the bottle horizontally on the bike better hope the have the tube cocked on an angle so when they take off they actually get their nitrous," says Pulde.

The second problem is that nitrous oxide isn't meant to be anything but a temporary power boost. "Nitrous is not something you'd want to leave on for a real long time," Pulde says, "because it'd be tough to meter it perfectly." That's because as the pressure in the bottle goes down, so does the pressure feeding nitrous to the engine — less pressure equals less nitrous equals less horsepower. Pulde explains, "A fresh bottle is what they call sweet nitrous, it has a lot of liquid still in it. The first couple of pulls on a bottle are fast."

That's not to say the average Harley rider with a bagger or Softail can't appreciate nitrous in everyday riding. The Edelbrock kit produces an extra 30

Nitrous on a 100-incher? Some would say overkill, others would just ask where the go-button is. The nitrous bottle on this bike is so unobtrusive you might miss it. They come in several sizes so you can even tuck them away out of sight altogether. (Dain Gingerelli)

- 35 horsepower, Pulde says, which comes in handy when you're passing a big truck on your heavily loaded bagger, or just looking to see the expression on your riding buddies' faces when you whack the throttle on the highway and leave them all in your mirrors.

Contrary to what many riders think, you can't, or more accurately, shouldn't, just activate the nitrous any time you want, at any engine speed. "The biggest problem we had in the past with nitrous kits is the guy who's riding down the highway in cruise mode with his girlfriend on the back. Somebody will pass him and he'll hit the throttle and then he'll hit the nitrous button, and next thing you know it blows the motor apart," says Pulde. A sudden shot of nitrous at low RPM puts a lot of liquid, both nitrous oxide and gasoline, in the cylinder, sometimes enough to result in hydraulic lock. "You want your engine speed up towards the top of the torque curve before you turn the nitrous on," explains Pulde. The Edelbrock kit comes with an RPM-sensitive switch that won't activate the bottle until the engine is at a pre-set RPM, no matter when you push the button.

That sudden rush of nitrous, with its rich load of oxygen, can lean out the engine to the point of fatal detonation, so the Edelbrock kit comes with a small fuel pump that's plumbed into the stock fuel system. The fuel pump kicks in a fraction of a second before the nitrous, sending enough extra gasoline into the cylinder to prevent the mixture from leaning out.

Depending on what you're doing with the bike (racing or just riding around) the amount of nitrous injected into the cylinder is adjustable. The feed line from the bottle goes to a plate that's inserted between the carb and the stock manifold. In the plate are tubes with tiny holes laser-drilled into them, similar to the injectors in a fuel-injection system. These tubes help atomize the liquid nitrous. On the outside of the plate is a place for a drop-in jet to meter the nitrous flow.

The adjustability has prompted some riders to go too far, which in turn prompted Edelbrock to supply only a few jets with each kit, jets they know work well on all the bikes they've tried them on. Pulde says incorrect jetting has done a lot of damage. "People don't realize that if you go from a .030-inch jet to a .045-inch jet, you're not just going up .015 inch, you're almost tripling the area size of the jet. When you're talking nitrous and gasoline, that's a big jump. A couple of thousandths makes a big difference, and when you hit the magic number one thousandth makes a big difference." As an example, he says, "We ran our bike at a dyno shootout and it was making 182 horsepower. I increased the jet sizes .004 inch per jet and made 197."

Pulde says nitrous oxide has gotten a bad reputation in some circles over the years because some of the companies that made kits didn't specify how or where to mount the components, they just sent out a bunch of parts in a box and left it to the customer to figure out. A common mistake was mounting the auxiliary fuel pump under the seat or in some other location far from the engine, and hiding the nitrous bottle close by. The drawback to this is that when you hit the nitrous button, the fuel pump (putting out anywhere from 5 to 9 pounds of pressure) just can't get gas to the engine before the nitrous bottle (charged at 950 psi) delivers its load. The result is a very lean mixture as you open the throttle, and sometimes a blown motor. Placing the fuel pump closer to the engine than the nitrous bottle gets around this.

A final note. You can buy nitrous oxide at many speed shops, but don't think it's exactly the same nitrous as you get at the dentist's office. Unlike medical-grade nitrous, the stuff you get for racing has sulfur dioxide added to it. You won't get happy if you huff it, you'll get very sick instead.

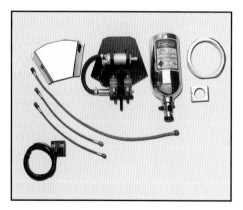

Edelbrock's nitrous kit is a bolt-on that promises a true 35-horsepower increase. An electronic module and RPM sensor activates the nitrous at 4300 rpm to reduce the chance of engine-damaging detonation. Nitrous bottles come in 12-ounce or two-pound sizes. (Edelbrock)

Nitrous plumbing can be installed in such as way as to be almost invisible to the casual observer. But nobody's going to miss the cloud of tire smoke you leave behind when you hit the go-button. (Edelbrock)

HEADS AND VALVETRAIN

CYLINDER HEADS

When you're modifying a stock Harley-Davidson, sometimes the temptation is to make a lot of small, inexpensive changes instead of big pricey ones. This is a good time to remember that there's a little bit of truth in every cliché, like "You get what you pay for." Cylinder heads are a good example. Lots of riders have their stock heads ported and milled and stuffed with valves the size of dinner plates, and still don't get the performance they're after. Worse, they end up spending more money modifying their stock heads than they would have buying new high-performance heads. Rod Sokoloski of Edelbrock explains why you're often better off shelving your stock Harley heads and choosing a set of well-made aftermarket ones.

The first problem with stock heads is that they're very limited in terms of valve size. During overlap, when both valves are open, stock-size valves clear each other as they protrude into the combustion chamber. The larger the valves, however, the more likely they are to collide. "That's why camshaft makers give you what they call a TDC drop recommendation," Sokoloski says. "When you go in and modify a Harley head, with a lot of streetable aftermarket camshafts you can safely go up to,

Port design has come a long way since the "bigger is better" school held sway with Harley racers. Today you can buy the experience of the industry's top tuners. (Jerry Smith)

Cylinder-head porting isn't for the faint of heart, or the short of experience. There are plenty of companies willing to sell you the benefit of their own experience, however, in configurations from mild to wild, like these heads from Zipper's. (Buzz Buzzelli/*American Rider* magazine)

Performer RPM heads from Edelbrock are available for 80- to 113-inch Evo and Twin Cam Big Twin engines, with combustion chamber volumes ranging from 72 to 92 cc. An Edelbrock manifold and modified or aftermarket pistons must be used. All are CNC-ported by Chapman Racing of NASCAR fame to Edelbrock specs. (Edelbrock)

Bolt-on cylinder heads come ported and equipped with top-notch valves, valvesprings, valve guides, and seals, and can be installed by anyone who knows which end of the wrench to hit the nail with. You can take them off when you sell the bike and put them on your new ride. (Jerry Smith)

say a 1.900-inch valve. But you have to relocate the valve, basically sink the valve into the seat, to reestablish valve-to-valve clearance. As a result of that, H-D has a recommended valve tip height from the spring pocket base up to the tip of the valve, which is like 2.0 to 2.15 inches. They even sell a service valve for when a guy sinks his valve job too deep, not necessarily as a result of a high-performance modification, but let's say the head has a few years and miles on it and he's sunk it a few times. They sell a shorter-than-normal valve called a service valve."

And it's not just valve size that holds stock heads back, but valve geometry as well. "If you're going to go after larger ports, and more RPM capability, you have to address the valve geometry. In our heads, and in most aftermarket heads, that's already been taken care of," Sokoloski says. "Our Performer head, our as-cast head, maintains stock Harley valve geometry, stock valve diameter, everything is stock. But when you get into what we call our RPM line, where it's CNC-ported, we actually go into the combustion chamber with a form tool prior to the CNC work and lower the top of the seats. We also design our valves specifically for a cer-

tain height requirement with the valve sunk in farther."

You could, of course, do the seat work and fit different valves to your stock head, but then, as Sokoloski points out, "you have to go in there and port the combustion chamber." That's because the sunk-in valves, even at maximum lift, are going to be partially shrouded by the combustion chamber. Sokoloski explains, "They're in a canyon, so to speak, which now requires you to go in there and do porting work because you have a larger combustion chamber and less compres-

Edelbrock Performer RPM heads for 1200 Sportsters are CNC-ported and fit 1986-1990 4-speed and 1991-and-later 5-speed XL models. An Edelbrock manifold and modified or aftermarket pistons must be used. The carb will mount higher and closer to the engine so to allow for clearance. (Edelbrock)

sion, so you mill the head." With every step forward, it seems, you take another step backward.

The advantage of buying an aftermarket head is that all the compromises are taken into account up front, and worked around in the design and manufacturing stages. For example, Sokoloski says, "Our combustion chamber, in an as-cast form, is automatically 10 cc smaller than a Harley head, so when you bolt our Performer head on you immediately take that stock 8.5:1 compression ratio and now you have 9.5:1. In an 80-inch Harley, 1 cc of combustion chamber volume equals a tenth of a compression ratio. So we have a 10 cc smaller chamber, and that results in a full compression point."

Starting out with a more or less clean sheet of paper makes it easier to design a cylinder head with attributes that are difficult to modify into a stock head. Sokoloski points to Edelbrock's D-shaped exhaust port as an example.

"Every port has what they call a long turn and a short turn, which is the roof and the floor," Sokoloski says. "The whole point of airflow is you'd like to try to equalize those two distances. When you put a D-port in there you're doing two things. First, you're in effect adding more material to the floor of the port, which is lengthening it to a minor degree." Why is it important to have the roof and floor of the port as close to each other in length as possible?

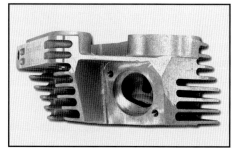

Edelbrock says its D-shaped exhaust port has more area than a round port, and also creates an intentional mismatch between the exhaust pipe and the exhaust exit to reduce reversion of the spent exhaust gas back into the engine. The result is better flow, more velocity, and a cleaner intake charge. (Edelbrock)

The flat floor of this rectangular Edelbrock intake port slows down the lower section of the intake charge as it crosses the lower short-side radius. This flow rate is equal to that of the upper charge as it moves along the top of the port, resulting in less turbulence and better atomization. (Edelbrock)

"If the floor is half the length of the roof, the column of air on the floor is going to get to the valve and into the combustion chamber first. So you have to do one of two things, speed up the roof or slow down the floor. I look at it the way you would look at the flow of a body of water. Let's say you have a river that's 200 yards wide, and then it necks down to 100 yards. It speeds up at that point. It might be flowing the same volume of water, but it's flowing faster. You can regulate speed by widening or narrowing the path. So getting back to the port, you can narrow the roof of the port to speed it up, which is sort of self-defeating because of the fact that you're trying to get higher volumes of air into the motor, or you can slow the floor down by widening it."

Sokoloski suggests drawing a simple diagram to better understand the analogy. "Draw a rectangle, and then draw a circle inside that rectangle. The rectangle is certainly a lot wider at the base than the circle." This results in a wider, and therefore slower port floor, which allows the flow along the roof of the port to catch up slightly. The bottom of a round port is narrower, and therefore faster.

The second important function of a D-port is to help prevent reversion and the adverse effect it has on combustion. Sokoloski explains, "Reversion is a reverse wave in the induction system. It

occurs during overlap, when both valves are open. It takes spent, contaminated exhaust gas and shoves it back into the combustion chamber. You can put a Harley motor with a larger-than-normal camshaft in it on a dyno and if you have a bad reversion problem you can run it up and see gas come backwards out the carburetor. Because reversion concentrates itself at the floor of the port, by putting a D-port in there, you put up that wall to discourage the reverse pulse. That's been in the automotive industry for years."

The combustion chambers in Edelbrock heads get the same careful treatment as the ports. "What you want to do in the combustion chamber is optimize quench. Quench is that area where the flat gasket surface of the head meets up with the piston — they'd hit one another if it weren't for the head gasket. It's where the 'squeeze' is. Squeeze is very important to torque. Detonation can occur in the quench area if it's designed wrong. But if it's designed right it can work for you. We have what we call a double quench combustion chamber. If you look diagonally you'll see where one side of the combustion chamber is sort of tucked in, and the other side is relieved. That's to accommodate the needs of the port. Of all the heads out there ours are very forgiving when it comes to detonation."

Not every engine works best with the same combustion chamber volume. "When we design our CNC combustion chambers we design them toward a specific compression ratio. When you get into larger motors, you can't put a 72-cc combustion chamber on them. We can on an 80-incher, because we sell a piston that matches that combustion chamber. But when you get into a 121-inch motor you're going to have to run something else. A 121 with an 83-cc combustion chamber and a flat-top piston is going to yield 10.3:1. We also sell a 92-cc combustion chamber so you can drop that down to 9-something. We juggle the factors to the point where we can accommodate a large variety of motor combinations. You go in and port a stock head, and if you want to

put that big a combustion chamber in it, there's only one thing you can do — start hogging material out of it," says Sokoloski.

Sokoloski has some advice for anyone looking at aftermarket heads, Edelbrock or any other: "Look for two things. First, call the company and ask to see some documentation or dyno sheets. Peak horsepower and flow numbers are basically just numbers. If you have a choice between giving up a flow bench or giving up a pair of calipers, put some wheels on the flow bench and get it out of there. I'm not saying it's not important, but it only tells you if you're going in the right direction. It's a measurement of potential. It doesn't tell you the end result. The second thing is you want something that produces a very broad torque range. Horsepower is a mathematical byproduct of the torque curve of the motor. Torque is what accelerates the vehicle. One of our design criteria for our Harley heads is we didn't want a guy to be riding up and hill and have to keep dropping gears."

There's also a danger in choosing aftermarket heads based solely on the peak torque and horsepower numbers advertised for them. Sokoloski explains, "During our Twin Cam development I modified two sets of Harley-Davidson cylinder heads to test the boundaries of port size. I had a conservative set and another set that was more aggressive. We

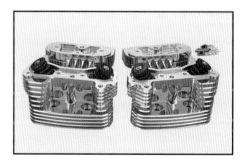

Pro-One's Proformance cylinder heads are machined from 6061-T6 billet aluminum and come with Ferrea severe-duty valves, ductile iron guides and seats, chrome silicon springs, and titanium retainers. Intake ports have a raised floor design and the exhaust ports are D-shaped for anti-reversion. Combustion chambers come in 72 or 80 cc. (Pro-One)

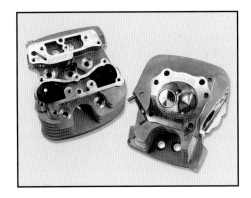

S&S makes cylinder heads that bolt onto stock engines and are compatible with stock exhaust systems, rocker covers and arms, gaskets, and venting hardware. For performance reasons, some special S&S parts must be used, and are available in the kit or separately. (S&S)

made 103 horsepower and 104 or 105 foot-pounds of torque, nice numbers to advertise. But — and this is very representative of what's out there — it only made 100 foot-pounds of torque for a total of 600 rpm. It fell off on both ends. But it made nice numbers, the kind that guys like to tell their buddies about."

Later on, however, "when we finished our CNC heads, we put them on there with our designs that made 104 horsepower. It won the AMA dyno shootout at Daytona that year in the Twin Cam class. The two runners-up were over 100-inch motors, and we won it with our 95. Our peak horsepower and torque numbers were about the same but we achieved over 100 foot-pounds of torque from 3700 to 5200 rpm. We nearly tripled the RPM range where it maintained over 100 foot-pounds of torque. The bottom line is the bike was going to accelerate tremendously faster," Sokoloski added.

Sokoloski has an engineer's unsentimental estimation of the basic design of a Harley V-twin. "With the stroke on a Harley, the motor should be pumping water into an irrigation ditch. It's basically an industrial motor." Which isn't to say it can't be made to run stronger — you just have to go about it the right way. "You can two things with a motor. You can try to eliminate its negative aspects, or try to enhance its positive aspects. Harley's

Zipper's Hammer 99-Inch Sportster

Had it up to here with those "chick bike" remarks when you pull up on your Sportster? Tired of Big Twin guys treating you like some little kid on a Big Wheel? Drop the hammer on 'em — the Zipper's Hammer, that is, 99 cubic inches of Evo-eatin', Twin Cam-trompin' XL power.

Sportsters are the logical choice for building low-cost, high-performance Harleys. They're easier to make faster than Big Twins because they start out that way. (Dain Gingerelli)

The Hammer 99-inch engine kit consists of parts any good garage mechanic can install, the only exception being the need to machine the crankcases to accommodate the 3-13/16-inch-bore cast-alloy cylinders with iron liners. A pair of CNC-ported Thunderstorm heads keep the pressure on forged pistons with a compression ratio of 10.7:1. Mixture is delivered via a Mikuni 45-mm HSR smoothbore carb.

The Hammer uses Red Shift 643 cams and features a forged-steel stroker crankshaft with heavy-duty rods for a stroke of 4-5/16 inches. The completed kit engine will slide right back into your stock Sportster frame, and to make sure it stays there, Zipper's provides special top and front engine mounts with the kit.

Good things (with 99-inch motors) come in small packages; this Sporty picks pieces of Big Twin out of its teeth. It shows what you can do when you start out with physics on your side. (Dain Gingerelli)

Aside from the Zipper's collector exhaust, there's not much besides the oversized cylinders to give away the Hammer's potential. With lots of low-end and midrange on tap, it purrs though everyday traffic. But when you twist the throttle wide open, those Big Twin riders will wonder who dropped the Hammer on them.

strongest feature has always been its ability to make tremendous amounts of torque in the low and mid-RPM ranges, and that's the feature you should build on and enhance," says Sokoloski.

What sort of power can you expect from a well-built engine? "Realistically if you get your money's worth, your engine should produce 1.1 horsepower per cubic inch. Our 80-inch RPM package will make 90 horsepower. Our 96

will make 106, the 121 will make 130-plus," Sokoloski responds.

Finally, Sokoloski offers an insider's advice for increasing a Harley's performance: "If you wanted to improve your Harley, and you had three paychecks to do it, you should do it in this order. First, put on a set of pipes. Second, put in a camshaft. You have to qualify the camshaft, though. Are you leaving your stock heads on, or are you

STD heads for Twin Cams are cast with 48,000-lb tensile strength aluminum and are available with a hand-blended valve job or with optional hand porting and polishing. The 78-cc combustion chambers work well with stock Twin Cams and larger 95-inch motors. (STD Development Company)

Evo Sportsters are famous for noisy cams. The stock gears are hand-fitted at the factory to reduce noise and lash. Aftermarket cam manufacturers like Andrews don't have that luxury, so their cams come with detailed and precise fitting instructions. Ignore those instructions at your peril — at your engine's peril, too. (Andrews Products)

Here in the cam chest is where many Harley riders make their biggest mistake — over-camming the engine. For streetbikes you'll almost always be happier with a little less cam than you think you need. (Buzz Buzzelli/American Rider magazine)

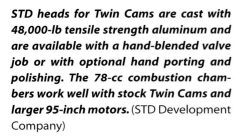

going to an aftermarket head? You want to do the heads and the cam at the same time so you don't get into the valve-to-valve clearance problem. Third, put on a carburetor. People have called and said they put a carb on a motor and didn't get a single horsepower. We ask what else they did to the bike, and they say nothing. We tell them to go put a set of pipes on it and get the cork out of it, and then go do that carb test again."

CAMS

The first step in choosing the right camshaft is to decide what you want it to do. If your answer is, "Make more power!" you're not alone. But the next question you need to ask yourself is where you'd like that power made. Aftermarket cams typically give you a powerband about 3500 rpm wide at best — some have powerbands that are so narrow that they're useless in real-world conditions. You can get that boost in the low RPM range, or the midrange, or way up there near the red part of the tachometer, but not all three. So it's important to think about how you ride, and where a camshaft's power boost will do you the most good.

The type of bike you ride will tell you a lot about how you ride. If you're a touring rider on a bagger, and you often carry a passenger and luggage, you're going to spend a lot of time at

relatively low RPM, say no higher than 3500. Since that's where most of your riding is done, that's where you'll want the most improvement. You might be tempted to get a cam that puts out more power at a higher RPM so you can pass trucks on the highway without downshifting, but such a cam will gut your low-RPM power in favor of a top-end

rush that you'll only use once or twice per ride.

Now let's say you ride a wide-tire Softail stripped down to the bare essentials, and you like nothing better than revving the engine at stoplights and dropping the clutch when the light turns green. You only ride the bike on weekends and never carry a passenger

As much fun as it might seem to go riding around all day testing new cams and other engine parts, it's not practical. This is what S&S does instead. This test stand can vary load and RPM to simulate thousands of miles of riding without ever leaving the building. (S&S)

The 1361 cam from JIMS is a bolt-in for 80-inch Evo Big Twins with stock heads. It works well with stock valvesprings and puts out good torque from 2000-6000 rpm. JIMS says it works best with a free-flowing air cleaner and exhaust system. (JIMS)

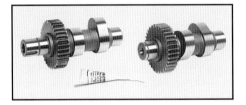

Andrews offers 19 different touring and performance Twin Cam grinds, ranging from bolt-in designs that work great with stock engines to high-lift models intended for use in high-compression motors with modified heads. The cams come with or without gears. (Andrews Products)

or luggage. You might even go bracket racing at the local drag strip on weekends. You don't mind lackluster low-end performance — it's that top-end rush that you live for. In that case, a cam that packs most of its wallop above 3500 rpm will suit you just fine

Finally, let's say you're Joe or Jane Average Harley rider, with a nice FXR or Sportster you ride to work and on weekends, and take on overnight trips now and then with your sweetie on the back and a T-Bag with a change of clothes for each of you. In this scenario you won't ever need to rev the engine past stock redline, and although you could use more low-end power for those two-up jaunts, most of the time it's just you and the bike and the open road, where you can let the engine wind up between gears. The cam for you is one

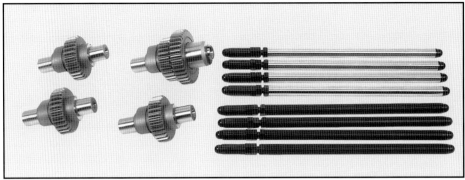

All but two of the more than a dozen Sportster grinds from Andrews can be used with stock pushrods. Adjustable models in chrome-moly or aluminum are available for the other two models, as are high-lift valvesprings and titanium collars. (Andrews Products)

The 510C cam from S&S fits Twin Cam models using the stock chain-drive cam system. It works best in stock or lightly modified engines and increases power across the range, but especially above 3000 rpm. An available camshaft installation kit comes with new gaskets and bearings. (S&S)

that packs its punch between about 2000 and 5000 rpm, with no dramatic bumps in the power curve, just a small but consistent improvement across the board.

Given the average Harley rider's eagerness to shelve stock parts in favor of aftermarket go-fast stuff, it's likely that a camshaft won't be the only high-performance mod on your bike, and if it's the first, it probably won't be the last. It cannot be said often enough that an engine is a system, and the various parts that make up that system need to work in harmony if you're going to get the performance you want. You might think that if you mate a low-end cam

with a set of high-RPM exhaust pipes, you'll get a bike that runs great at both low and high RPM. In fact, what you'll get is a bike that runs poorly at just about every RPM as the two incompatible components hold each other back. When you're looking for the right cam for your bike, you need to take into consideration all the others modifications that cam has to work with, including but not limited to the air cleaner and exhaust system; whether the engine is carbureted or fuel-injected; any cylinder head modifications such as porting, bigger valves, or a higher compression ratio; displacement; and your final-drive gearing.

You sometimes hear an engine referred to as a "mill," but the more appropriate image is that of a pump. The whole idea is to move the air-fuel charge into and out of the engine as quickly as possible. The more you can move through it in a given amount of time the more power the engine will produce. The camshaft orchestrates the entry and exit of the charge. There are lots of subtleties to camshaft design that don't need to be explored here, but two characteristics are worth mentioning.

The first is duration. This is a measurement of the amount of time either valve is open, expressed in terms of crankshaft rotation. In general, the longer the duration, the higher the RPM the engine operates at. Big, heavy touring bikes and bikes often ridden at low RPM work best with cams with shorter duration, while hot-rod Harleys thrive on long-duration cams.

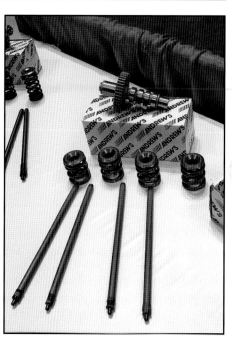

Edelbrock cams have been tested and dyno-matched to work best with Edelbrock cylinder heads and manifolds, and Edelbrock/JE pistons. They're available for stock-displacement and big-bore Evo and Twin Cam Big Twins, and for 1986-and-later Evo Sportsters, to complement Edelbrock's Performer-Plus and Performer RPM heads. (Edelbrock)

is higher in the cylinder before the valve closes and traps the charge. Compression is a function of how much the charge is compressed, and the longer the intake valve remains open as the piston rises, the less compression occurs once the valve finally closes. This is why most bikes with long-duration cams will also need more compression from milled heads, high-compression pistons, or both.

VALVETRAIN COMPONENTS

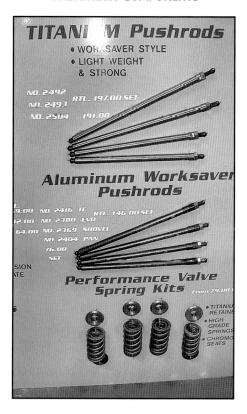

The second characteristic is lift. This is how far the valve opens measured in thousandths of an inch. The more lift a cam produces, the bigger the volume of charge can be sucked into and pushed out of the combustion chamber, which results in more torque. There are mechanical limits to lift, however, such as clearance between the valve and the piston, as well as clearance with the other valve. Too much lift and the valve will hit one or the other or both, with disastrous consequences. High-lift cams also put a lot of stress on valvesprings, which have to compress farther and be stiffer in order to bring the valve back to the valve seat as quickly from a larger distance.

Large-displacement engines work well with long-duration, high-lift cams, because the bigger cylinders need more air-fuel mixture. Such engines will also have modified exhaust and intake systems, too. For stock or mildly modified engines, stick with a cam with mild duration, and complement it with a free-flowing air cleaner and exhaust system.

Another aspect of cam timing that many people overlook is its effect on compression ratio. If you lower an engine's compression ratio, the invariable result is less power. Because long-duration cams leave the intake valve open longer than stock cams, the piston

When you change cams you have to change the pushrods, too. Adjustable pushrods make the job easier by allowing installation without taking off the top end of the cylinder. (Mark Tuttle Jr.)

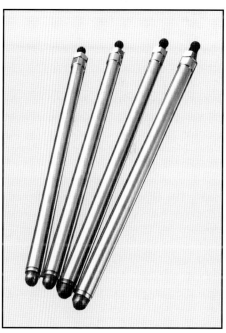

Valvetrain components are the Rodney Dangerfields of high-performance tuning. They aren't sexy, or shiny, but they can help a modified engine make good power. Don't cheap out on them. (Mark Tuttle Jr.)

In any high-performance upgrade you have your star players — the big pistons, the hot cams, the ported heads — and your supporting cast, like pushrods, valves, valvesprings, lifters, and rocker arms. None of these by itself is a major contributor to increasing an engine's power output, but they all perform critical tasks, and those tasks become more important the higher the engine's output becomes.

JIMS titanium pushrods are made of gun-drilled bar stock and can be installed without removing the top end. At 67 grams each, they're lighter than stock, and that means reduced valvetrain mass for quicker acceleration. They're available for most Evo and Twin Cam Big Twins, and Sportsters. (JIMS)

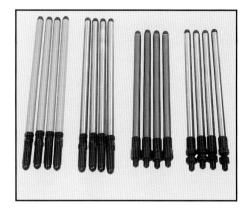

Andrews makes anodized aluminum and chrome-moly steel pushrods for Big Twins and Sportsters. The EZ-install version comes with adjustable tips, so you can install them without removing the rocker boxes or gas tank. (Andrews Products)

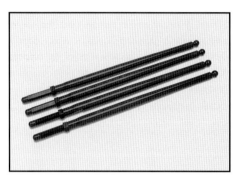

Rivera's Taper-Lite pushrods can be installed in any Big Twin engine without dismantling the top end or removing the lifter blocks, and their special design allows them to be used with high-lift cams and related valvetrain components. The adjusters use 3/8 x 40 threads so every full turn equals .025 inch of adjustment. (Rivera Engineering)

Pushrods

"On a Harley, you don't change the pushrods unless you go to an aftermarket camshaft or an aftermarket valvetrain," says Rick Ulrich, motorcycle products manager at Crane Cams. "The factory Harley pushrod is non-adjustable, but it is the proper length for the setup unless you make some change in the motor. If you change anything, you have to go to an adjustable pushrod, especially if you go to a high-performance camshaft where generally the base-circle diameter is a little bit

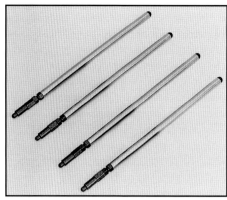

High-lift cams and stronger valve-springs require high-strength pushrods like these adjustable units from Crane. They fit all Twin Cams and are made from 3/8-inch chrome-moly steel tubing with ends that are heat-treated and hardened. (Crane Cams)

smaller so your lifter will drop down into the engine farther. That's why you have to have an adjustable pushrod, to compensate and maintain the proper preload on your lifter."

Crane makes its Big Twin pushrods out of 4130 chrome-moly, heavy-wall tubing, in 3/8- or 7/16-inch diameters. "Our 3/8 one is basically a two-piece adjustable pushrod, but you have to either take the top end of the motor off or take the camshaft out in order to install it. Our 7/16 pushrod is called the Time Saver. It has a sleeve welded on the end of it that's drilled and tapped, and then there's a hardened 9-mm-thread adjuster that's about three inches long. The advantage of having that is you can turn that adjuster all the way inside the pushrod and set the pushrod in the rocker box and swing them over the tappet block, or the lifter cover on a Twin Cam, and adjust it without taking any of the rest of the motor apart. It saves you three or four hours of labor by not having to take off your rocker boxes, break all your gaskets loose, and take off your tappet block," says Ulrich.

Since a pushrod is a reciprocating part, you'd think lightness would be an important feature in a high-performance pushrod. But Ulrich says that's not necessarily the case. "The weight doesn't have as much bearing as you'd

think, because the weight is under the valve, not over it. It makes a lot of difference when you have a lot of weight over the valve in terms of the moment of inertia and the mass." For those who just have to have a light pushrod, Crane makes them out of aluminum. "We use a .065-wall T6061 aircraft-quality aluminum. It's the same basic pushrod as our 3/8 adjustable. It is lighter, but you get a little more flex with it because it's not as rigid as steel. Still, some people believe in them because they grow at almost the same rate as the expansion of the motor because they're a similar material to the cylinders and heads," explains Ulrich.

For a stock motor, however, the stock pushrods are fine, says Ulrich. "The factory pushrods are basically okay for a regular motor. Unless you change something and raise the RPM level or the performance of the motor, there's no real need to change the pushrods."

Valves

Like the stock pushrods, Ulrich says, the stock valves are pretty good pieces. Their only drawback is they're not big enough for ported heads. "Most people don't even bother to go to an aftermarket valve until they want to port the heads or add displacement or compression. What

JIMS Black Tulips are forged, one-piece valves made from a racing-grade stainless-steel alloy. They're heat-treated for better wear resistance, and a special micropolished 45-degree angle just below the lock groove prevents excess stress on the valve. They're available for Evo and Twin Cam Big Twins, and 883-to-1200-cc Sportster conversions. (JIMS)

These swirl-polished stainless steel valves by Head Quarters have hard-chrome stems and are flow-bench designed and CNC-ground for concentricity. They're available for 1984-2003 Evo and Twin Cam Big Twins and 1986-2003 Sportsters. (Drag Specialties)

they'll do then is port or flow the heads, get the intake and exhaust ports flowing the best they can for the amount of lift they want to put into the motor, and then sometimes they'll put a .060-inch bigger intake or exhaust valve in that'll flow a little but better."

Valvesprings

"The main reason to change springs is to make sure you have a sufficient amount of travel when you go to a ported head or a higher-lift cam," says Ulrich. "You want to make sure you have sufficient spring travel, the proper seat pressure — both open and

closed pressure — and the right amount of clearance between the retainer and the guide. You also want to make sure you stay at least .100-inch away from coil-bind."

The material a spring is made of can affect its performance. As an example, Ulrich says, "We have a dual spring made out of H11 tool steel that installs at 1.800-inch at 180 pounds on the seat, and about 480 open. Our standard spring, a chrome-silicon spring that's the same basic OD (outer diameter), ID (inner diameter), and (wire) diameter, at the same installed height, is 155 (pounds) on the seat and probably less than 400 (pounds) open."

Hydraulic Lifters

The difference between a stock lifter and an aftermarket one is subtle, and not always visible just by looking at it. "The stock Harley tappet has a little flat wafer on the bottom of the high-pressure chamber. The flat wafer has a little spring under it and it opens and closes as oil flows in and out of the lifter. It can get bent, or get some dirt under it, or simply rust, and then it doesn't seal properly. Our Evo tappet is a machined steel tappet instead of an investment-cast body. The high-pressure chamber in our lifter has a ball-check valve. The ball itself is self-rotating and self-cleaning so it always has a positive seal. Even at high

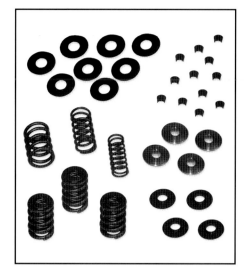

S&S valvespring kits simplify high-lift cam installation by eliminating most of the complex procedures and special tools needed to prepare the head for a high-lift cam. Most Evo street cams will require no headwork, and in some cases these springs can be used in stock rebuild applications. (S&S)

RPM you always get positive sealing, and you always get full valve lift," explains Ulrich.

Rocker Arms

Stock Harley rocker arms have solid tips that generate a slight sideways pushing motion against the tip of the valve that is transmitted to the valve guide. This pushing motion not only promotes

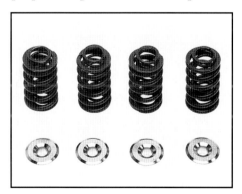

Andrews's high-lift Twin Cam valvesprings are designed for valve lifts up to .560 inch, and require no machining of the head. Titanium upper spring collars provide .050 inch more spring travel than stock collars, and are 50 percent lighter. (Andrews Products)

Crane roller tappets are available for 1999-and-later Twin Cams, and 2000-and-later Sportsters and Buells. They have a hardened ball-type check valve and a self-cleaning valve seat. The lifter body and roller wheel are heat-treated, and the plunger is made to tight tolerances that promote quiet running. (Crane Cams)

This higher-ratio rocker arm from Crane increases the stock 1.60:1 ratio to 1.75:1 for .030-.035-inch more valve lift without changing cams. They're investment-cast from 4140-alloy steel, and then CNC-machined and heat-treated. The fulcrums are bushed and Crane's oil metering system lubricates them and the roller tip. (Crane Cams)

valve-guide wear, it also creates friction. The high-performance solution to the problem is to put a roller tip on the rocker arm. "The roller tip stops the sliding or pushing motion against the side of the valve guide you get with a flat-faced rocker arm, which tries to push the valve one way when it opens and the other way when it closes," says Ulrich. "The roller tip will roll over the stem and the stem moves freely up and down without that pushing motion."

Crane's roller rockers offer another advantage. "We set up our roller tip to

JIMS Twin Cam roller rocker arms are made of 4340 chrome-moly steel and come in two ratios, 1.625:1 (stock) and 1.745:1. Both feature full oiling of the roller tip and 660 bronze bushings to meet Harley-Davidson specs and for the best wear resistance and oil control. (JIMS)

S&S forged steel roller rocker arms are designed to eliminate the failure-prone stress areas found in some other rockers. They're heat-treated and shot-peened and use 3/4-inch-long bronze bushings instead of the more common 1/2-inch ones. A modified lubrication system gives unrestricted roller oiling. (S&S)

get the valve off the seat a little bit faster. But at wide-open valve lift our rocker ratio is basically equal to the factory geometry. If you don't do that you end up with problems when people put on your rockers and they don't know that all of a sudden they have more lift, and they have a problem with valve-to-piston clearance or valve-to-valve clearance. We do sell a rocker that's a higher ratio," says Ulrich, "so if you want to change your rockers and not change your cam, you can gain .030- to 035-inch of lift just by changing the rocker arms from a 1.65 to a 1.75 ratio."

The bottom line on all of these valvetrain parts, says Ulrich, is "Changing the cam from stock is always a great way to increase power. If you're going to change the camshaft you should also change the valvetrain components. This is generally required, and will allow your engine to take advantage of the

increased horsepower that the cam is capable of producing. After the cam, the first thing to consider changing is the rocker arms. Going to roller rockers is a proven way to reduce friction and add power. Changing the lifters is also a good idea. If you install a performance cam it's going to have higher valve lift than stock. This means you also have to replace the valvesprings with performance-designed springs that have the increased pressure and travel your new cam requires. This also requires a change in pushrods. With these modifications you'll be amazed at the gains in horsepower, torque, and RPM your bike will deliver."

GEAR-DRIVE CONVERSIONS FOR TWIN CAMS

As the name implies, the Twin Cam 88 has two camshafts instead of the sin-

High-performance Twin Cam engines put a lot of stress on the stock cam chain and tensioner shoes. Converting to gear-drive cams eliminates the possibility of shoe wear affecting cam timing, or debris from a worn shoe contaminating the engine. (Dain Gingerelli)

This gear-drive cam kit for Twin Cam motors from S&S replaces the stock chain and tensioner, reducing friction and eliminating the timing error that can come from a loose chain. A variety of different cams are available with the kit. (S&S)

gle cam in the earlier Evolution Big Twin motors. The crankshaft drives the rear cam via a chain, and the rear cam turns the front cam, also via a chain. Both chains use spring-loaded slipper-type tensioners to reduce slack and keep the valve timing consistent. It's a neat and inexpensive engineering solution to the problem of driving two camshafts, and it has the added advantage of being fairly quiet, which is important in an air-cooled motor that lacks a water-cooled engine's sound-insulating water jacket.

This set-up has its drawbacks, however, when it comes to high-performance engines, especially those equipped with heavier-than-stock valvesprings. Under these circumstances, the cam drive chains and chain tensioners are subjected to more stress. This results not only in the accelerated wear of the components themselves, but it can alter cam timing by a few degrees, enough to make a noticeable difference in performance. The chain tensioner pads can wear more quickly, dropping potentially destructive particles into the engine oil. The tensioner springs get more of a workout, too, and if they break, all bets are off.

S&S designed a gear-drive system that eliminates all these problems. It consists of two sets of gears, one set to

Branch Flowmetrics' Extreme Velocity Gear Drive cam kit fits 1999 and later Twin Cam engines. The cams increase power from idle to 6000 rpm and have .560-inch lift and 255 degrees of duration. The gear-drive system gives more accurate cam timing. (Branch Flowmetrics)

replace the pinion gear on the end of the crank and the rear cam's drive gear, and the other set pressed onto a pair of S&S cams. The cams are specially ground for the gear-drive kit because they rotate backwards compared to chain-drive cams. This backward rotation provides more operating clearance between the lobes of the two cams, permitting taller lobes and higher lift than you could use with the stock Twin Cam arrangement. Without chains, the tensioners are no longer needed.

Converting a Twin Cam to gear drive results in more consistent cam timing, since the slack of the chains is removed, and more power — S&S says up to four rear-wheel horsepower are lost to sloppy timing induced by the chains and the tensioners. Just about the only downside of the conversion is the possibility of a little more gear noise coming from the cam chest. If it really bothers you, S&S will be happy to sell you oversized or undersized gears to achieve the correct lash for quieter running. S&S also makes gear-drive cams without gears so you can change cams down the road without having to buy new cams gears.

IGNITION SYSTEM

IGNITION COILS

When you're a rider building a high-performance bike in your garage, you can afford to splurge here and there. When you're Harley-Davidson, cranking out more than 200,000 bikes every year, you have to cut the occasional corner to keep costs in line. One place where Harley saved a few bucks is the single-fire coil used on carbureted

Evolution models. "The advantage from the factory's standpoint is simplicity," says Scott Valentine of Dyna Performance Electronics, makers of high-performance ignition systems and parts. "There's only one coil, and there's very little circuitry involved."

In a single-fire system the spark plugs in both cylinders are fired at the same time by a single coil with two outlets. "You have a spark on compression

Going from a single-fire coil like the one that comes stock on Evo Harleys to a dual-fire model gives you better combustion, a smoother idle, and better fuel economy. It also helps prevent "sneezing" through the manifold with high-lift cams. (Jerry Smith)

Spark, at the right time, is essential for good performance. Spark at the wrong time can be one of the most destructive forces inside an engine. (Ron Goodger)

High-compression engines require more voltage to jump the spark-plug gap and light the fire in the combustion chamber. Aftermarket high-voltage coils are hotter than stock. (Jerry Smith)

Installing aftermarket ignition coils is simple and brings with it big improvements in performance on high-performance engines. Stockers don't benefit much unless the stock coil is weak. (Jerry Smith)

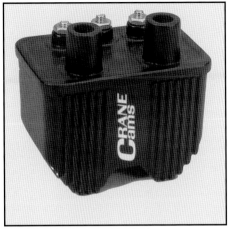

The FireBall Hi-Intensity Single Fire coil fits under the stock coil cover and is both lighter and smaller than the stock coil. It produces a 50 percent longer spark duration and 15 percent greater spark current than stock. It fits 1970-1998 (and some 1999) carbureted Big Twins and 1971-and-later Sportsters (except the XL1200S). (Crane Cams)

ACCEL's Power Pulse coil features greater spark voltage, faster rise time, and longer spark duration than stock coils. It gives better starting, midrange throttle response, and top-end acceleration when used with ACCEL ignition wires, U-groove spark plugs, and an ACCEL ignition. (ACCEL)

in one cylinder and a small, low-voltage waste spark in the cylinder that's on its exhaust stroke," Valentine says. "The physics of it works like this — the majority of the spark goes to the cylinder under compression. If you have 30,000 volts available you'll get maybe 28,000 to the cylinder under compression and a couple of thousand to the cylinder on the exhaust stroke."

Economical, yes, but when you start bolting high-performance parts onto the engine, the drawbacks of the system start to emerge. "If you have a real big cam in the motor with a lot of overlap, you can get a little sneeze out the carb on overlap with a dual-fire system," Valentine warns. The "sneeze" is caused by the waste spark lighting trace amounts of fuel-air mixture suspended in the intake manifold. "Converting to single-fire will eliminate that," he adds.

A single-fire system separates the spark functions of the two cylinders, giving each one its own coil so each cylinder fires independently of the other. Dyna's dual-fire coil is two coils in one compact body, so you can mount it where the smaller stock coil goes. In addition to fitting in the stock location, the Dyna coils put out almost twice the voltage of the stock coil. This allows the spark to ignite more readily under less-than-ideal circumstances, resulting in better performance and fuel economy, and easier starting.

Not all the voltage is needed at any

one time, though, according to Valentine. "Generally a coil only puts out the amount of spark voltage that's required to jump a given plug gap. If it only requires 20,000 volts to jump the gap, that's all the coil will put out. If you have a high-compression engine — blower, turbo, nitrous, anything that raises cylinder pressure — those usually require a higher voltage to jump that gap. Just putting a high-voltage coil on a stock bike doesn't necessarily increase performance. It only comes into play if the stock coil isn't doing the job."

IGNITION MODULES

Other than fuel injection, nothing gave Harley old-timers more fits than the introduction of electronic ignition. But even though electronic ignition is more mysterious than its predecessor, like fuel injection, it has proven itself to be tough, reliable, and extremely adaptable to different tuning requirements. And like just about every other stock part on a Harley, the factory ignition system has limitations in high-performance tuning applications.

Scott Valentine, who handles customer service and tech support at Dyna

Adjustable ignition modules let you tailor the spark curve to accommodate different states of tune, types of riding, and even loads. You can put one on a fairly mild engine and tweak it as you add more high-performance goodies. (Ron Goodger)

Performance Electronics, says the primary drawback of the stock Harley ignition is its lack of adjustability. "When you start making performance modifications to the bike, you start running up against those limitations," he

Different riding situations — two-up on a steep grade in 90-degree weather versus solo touring in the fall — require different ignition advance curves to account for load and temperature. An adjustable ignition module lets you adjust for conditions. (Jerry Smith)

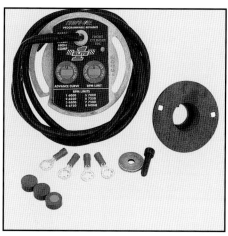

Elite 1 ignition modules from Compu-Fire mount in the nose cone and feature selectable advance curves — eight in either single- or dual-fire operation — and eight RPM limits. Models are available for stock or slightly modified engines, high-compression engines, and race engines. (Compu-Fire)

Crane's HI-4 PowerLink programmable ignition fits 1970-1999 carbureted Big Twins and 1971-and-later Sportsters (except the XL1200S). A PC is used to program one of 10 custom advance curves. The unit allows both single- and dual-spark running, and has an adjustable rev-limiter. (Crane Cams)

The Intelligent Spark Technology module from S&S detects engine knocking and automatically adjusts ignition timing to eliminate it. It even "remembers" the conditions under which knock occurs and automatically adjusts timing to prevent it in future situations by writing a custom ignition map. (S&S)

says. "Particularly on the Evos, the stock ignition limits the stock engine. I've seen several bikes make peak horsepower at 5700 rpm, but the stock rev limiter is set to 5200. Just being able to raise the rev limit would pick up performance. Also, the advance curves in factory modules are not always set up for performance."

Advance, as the term applies to ignition timing, refers to when the spark is ignited in the combustion chamber relative to engine RPM and the degrees

of crankshaft rotation before the point where the piston arrives at top dead center in the cylinder. The higher the engine revs, the more advanced the timing needs to be, because even though the piston is approaching top dead center more quickly at higher RPM, the fuel-air charge burns at a fixed rate. If the charge isn't ignited earlier at higher RPM, the piston will have already moved past the optimum position in the cylinder.

"The whole idea behind ignition timing is to get the peak cylinder pressure to occur at a specific point after top dead center," Valentine says. "That's where you get the best drive on the piston as it's moving down. The burn starts as the piston is coming up on the compression stroke. That spark occurs at 35 degrees before top dead center, let's say, but there's still compression going on. Cylinder pressure is building, but peak cylinder pressure, if everything is right for that combination, is going to occur at some point after top dead center. Some engines might run better at 30 degrees, others at 35. There's no real way to tell which is better without trying it. Engine builders spend hours on the dyno trying to find that optimum setting."

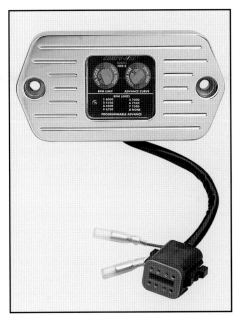

Compu-Fire makes a chrome billet plug-in module that replaces the OE Harley unit. It has selectable advance curves in single- and dual-fire modes, adjustable RPM limits, and dual-range VOES operation. This module is for carbureted bikes only. (Compu-Fire)

They don't spend all that time researching the right advance curve just for fun — it really makes a difference in the way a high-performance engine runs. "Advance is fairly critical, even in the case of a stock engine," Valentine says. "The stock advance curve is there for a variety of reasons — sound requirements, emission requirements — and performance is usually on the bottom of the list. Harleys with high-performance bolt-ons respond very well to changing the curve to something other than the stock curve. If you can advance or retard the timing you can match the curve to whatever modifications have been done to the bike, like different cam profiles, different exhaust systems, different carbs, and definitely when you get into high-compression engines on pump gas. When you try to run pump gas in high-compression engines you want to be able to bring that timing in slower and more retarded to prevent pre-ignition."

Valentine says that the type of gas you use, not just the kind of bolt-on performance parts your engine has, can

dictate a change in ignition timing, too. "High-octane gas has a slower burn rate. If you're running high-octane pump gas in an 11:1 compression engine, you need to retard the timing because it's going to detonate. If you change that fuel to 100 octane, you can probably run conventional timing. If you take that same 11:1 engine and put 116-octane fuel in it, it's going to run like a dog because you just can't advance the timing enough — the fuel burns too slowly for that combination. You have to match the fuel to your combination."

Like most high-performance ignition modules, Dyna Performance modules all come with several advance curves, some as many as eight, to let you pick the curve that works best with your particular combination. The Dyna 2000, for example, is a direct plug-in replacement module for 1991-1998 model Evos and some XLs. For 1990 and earlier models without plug-in modules, Dyna makes the 2000i to replace the hard-wired stock unit. The 2000i fits in the nose cone on the right side of the engine.

Choosing the right advance curve for your engine is easy, says Valentine. "Our general rule of thumb is to run the most aggressive — the most advanced — curve you can that doesn't result in detonation. In the case of the Dyna 2000 you have four curves. Curve one is the most aggressive; curve four is the least aggressive. You run curve number two as a starting point for most basic bolt-on applications. If it works okay, you run curve number one, and if that runs okay, the bike's running well, you're not feeling any degradation of performance, it's not pinging, we say go with that. If you put it on curve one and it starts to rattle a little bit as you roll on the throttle, then you go back to curve number two."

Some engines require special timing curves, so Dyna has a feature it calls a retard mode. "Both the 2000 and 2000i modules offer a kind of selectable retard mode," Valentine says, "using the VOES input circuit for nitrous and turbo applications where under boost or under nitrous operation you want to

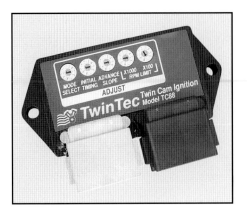

The Daytona Twin Tec module comes with two advance curve families that are adjustable to accommodate both stock and modified engines. Four rotary switches let you dial in timing, single or dual sparks, and RPM limit. (Daytona Twin Tec courtesy Drag Specialties)

retard the timing more than an normal curve would do. Rather than just slowing the advance down, you need to go from say 35 degrees total advance to 25 degrees because of the added cylinder pressure. In the case of a turbo or a blower you'd add a pressure switch into the system that would ground the input wire at a predetermined boost pressure. With a nitrous system you'd just wire it into the nitrous activation circuit and when you activate the nitrous it retards the timing."

SPARK PLUG WIRES

It takes a good, hot spark, delivered at just the right time, to light the fire in a high-performance engine. Like any other system in the engine, every component of the ignition system has to be in top condition so every other component can do its job. Even small, seemingly insignificant components like spark plug wires can have a big effect on performance — and not always in a good way.

Spark plug wires consist of an outer layer of insulation and an inner core. There are three basic core constructions. The first, solid-core wires, use a solid wire of copper or stainless steel to conduct the electricity necessary to make a spark. The upside of solid-core plug wires is they have very low resist-

Spark plug wires and caps can be pulled apart if you're not careful. Each time you yank the plug cap to check the spark plug, grab the cap itself and not the wire, otherwise you could pull the wire out of the cap. (Jerry Smith)

ance, and so deliver the maximum spark energy to the plug. The downside is that in electrical terms, they're very noisy, which is to say they emit a lot of electromagnetic radiation of the sort that causes nearby car radios to sound like they've been tuned to the all-static station. Coincidentally, the static you hear over the radio might be pretty much what the microprocessor in your electronic ignition is hearing, too. In fact, the interference caused by solid-core wires can be strong enough to cause a malfunction in the ignition. On bikes with analog ignition, which is to say contact points, solid-core wires won't be a problem. But if you're building a high-performance motor with points, you already have other problems.

The second type of spark plug wire, called spiral-coil wire, is a bit of a compromise compared to solid-core. Spiral-coil wires use a core of a carbon- or graphite-type material wrapped with a coil of solid wire. They have a little more electrical resistance and a little more noise suppression than solid-core wires.

Ordinary solid-core spark plug wires emit lots of electromagnetic radiation that interferes with radios and televisions. Be nice to your neighbors by using suppressor spark plugs wires like these from ACCEL. (Jerry Smith)

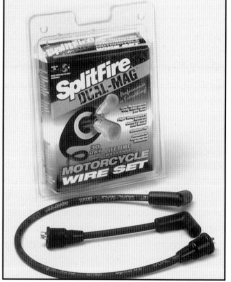

SplitFire's Dual Mag plug-wire sets use 100-percent silicone jacketing and high-heat boots. Two Kevlar fiberglass-reinforced magnetic suppression cores are individually wrapped in a stainless-steel winding. Dielectric grease and installation instructions come with each set. (SplitFire)

The third type of wire is called a carbon-core wire. Think of it as spiral-coil wire without the spiral part, just the carbon core. Carbon-core wires are the noise-suppression champs — neither the microprocessor in your ignition nor the stereo in the car in the next lane will be bothered by them. Of the tree types of spark plug wires, carbon-core has the highest electrical resistance, and cuts into the spark output more than either solid-core or spiral-coil wires. It's interesting to note, however, that most of the current record holders in Funny Bike, Pro Stock, and Pro Modified classes — in fact just about anything short of Top Fuel Harleys — use carbon-core wires, so they'll probably work just fine in a street-ridden high-performance bike. The one downside to carbon-core wires is they tend to wear out a little bit more quickly than other types.

SPARK PLUGS

Big-bore cylinders and CNC-ported heads get all the glamour, and fat header pipes snaking back to chromed mufflers get the attention, but none of it would do anything but look good without spark plugs to light the fire in the combustion chamber. Yet despite the importance of this often-neglected little device, few riders know much about them. And this is one of those instances where what you don't know can hurt you, or more accurately, hurt your bike's performance.

If there's any one property of spark plugs that most riders have at least heard of, it's heat range. A plug's heat range indicates its ability to transfer heat out of the combustion chamber through the cylinder head. A "hot" plug has a long, thin insulator — that ceramic tube around the center electrode — which, because it has a lot of surface area exposed to combustion gases, keeps the temperature of the plug higher overall. This is handy for bikes that are ridden in stop-and-go traffic and other everyday riding situations, and helps prevent fouling.

A "cold" plug's insulator is shorter and thicker. This minimizes the amount of surface area exposed to hot combus-

Dave Perewitz Custom Bagger

Packed with custom and performance touches, this Perewitz Road King just might be the Rolls-Royce of touring bikes. If you have to ask how much it costs, well, you know…
(Dain Gingerelli)

Maybe it's the general graying of the motorcycle-riding population, or just a desire to get more out of a custom bike than the envy of their riding buddies, but these days more Harley riders who want custom bikes are having them built on baggers instead of Softails. And who can blame them, when with a single bike you can look good and go far, and do both in comfort?

Dave Perewitz, longtime custom builder and owner of Cycle Fabrications in Brockton, Massachusetts, sees no reason why good looks and a good ride can't go hand in hand. At least one of those hands better be full of cash, however, because Perewitz's bagger conversion doesn't come cheap — it'll run you more than the

cost of the bike, which you have to supply, and that doesn't include any options you might want him to add to the job list.

This example rolls on Performance Machine wheels and brakes with braided steel brake lines. You get your choice of 16- or 18-inch wheels shod in Avon tires. The Twin Cam engine is punched out to 95 cubic inches and the cylinder heads have been ported by Tom Pirone of TP Engineering. A set of mild performance cams tells a rebuilt carb with a Cycle Fab stretched air cleaner when to inhale. The ignition is by Power Commander, and the pipes — true dual headers with rolled-oval mufflers — are made by Samson. A Baker 6-speed transmission tops off the drivetrain.

tion gases, and transfer heat out of the combustion chamber to the cylinder more quickly and efficiently than a hotter plug. Cold plugs work best in racing or very high-performance applications where you want to keep the combustion chamber cool to prevent detonation, pre-ignition, and heat-related engine failure. For everyday street riding, though, a cold plug is more likely to foul than a hotter one.

You shouldn't make big changes in a spark plug's heat range without a very good reason, such as converting a street

engine to a racing powerplant. If, for example, you switch to a colder plug in order to cure what you perceive as overheating at high RPM, you could be trading slightly cooler running up in the top of the rev range for frequent plug fouling down low. Inversely, putting hotter plugs in an engine prone to plug fouling might only take care of part of the problem. At high RPM, they'll run too hot, and you'll risk engine damage from overheating.

Spark plug manufacturer Denso says of the heat generated by combus-

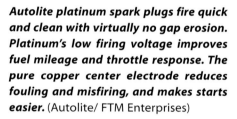

Autolite platinum spark plugs fire quick and clean with virtually no gap erosion. Platinum's low firing voltage improves fuel mileage and throttle response. The pure copper center electrode reduces fouling and misfiring, and makes starts easier. (Autolite/ FTM Enterprises)

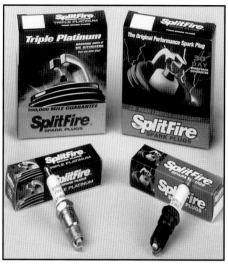

SplitFire Triple Platinum spark plugs combine the SplitFire's split "V" side electrode design with a fine-wire center electrode and three separate points of platinum, more than any other plug, for longer life and a hotter spark. (SplitFire)

Denso Iridium spark plugs use a center electrode made of iridium and rhodium for extremely long life and excellent electrical conductivity. The thin, fine-wire electrode design and tapered, U-groove ground electrode give a hotter spark with less voltage draw. (Denso)

tion, 20 percent is absorbed by the incoming fresh charge of the next intake stroke, 58 percent is absorbed by the walls of the cylinder head, and 20 percent is absorbed by the spark plug's insulator and side walls, with the final 2 percent absorbed by the spark plug wires.

Twenty percent of the heat of combustion is a big chunk, but of course helping to cool the engine isn't all the spark plug does — it plays a pivotal role in getting it hot in the first place. The materials used in the plug make a difference not only in terms of ignition, but longevity, too. Take your average spark plug, which has a center electrode made of copper and a ground electrode made of a nickel composite, as an example.

"Copper is a relatively good conductor of electricity," says Denso's Aaron Block, "but it's not very durable in terms of longevity." The result of this is that heat and electricity act together to erode the copper center electrode

over time. The more the copper erodes, the wider the spark plug gap becomes. If the gap gets too wide the ignition system won't be able to produce a spark strong enough to bridge the gap, and the result is a misfire. "The other thing that also happens, which a lot of people might not be aware of, is the corners of the center electrode start to round off. When it rounds off, it makes the gap larger, and you don't get as crisp a spark," adds Block. And when the flat surface of the center electrode's tips becomes rounded, the plug can't produce as wide a spark, either, so performance suffers.

Over the years, spark plug manufacturers experimented with different materials for the center electrode. Platinum was found to last longer than copper, but there was a drawback. "Platinum isn't a very good conductor of electricity," says Block. "It is, however, a perfect material for the center electrode of a plug for someone who just wants a spark plug to last a long time. We sell lots of platinum plugs, but if you're looking for performance that's not really where you're going to get it." Denso's solution was to use an alloy of iridium and rhodium, an alloy that has excellent conductivity and longevity.

It was also strong enough to allow Denso engineers to make an extremely thin center electrode that would still stand up to the pressures inside the combustion chamber. "Everyone knew the finer the center electrode the better the spark you get — it takes less voltage to fire a smaller electrode — but no one could manufacture a plug that had any kind of longevity and could be used in everyday applications," says Block. "Many of the old-time racers knew that a smaller center electrode was better, so they'd file down the copper ones to a smaller point. In doing this, they got better performance, but the plug only lasted for maybe a race, because the copper wasn't strong enough and would burn away." With the development of the iridium-rhodium alloy, Block says, "we got the durability that's missing in copper, and the attributes of the fine-wire center electrode."

The ground electrode also plays a part in spark plug performance, although it hasn't been necessary to resort to exotic materials for its construction. "Those are pretty much all made out of a nickel composite material. It's pretty standard across the industry," says Block. While the ground electrode is subject to the same erosion as the center electrode, using a more erosion-resistant center electrode material slows the widening of the gap and increases the service life of the plug.

But there are still ways to increase a plug's performance and life by modifying the ground electrode's design. Block explains, "What we did is put a taper and a U-groove on the ground electrode. The point of the taper is it gives the spark only about one or two places to fire to, so you know where that spark is going every time. With a standard flat ground electrode, it quenches the flame front. But the U shape allows the flame to get even larger."

Some plug manufacturers have sought to increase performance by using more than one ground electrode, but Block is skeptical of some of the claims made for these plugs. "They'll last a little bit longer, because the spark has more points to fire to," he says. "But the spark won't fire to two places at once — it's just not possible. You'd have to have two center electrodes and two wires going to it."

Regardless of its design, there are attributes that any plug you put in a high-performance engine should have, the first being consistency. "You want the most consistent plug possible, one that has the least amount of misfires. Inherently every spark plug will misfire under certain conditions, like high compression and lots of cylinder pressure, even our iridium plug," says Block. He offers a rough guideline: "A copper plug will fire 80 percent of the time. A platinum plug with a fine-wire electrode will fire 90 percent of the time. An iridium plug will fire about 97 or 98 percent of the time. It's impossible to say the iridium plug won't misfire, but it will misfire less frequently than anything else."

A tip-off to how well your spark plug resists misfiring can be heard without even touching the throttle. "Listen

---

Doing it by the Book

No matter how good a mechanic you think you are, get a shop manual before you tear into your bike. Even many factory-trained Harley wrenches refer to them while they're working on a bike. (Jerry Smith)

Some high-performance projects go more smoothly than others, but they all seem to have a few things in common. One of them is finding yourself alone in your garage on a Saturday night, with your bike in pieces all over the garage. You're staring at a lone, tiny spring or bolt on the workbench that doesn't seem to belong with anything else, and you ask yourself, "Where does that go?"

The whole idea behind increasing the performance of your Harley is to be able to ride it and enjoy the fruits of your labor, so any unnecessary downtime that can be eliminated from the building process translates into more time on the road. That's why in among the exotic go-fast parts you cart home to bolt onto your bike, you should get a factory shop manual and a parts catalog.

The reason for getting a shop manual

should be obvious. First, you'd know where that spring goes, and second, you'd know how to install it, and check it to see if it's within spec. And just as important, if you'd read the section relevant to the job you're doing before you started, you'd know you needed a special Harley tool to do it, and you'd have already bought it instead of realizing that the dealer doesn't open again until Tuesday morning.

It might not seem like a parts catalog would do you much good — after all, if you want to order a part, the dealer can do that for you, and pick the numbers out of the catalogs there — but parts catalogs aren't just lists of part numbers. To begin with, they're full of very detailed line drawings that you won't find in the shop manual. Those drawings can show you, sometimes in a way far more easy to understand than the shop manual, how things go together, and how many of each part are required.

The listings of part numbers can come in handy, too, when you need to order something. Aside from being able to phone the dealer and tell the parts department the number of the part you need, you can compare part numbers to those of parts you might already have, possibly saving yourself the hassle of ordering it. Many large aftermarket companies list the OE part numbers with their own, too, so you can be sure the high-performance part you're ordering is the correct replacement for the stock part.

And finally if you ever sell your bike, it really sweetens the deal to throw in a shop manual and parts catalog.

---

to the idle to see how smooth it is. If your plug is misfiring up high, it'll probably misfire at idle, too," Block explains. Finally, Block says, a lot of riders who buy expensive high-performance ignition systems to clear up a misfire might only need a better set of properly gapped spark plugs.

STARTERS

Sometimes it's so easy to get caught up in the dazzle of building a high-performance engine that you forget the fundamentals. One very fundamental aspect of high-performance tuning is you have to start the engine first. While

Don't get all the way through a high-compression or big-bore motor project and find yourself unable to crank that bad boy over. Replace the stock starter with a beefier aftermarket unit. (John Hyder)

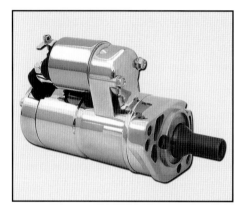

Big-inch or high-compression engines sneer at wimpy stock starter motors, so Compu-Fire made the Gen II to get their attention. They're new, not remanufactured, and feature a 6:1 gear ratio, a six-pole permanent magnet field, and a super-duty clutch. The starter body is polished with chrome end caps. (Compu-Fire)

the stock starter is adequate for most engines with mild performance mods, big-bore, high-compression engines are harder to turn over than stock ones, and place far higher demands on their starter motors than you'd think.

The stock Big Twin starter is rated at 1.2 Kw and is well matched to the stock battery. The bigger the engine, though, or the higher the compression, the more torque the starter motor needs to produce. The limiting factor, however, isn't just the starter itself, but the stock battery, which doesn't have the juice to power any starter rated much higher than the stock one. For example, a 2.0-Kw starter requires 540 amps to

Python performance starter motors from Drag Specialties are new, not remanufactured, and come with a heavy-duty starter clutch and a polished billet end cover. They put out 1.5 kW of power, more than enough to crank over the biggest big-bore engine. They're available in chrome and black. (Drag Specialties)

achieve its rated torque, but the stock battery is limited to 350 amps.

"Hard starting and kick-back on big-inch motors is caused by the starter motor drawing current out of the battery," says Martin Tesh of Compu-Fire. "This condition makes the voltage drop in the battery. When the voltage drops below the minimum needed for the ignition module, the module turns off, interrupting the current flow through the coils. This makes the coil discharge a mis-timed spark and a kick-back."

Aftermarket started motors like the Compu-Fire Gen II have a lower gear ratio from the output shaft to the armature. The lower gear ratio gives the starter more leverage when turning over a high-compression engine through the compression stroke. It also has a permanent magnet field design that allows it to produce its rated torque without straining the battery. Compu-Fire also has a Gen II HT starter that makes a claimed 30 percent more power without any additional battery current draw. It accomplishes this by using powerful neodymium magnets in a new field housing and a beefed-up clutch to handle the increased torque loads.

BATTERIES

If you've been paying any attention to motorcycle batteries over the past few years — and don't feel bad if you haven't, because almost no one ever does anyway — you've noticed that you don't have to pay as much attention to

them as you used to. In the old days, you had to check the electrolyte level regularly, and add distilled water if the level got too low, and watch out for that cloudy white build-up on the plates that more often than not signaled the end of your battery's life. In recent times, however, the old "wet" batteries — like the one that's still in your lawn tractor or that old ATV the kids don't ride any more — have been replaced by maintenance-free batteries that not only don't need water added, but won't let you, because they're sealed after they're activated and can't be opened without letting the electric genie escape.

The chemistry going on inside both types of batteries is pretty much the same. The heart of a battery is pairs of lead plates, one plate charged positively and one negatively. Each pair is worth about 2 volts of output, so a 12-volt battery has six pairs. All the positive plates in the battery are connected to each other, as are all the negative plates. An insulator made of treated paper or fiberglass is placed between the plates to keep them from touching. A battery's cranking power goes up with the number of plates, or the size of the plates.

The plates are immersed in a current-conducting solution of sulfuric acid and water, called electrolyte. A chemical reaction between the lead

The new generation of maintenance-free batteries is tougher than ever, more able to resist the vibration of even solid-mounted Sportster motors. Some are even made extra-strong to turn over pumped, high-compression engines. (Jerry Smith)

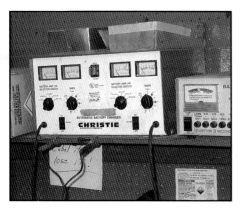

You don't need anything as elaborate as this shop-grade battery charger to keep your bike's battery in good condition, but an occasional boost charge helps it last longer and work better, especially if most of your rides are short. (Jerry Smith)

In the old days your leg provided the starting power and the battery did little besides blinking the taillight and honking the horn. Today's bikes ask far more of batteries, and those batteries ask more of riders. (Jerry Smith)

plates and the sulfuric acid changes the lead to lead sulfate, and at the same time leaves free electrons on the positively charged plates. When you put a load on the battery (when you turn on the ignition switch, for instance) the electrons move from the positively charged plates to the negatively charged ones, and in so doing produce electricity.

This electricity-producing phase is called the discharge cycle. During the discharge cycle, the electrolyte gives up its sulfur to the lead plates in the cell, turning them into lead sulfate. The more sulfur it gives up, the closer to plain old water it becomes. During the charging phase — when your bike's electrical system is putting voltage back into the battery, or when you put it on an external charger — the sulfur returns to the water, turning it back into electrolyte, and changing the plates from lead sulfate back to lead.

The sulfur in the electrolyte isn't used up during this migration from the electrolyte to the plates and back again. But the charge cycle breaks down some of the water in the electrolyte to its components gases, hydrogen and oxygen, which escape through the battery's vent tube. Over time, enough water vapor is lost that the fluid level in the battery goes down visibly. With old wet batteries, this was the time to add more water to bring the electrolyte level back up. In maintenance-free batteries such

as Yuasa's VRLA battery, the hydrogen and oxygen gases react with materials inside the battery to recombine into water. Yuasa calls it "gas recombinant technology," a tongue twister that means you never have to add water to the battery.

Maintenance-free batteries have other advantages, too, especially for Harley riders. Vibration used to be the number one killer of Harley batteries, but the insides of a maintenance-free battery are so tightly packed in that nothing much can move at all. Because they don't need to be checked for electrolyte level, they can be put in places on customs and high-performance bikes that would make them very awkward to service otherwise. They've become so popular, in fact, that Yuasa is making a line of high-performance maintenance-free batteries called, not surprisingly, the High-Performance line. They're a direct response to customer complaints that stock batteries wouldn't crank over big-bore, high-compression engines.

Maintenance-free batteries can't be ignored completely once they're put into service, however. Short rides don't charge them back up enough to prevent a gradual loss of cranking power, and all

The Yuasa High-Performance maintenance-free battery doesn't require periodic electrolyte checks, and only asks for an occasional charge to keep it in top shape. It's designed with more cranking power to start high-compression Harley engines. (Yuasa)

batteries, no matter what type, self-discharge over time. Charge them occasionally, watch out for leaks from external damage to the case, and keep the terminals clean and the battery cable bolts snug. It's a small price to pay for not feeling like a chump when you hit the starter button and your big-inch motor clicks once and refuses to start.

RECIPROCATING PARTS AND LUBRICATION

BIG-BORE STROKER KITS

One of the aims of this book is to show you ways to improve the performance of your Harley-Davidson without sending major components off to be machined, which can involve a lot of expense and annoying downtime. When it comes to most big-bore kits, however, expense and downtime are pretty much unavoidable, because they require you to strip the engine to the

bare cases, and then have the cases bored out to accept larger cylinders. But there are a couple of Harley models whose displacement you can bump fairly cheaply and easily, and only bend the no-machining rule slightly, by boring out the stock cylinders.

There's not enough meat in an Evolution Big Twin cylinder to make enough of a difference to justify the procedure. Evo 883 Sportsters are a different matter. The stock 883 liners are

Stock bore or big bore, S&S makes them all for Evos, Twin Cams, and Sportsters. They gave thicker sections than stock cylinders in critical areas and more fins for better cooling. Stock-bore cylinders are the same height as stock. They can be used with any stroke with the proper pistons. (S&S)

very thick — thick enough, in fact, that they can easily be bored out to accommodate 1200-cc pistons. This, and the fact that there are plenty of unloved and low-priced 883s out there, makes the 883 an attractive starting point for custom or high-performance Sportster projects.

The Twin Cam 88 is another good candidate for a quick displacement fix via a bore job, says Bruce Tessmer of S&S. "When you get into the Twin

The heart of any Harley is its V-twin engine. Anyone can make it loud and shiny. Only a select few can make it fast and reliable. (Ron Goodger)

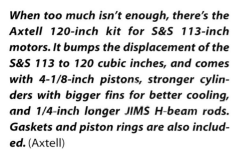

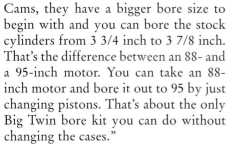

When too much isn't enough, there's the Axtell 120-inch kit for S&S 113-inch motors. It bumps the displacement of the S&S 113 to 120 cubic inches, and comes with 4-1/8-inch pistons, stronger cylinders with bigger fins for better cooling, and 1/4-inch longer JIMS H-beam rods. Gaskets and piston rings are also included. (Axtell)

JIMS makes a wide variety of stroker kits, including this one for Twin Cam FL and Dyna models. Each kit is shipped pre-balanced and is assembled with a hollow, press-fit crank pin. The cast aluminum cylinders come in plain or wrinkle-finish black. (JIMS)

This 89-inch Evolution stroker kit from S&S includes 4-5/8-inch flywheels, assembled and balanced rods, 9.25:1 pistons, and sprocket and pinion shafts. It uses the stock heads, cylinders tappets, pushrods, carb, and manifold. It fits 1984-1999 Evo Big Twins. (Drag Specialties)

Cams, they have a bigger bore size to begin with and you can bore the stock cylinders from 3 3/4 inch to 3 7/8 inch. That's the difference between an 88- and a 95-inch motor. You can take an 88-inch motor and bore it out to 95 by just changing pistons. That's about the only Big Twin bore kit you can do without changing the cases."

As easy and cheap as this is, Tessmer says you get the most bang for your high-performance buck with stock-bore stroker kits. As the name implies, the bore remains stock, while the stroke is increased. This is done by using stock-length rods but different crankshaft flywheels, which locate the crankpin farther away from the center of the flywheel. The farther away it is, the longer the stroke of the engine is. Special pistons are needed with a shorter deck height measured from the wrist pin to the top of the piston, and a shorter skirt to keep the piston from hitting the flywheel or the other piston at bottom dead center. And maybe the best part is the job is a true bolt-in. Just take out the stock crank, replace it with the stroker crank, and replace the stock pistons with the stroker pistons. S&S has a 106-inch stock-bore stroker kit for the Twin Cam that bumps horsepower to about 110.

"The cool thing about stock-bore strokers is the longer stroke gives you more torque," Tessmer says, "and that's what you feel in the seat of your pants when you twist on the throttle. Torque is what people really need to look at when they look at dyno numbers. Horsepower will tell you how fast you can go on the top end. Torque is how fast can accelerate."

Tessmer says engines with an extremely long stroke can suffer in terms of longevity. "If you get up to like a 5-inch stroke, those motors don't last very long because the piston speed is really high, and the rod angle is pretty steep. They're hot rods, there's no two ways about it. You might get 25,000 or 30,000 miles out of one of those." But most of the stock-bore stroker kits on the market, including S&S's own kits, tend to live as long as well-maintained stock motors. "Of course there's the beat-it-up factor to be considered," Tessmer points out, "because people don't buy high-performance engines just to look at them."

Evolution Sportsters present a special challenge when it comes to stroking them. "The problem with Evo Sportsters is they have very short rods, and in order to make a stock-bore stroker kit you have to make a shorter piston. Your rod angle gets way out of whack, and you're making some serious thrust to

the front and rear of the piston," explains Tessmer. For that reason, and because the demand just isn't there, Tessmer says S&S doesn't offer many Sportster kits. "Probably the most popular kit we sell for Evo XLs is the 89-inch big-bore stroker kit. It uses a set of flywheels with a 4 5/16-inch stroke, and a set of 3 5/8-inch cylinders. You can use our heads with that, of course, for even better results. This is the biggest motor we can make in that size that fits in the stock frame. We make a 103-inch kit for XLs, too, with a 5-inch stroke, but it requires that you cut your frame and modify it," says Tessmer.

PISTONS

When you're looking at replacement pistons, either for your stock engine or for that high-performance upgrade you're planning, the first — and in many ways the most important — question that comes up is whether to get cast or forged pistons. Like so many questions of this type, the answer is "It depends."

First you need to know the fundamental difference between cast pistons and forged pistons. Dave Fussner is the research and development manager of Wiseco Piston, Inc., makers of some of the best pistons in the world, not only

They're small, they're round, what's so complicated about making pistons? Well, first off, you need one of these babies to make good ones. The precision machining on a forged piston blank is what turns a slug of metal into a high-performance part. (Wiseco)

Wiseco pistons are forged for long life, maximum strength, and high heat resistance, and then machined to spec. Applications are available for all Harley models, and custom designs are available on special order. (Wiseco)

High-performance tuning moves from the garage to the office cubicle. Computer simulations let piston engineers test new designs in virtual reality, pushing them to failure in the computer so you don't have to do it in your engine. (Wiseco)

for motorcycles but NASCAR, Formula One, and just about any other high-performance application you can think of.

"Cast pistons have some good qualities," he says, "and if that weren't so, there wouldn't be billions of them on the road. Almost every car comes with cast pistons, and the main reason is twofold. First, they're cheap, and second, as long as they're operated in a controlled, low-performance environment, they work very well."

The casting process begins with a mold that molten metal is poured into. The mold can be used over and over, and so you can make a lot of pistons fairly inexpensively. "Another of the advantages of casting is you can cast in a lot of the features if they don't have to be real accurate," Fussner says. "The downside is when you pour the metal in you get a random grain structure." This randomness affects the piston in ways that become critical the more stress it's subjected to.

"Think of a cast piston as being a china dinner plate. If you tried to bend it you'd find it's pretty strong. As long as you didn't exceed the yield of the material, you'd be in good shape. But when you did, it would be a very fine line separating the point where the plate held and where the fracture would occur, and it would probably break into several pieces. The reason is the china dinner plate has very low ductility, which is the ability to distort and return to close to its original shape. It's very strong, right up until it reaches its yield point," Fussner explains. The same goes for cast pistons. "The reality is the cast piston is always offered as a low-price alternative. You will never see a cast piston in any kind of legiti-

mate racing engine. You won't see it in Winston Cup, or at Indy, or in Formula One, because they know it's just not going to work."

Forging eliminates a lot of the problems that cast pistons have, although at the cost of a more complicated manufacturing process. "We start out with an extruded round bar of certified aircraft-grade bar stock and cut it to lengths called pucks. We use a 2000-series alloy and a 4000-series alloy. The 2000-series is the same that we use in all our Winston Cup and Indy car pistons," says Fussner. "It has great heat resistance, and can withstand a lot of sustained heat. On a superspeedway, those guys hardly ever lift the throttle. That's really high heat input."

The pucks are then warmed in an over to a temperature Fussner won't reveal — it's a trade secret — but which it's safe to say leaves them much softer than they'd be at room temperature. Each puck is then placed in a die, and a punch on the end of a rod connecting to a flywheel — much like a connecting rod on a crankshaft — hits it and shapes it into it raw form. "By taking the raw material and shoving into a smaller form," Fussner says, "you're making the material more dense," avoiding the

JIMS Evo Big Twin piston kits are CNC-milled from forged, high-silicon aluminum alloy. They're available in bores sizes from 3 1/2 to 4 1/4 inches, all with common oversizes, and in compression ratios from 9.25:1 to 10:1. They also have pistons for big-bore motors up to 132 cubic inches. (JIMS)

random grain structure that results from the casting process.

Unlike casting, it's much harder to forge a piston close to its finished form. Instead, the forging blank must be machined into its final form. In fact, this is a good thing because you can be a lot more precise with a CNC mill than you can with a mold. "More chips have to fall off of a forged piston to make it, but in the end a forged piston can stand considerably more distortion and return without breaking," says Fussner, "And because forgings are densified, they can be made thinner in sections generally than a cast part. With com-

S&S makes both cast and forged replacement pistons for Evo and Twin Cam Big Twins and Evo Sportsters with stock cylinder heads. They also make pistons to go with their own Sidewinder engines and Super Stock heads. (S&S)

pletely CNC-controlled machining process, you get very high accuracy, whereas you get what you get with a casting. They're not as precise."

The higher your engine revs, the more important this becomes. "As long as you stay below the parameter of fracture of a cast piston, you're okay," Fussner says. "But in a high-performance application like a stroker motor, the longer the stroke the faster the piston has to go in order to make one revolution, covering more distance in the same amount of time. Any piston, cast or forged, must come to an absolute stop at top and bottom dead center. The faster the piston goes, the less inclined it is to stop, and the more force is required to stop it. That's where areas like the pin boss take a lot of load to stop a piston."

Stock Harleys come with cast pistons, but as Fussner points out, "Harleys are all rev-limited, and in terms of horsepower per cubic inch they're pretty docile in stock form. All the cast pistons out there that are designed by the OEM are not on the edge of fracture in their intended application," he says, though he adds, "Harleys are pretty hard on pistons, because of being an older design and because of that long stroke. These guys rev these things pretty good — not compared to a Japanese engine that revs 12,000 rpm, of course, but while a Harley revving 7,000 rpm doesn't sound like much, you have to realize the Harley has twice the stroke of the Japanese bike which makes its piston speed just as high or higher."

By now it's obvious that forged pistons are the way to go in any but a bone-stock engine. "If you have any doubts at all, put a forged piston in there, and you won't have to worry about the thing flying apart," Fussner says. It's only natural, too, that he thinks Wiseco forged pistons are the best you can get, and he makes a compelling argument. "Wiseco is the only aftermarket piston manufacturer in the U.S. that builds all of its own tools and dies to forge the pistons. Every other company buys its forging blanks from someone else, and then machines them

Edelbrock/JE high-compression (10.5:1) pistons are designed to match the unique combustion chamber of Edelbrock cylinder heads. They come with wrist pins made of heat-treated chrome-moly bar stock, top piston rings made of moly-faced ductile iron, and second rings with an anti-blowby twist taper design. (Edelbrock)

in-house. They don't forge or heat-treat their blanks. We take the raw material and forge and heat-treat it ourselves, on tooling built by us. It's all done in-house. Everyone out there except Wiseco is a machining center. They machine their pistons, they don't make the forgings."

Making its own forging blanks and tools gives Wiseco a flexibility others company don't enjoy. "We do a lot of what we call dedicated forging," says Fussner. "A piston will have a dedicated series of tools just to build that part." The opposite of dedicated forging is multi-purpose forging, where you start with one forging and try to make several different pistons out of it. It doesn't always work well. Some pistons end up a bit too thin here or a little too thick there — compromises for the sake of economy. The final machining, too, might actually weaken or compromise the piston in some way that a dedicated forging won't.

"That's not to say we don't have an array of multi-purpose forgings," Fussner says, "but we use them for things like guys with '32 Fords who want to replace the worn-out cast stock pistons."

CRATE MOTORS

Building a high-performance engine takes time, experience, and more than a little bit of money. And there are plenty of opportunities along the way to make some small mistake that will necessitate taking it all apart and doing it again — with luck before you've bolted it into the frame. Fortunately for the ten-thumbed and luckless among us, there are several companies who manufacture complete, ready-to-install engines, called crate motors, in a variety of displacements and performance levels.

The 800-pound gorilla of the crate-motor industry is S&S, which began making bolt-on high-performance parts 45 years ago, and later began turning out complete engines. You can't go to a rally and not see an S&S engine in just about every third or fourth bike. Take a close look at the engines in a lot of V-twin manufacturers' bikes, and you'll

Why do you think they call them crate motors? The price of a complete, assembled engine might seem steep, but compared to doing it yourself, bit-by-bit, it's a screaming bargain, especially since you can get it made to order for the kind of riding you intend to do. (Ron Goodger)

see the S&S logo, too. Bruce Tessmer of S&S says the company will be more than happy to sell you an engine in displacements ranging from stock on up to 113 cubic inches and higher, built to levels of performance suitable for everything from cruising the main to racing for pinks. But first he wants you to think hard about what you need, as opposed to what you think you want, in an engine.

"A lot of guys say they want the most horsepower they can get," Tessmer says. "From us, that's going to be a 124 cubic inches, with 130 horsepower and 140 foot-pounds of torque. But let's say the guy is going touring with his bike. He doesn't really need that kind of motor. Ask yourself you're really bad ass enough to warrant a 124-inch motor. Are you a hardcore performance guy or do you just want to get out on the highway and pass semis without downshifting?"

Cost is a big factor, too. Depending on how much work you want to do to your stock engine, you might get more bang for your buck by carefully choosing a few key components rather than replacing everything. If all you're after is a modest improvement, say for better passing power and more low-end

torque, then a crate motor might not be the best option for you. "Let's say you have a stock TC and by adding a carb and a set of our cams, you can add 20 horsepower — the bang for the buck is way bigger than buying a big-bore motor," Tessmer says. "You can save some money if you don't need all that power, and of course a less-powerful engine is going to last longer."

On the flip side is the guy with a worn-out stock engine, or a hankering for big horsepower numbers, or both. "Our 113-inch engine retails for around $6500. By the time you put a big-bore kit in your stock motor and send your heads out for porting or buy new ones, it's getting iffy, especially if you have early 1990s crankcases and you don't know if you want to bore them — they're bad enough as they are. You've already replaced just about everything in there anyway, so you might as well get a complete engine," says Tessmer.

After you decide what you want, think about who to get it from. Tessmer says there's more to it than just picking a part number out of a catalog. "Look at the company that makes the motor," he says. "You can't manufacture everything perfectly all the time, so things will hap-

Ready-built high-performance engines like this RevTech 100-incher save you the hassle of ordering from a dozen different companies and suffering through half a dozen backorders. Just order one part number, write one check, and start wrenching. (Jerry Smith)

pen. Is the company going to back up its products if something goes wrong?"

Another tip-off is to see whose motor aftermarket bike manufacturers use. The majority buy their engines from S&S, and Tessmer says it's because they can't afford a lot of problems. "Those guys have a lot of exposure as far as warranty and customer satisfaction. If they're selling $60,000 motorcycles and people aren't happy with them, is that going to fly?"

With the exception of a few parts like pistons, valves, and bearings, S&S makes all the parts in its engines. That's important because if you have a problem with an engine built by a company that buys a lot of its parts from an outside supplier, you could find yourself dealing with a third party that doesn't really care about your problems.

S&S

S&S Cycle started out making bolt-on high-performance kits — carbs, flywheels, rods, and stroker kits — for stock engines. "The next thing you do is make more power, and next week some part breaks, so you make a better one," says Bruce Tessmer of S&S. "For example, we were making big-bore kits that were making so much power they'd bend the stock rods. So then we had to start making connecting rods. These days everything we make is over-engineered so it can take a lot of power."

Got some time to kill? Feeling that old do-it-yourself urge? You can get engines from some companies in kit form. This TP Engineering kit includes everything you need, right down to the spark plugs. (TP Engineering)

S&S pretty much pioneered the crate motor industry for motorcycles, and offers a huge selection of displacements, options, and finishes on its assembled, drop-in Evolution Big Twin-style engines. You can also get basic long blocks and add your own top-end parts. (S&S)

Odds are pretty good the next non-Harley-built V-twin you see will have an S&S engine. S&S supplies several well-known "clone-bike" manufacturers with ready-made engines in varying displacements and states of tune. Many backyard builders choose S&S engines, too, for their reliability and great factory support. (Ron Goodger)

Merch 120-inch FLHTC

Hindsight is often 20-20. If you're one of those riders who has looked back after a long and expensive high-performance project only to wish you knew then what you know now, next time you think about building up an engine a piece at a time you might want to consider the crate motor option instead. Buying a turnkey engine assembly that's already brimming to the rocker covers with power not only makes financial sense, it's a great time-saver, too. Choosing a crate motor puts you on the road at the helm of your new high-performance bike a lot sooner than if you built it yourself.

This FHLTC has a 120-cubic-inch Merch and a 6-speed Baker transmission. The 120 Merch motor has square bore and stroke dimensions — 4.25 inches for both — and delivers 100 horsepower and 135 foot-pounds of torque, with a little help from a CompuFire ignition and a Crane Single Fire coil. It can be lugged down to 2,000 rpm in sixth gear, then with a gradual opening of the throttle, motored on up to well over 100 mph with nary a twitch or a shudder.

So let's review — buy a truckload of parts from a dozen different aftermarket manufacturers and spend weekend after weekend trying to make them all work right together, or order one part number, spend Friday and Saturday night bolting it into your frame, and be on the road Sunday morning. It's your call.

As the S&S catalog filled with replacement parts like crankcases, stock-bore cylinders, and cylinder heads that were all stronger than stock, the light bulb went on. "We thought, hey, we could make a motor here," Tessmer says. "Actually, it was always in the back of our minds, but we finally got to the point where we could put motors together."

As you might expect, an engine made entirely of parts that are better than stock performs better, too, "because our heads flow so much better, and it's going to have a little higher compression, and of course our cam and carb combination is all high-performance stuff. Instead of a stock Evo with 50-55 horsepower, ours makes around 80 or more from an 80-inch displacement," says Tessmer.

Mid-USA

The Powerhouse 114 from Mid-USA isn't just another Evo-clone. The 114-cubic-inch motor puts out a claimed 135 horsepower and 130 foot-pounds of torque with an S&S Super G carb and Cycle Shack pipes with the baffles removed, and Mid-USA says it can spin to 7300rpm safely.

If you've got it, flaunt it — and no fair buying just the air cleaner cover. Besides, once you've pulled the wires on a 120-incher, you'll agree it's worth whatever it costs. (Dain Gingerelli)

Big bikes need big engines. Riding a bagger with a 120-inch motor means never having to leave anything at home when you hit the road. (Dain Gingerelli)

S&S complete long blocks for Sportsters come in 91- and 100-inch displacements. Cylinder length is stock so the engine fits in stock frames with little or no modification. Primary components, a charging system, an ignition system, an oil pump, and transmission parts are not included. (S&S)

The Powerhouse 114 lives up to its name with a claimed 135 horsepower on tap. It's built with some of the best parts the aftermarket has to offer, and throws in some unique tricks of its own compared to the competition. (Mid-USA)

Several technical features make the Powerhouse stand out from the crowd of crate motors. The most obvious is the Falicon crankshaft with hardened and tempered forged halves and integrated sprocket and pinion shafts. A 2-inch crankpin is made from billet, then tempered, hardened, and hard-chrome plated before being welded in place. Instead of the traditional knife-and-fork rod arrangement riding on split roller bear-

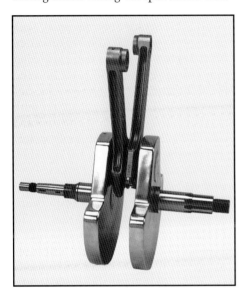

The Powerhouse 114 crankshaft uses rods with split bottom ends that ride on plain bearings. The rod small ends are offset so the rods can clear each other and still place both cylinders in line, just the way traditionalists like them. (Mid-USA)

ings found in Harleys and aftermarket crate motors, the Powerhouse uses a pair of side-by-side Carrillo connecting rods with split big ends that run on automotive-type plain bearings. The H-beam rods have offset wrist pin supports so the cylinders remain in line, retaining the 45-degree V-twin look. The Delkron crankcases that hold all this together have a minimum wall thickness of 1/2 inch.

KB Performance pistons ride in sleeves made by L.A. Sleeve. The cylinders are cast around the sleeves for a no-slip fit. Inside the billet, dual-plug, high-flow cylinder heads are stainless steel valves, JIMS roller rockers, and Rowe cast-iron valve guides.

The Powerhouse 114 will fit Evolution frames and comes with an electronic advance ignition, but without a carburetor or charging system.

Midwest Motorcycle Supply

Midwest Motorcycle Supply's El Bruto engine series comes in displacements ranging from 110 to 127 cubic inches, with a claimed 140 horsepower and 145 foot-pounds of torque available from the 127-incher. Ken Francis, Midwest's vice-president of engineering, says the idea behind these motors was "to deliver at least one horsepower per cubic inch to the rear wheel for less money than anybody else out there. At this point I think we've succeeded."

Midwest uses C355 alloy in its engines, which has a little more copper in it than other commonly used alloys. "We use the same alloy on our cylinder head and cases," says Francis, "which is not the norm for most guys out there. The advantage of this alloy is its stability over heat cycles. It's very stable, and doesn't have much creep." What's creep? "You'll take a casting, bore a bunch of holes in it, and heat-treat it, and it's pretty stable at that point. But when you run it through a few heat cycles, typically some of the casting will move around — creep — ever so slightly," answers Francis.

In addition to its stability, there's another reason C355 is used for the heads and the cases. "When you go and polish a motor, we want you to see a good matching set," says Francis.

Compared to a stock Harley-Davidson Evolution motor, Midwest's motors are improved in almost every way. For example, they have more fins for better cooling, something Harley addressed with the Twin Cam engine. "We also put in valves big enough to make power," adds Francis.

El Bruto engines from Midwest Motorcycle Supply are designed to put out one horsepower per cubic inch, and do it for less money than anyone else. Just about everything on it is an improvement over the Evolution motor it's based on. (Midwest Motorcycle Supply)

The beautiful Carrillo rods in the Powerhouse 114 are made with an H-beam section, and feature split big ends so you can swap them out without taking the crank apart. The plain bearings are easily replaceable, too. The hard-chromed crank pin is welded to the halves after assembly. (Mid-USA)

Francis makes a good case for aftermarket engines: "When you play with all these performance improvements or upgrades on your Evo, when you're done you'll have a marginal life engine, because the components in that engine were designed for a much lower performance engine. Why not go ahead and buy a motor that's built for it?"

Merch Performance

When it comes to discussing his engine's performance, Jim Sekora of Merch Performance is clear. "We don't talk horsepower," he says, "we talk torque, we build torque. We know people ride torque. Our engines are hard on stock clutches. They run 100 foot-pounds of torque just off idle."

Merch makes four engines, a 100-incher that uses Twin Cam barrels and heads, and 120-, 125-, and 131-inchers based on Merch's 4 1/4-inch-bore crankcase. That bore might sound familiar to car buffs, and in fact, as Sekora points out, "That's the same bore as the 454 Chevy or the 426 Dodge." The pistons for these motors are re-machined car pistons, adapted to use a .927-inch wrist pin. There are other automotive parts inside Merch engines, too.

Merch crankcases are reinforced with a patented process that places cylinders of stainless steel called bullets at the base of each cylinder stud, inserting perpendicular to the stud. The bullet is drilled and tapped, and the stud is threaded into it. This "T" structure is just about impossible to pull out, Sekora says.

Merch flywheels are 8.25 inches in diameter, slightly smaller than stock Harley-Davidson flywheels, which allows the crankcases to be thicker and the piston skirts to be longer. While Merch initially duplicated the stock Harley crankcases, they've made about 40 improvements to them since then. Cylinders, heads, rocker covers, flywheels, and connecting rods are made in-house for better quality control.

Most engines are pre-run, turnkey assemblies. Each comes with a Mikuni carb and air cleaner, Andrews cams ground specially for Merch, and a Daytona Twin Tec ignition programmed for the engine. Many Evo gaskets are used for easy rebuilding.

"We have some motors out there with 100,000 miles on them," Sekora says. "They're very streetable, quiet in town and yet powerful on the highway."

TP Engineering

Tom Pirone, owner of TP Engineering, has a simple goal: "I want to be the Ferrari of the industry," he says. He started his company, originally a speed shop, in 1984, with 99 percent of the work geared toward engines. "I started doing a lot of machine shop work for other shops that didn't have the equipment I did. In the early 1990s we started building crate motors out of everyone else's components, and in 1996 I started developing my own product line."

In addition to a desire to emulate Ferrari, Pirone has another goal, one that's perhaps more down-to-earth. "What I strive for at this company is an improved engine." In the years since he started building crate motors, he has done just that, tweaking and refining just about every part in them to work better in high-performance applications.

Take the TP oil pump, for example. Pirone explains, "We have a patented oil pump that completely changes the way the motor oils. It's a three-valve system that delivers oil to the crankshaft at all RPMs, including at idle. A standard Evo oil pump shuts off the supply of oil to the crankshaft at low RPM, and doesn't start oiling again until about 2000 rpm. For 80-inch motors that's fine — there's a lot of splash coming down from the top end —but for performance motors it's not a good thing."

The 100-inch Merch engine uses a modified Twin Cam top end and 3.875-inch pistons. It has a 9.7:1 compression ratio for easy starting and comes pre-run. Available finishes include machine, black, and polished. (Merch Performance)

Merch's 131-inch engine comes in three stages and is .440 inch taller than a stock motor. In its strongest state of tune it puts out a claimed 140 horsepower and a whopping 150 foot-pounds of torque at the rear wheel. (Merch Performance)

TP Engineering makes all the parts that go into its engines, and offers displacements from 100 to 124 cubic inches. They feature a redesigned oil pump and breather system, and use special slipper pistons made for TP by Wiseco. (Drag Specialties)

Other improvements include a 1 5/8-inch pinion shaft. "It supported the flywheel better than what we were using, and we developed — by accident — a much smoother motor. Wiseco helped us develop a slipper-type piston, and right now we're the only one in the industry using it. And I spent a lot of time getting the perfect rod-to-stroke ratio on our big-inch motors, which also has a lot to do with how smooth they are," says Pirone.

Pirone's research allowed him to do away with a perennial trouble spot in the Evo motor. "If you start doing performance mods to an Evo or a Twin Cam, you're going to get oil in your air cleaner. By redesigning the way the air leaves the motor, through our Pro Vent rocker boxes, we've eliminated oil in the air cleaner. It works so well I was able to remove the breather gear and achieve two pounds less crankcase pressure."

Pirone is proud to say that TP Engineering manufactures every part that goes into its engines, even the rods. "We offer motors from 100 to 124 inches, and our 124 will fit into a stock frame. With our 121 and 124 motors, pretty much out of the box you're going to experience 120 foot-pounds of torque at 2200 rpm." Maybe that Ferrari fantasy isn't so wacky after all.

LUBRICATION SYSTEM

Evolution Big Twins

Few aftermarket companies have done as much research into the Evolution Big Twin engine as crate-motor manufacturer TP Engineering. TP's Tom Pirone didn't just want to build a replacement Evo motor, he wanted to build a better one, so he took a look deep inside the stock motor and found ways to improve just about every part, including the oiling system.

Pirone thinks the stock oiling system is just fine — for stock engines. "Otherwise there'd be an awful lot of 80-inch Evo motors burning up, and that's not the case," he says. But when it comes to an Evolution-style engine, whether from Harley or an aftermarket company like TP, with increased performance, Pirone thinks there's room for improvement.

TP Engineering started out building engines from other companies' parts, and look where they are today. Every part in a TP engine is manufactured in-house, even the connecting rods. Try making them at home. (TP Engineering)

TP makes engines from 100 to 124 cubic inches. Based on the Evolution 80-incher, they've been relentlessly improved so every part is better than the original. Why rebuild when you can replace? (TP Engineering)

Stock or lightly modified Evo motors work fine with the stock oil pump. Add horsepower, however, and you add heat, and the more heat the engine puts out, the more oil the crankshaft needs at low RPM. (Jerry Smith)

Oil reaches the top end of an Evolution engine by being pumped first through the hydraulic lifters, then through the pushrods, and finally through the rocker arms. At cruising speed, the oil pump also feeds the crankshaft's roller bearings, aided by splash coming back down from the top end. The problem with the Evolution engine, according to Pirone, lies in the fact that the crankshaft uses roller bearings, instead of the sort of high-pressure plain bearings found in cars and many imported motorcycles. "Because these motors run roller crankshafts and not flat babbited bearings like a car, it's very difficult to hold oil pressure. In any motor, oil will always take the path of least resistance. So if you have two paths for oil to take from a pump, and it can either go upstairs to the cylinder head, or through the crankshaft, most of the oil is going through the crank because it's easier."

Harley's solution was to literally shut off the oil supply to the crankshaft at low engine RPM, and rely on splash from the top end to lubricate the crank. "The stock oil pump uses a long plunger and a spring," says Pirone. "At 1800 rpm and below, when the pump is mov-

ing less oil and making less pressure, the plunger spring is strong enough to overcome the oil pressure, and it closes off the oil going to the bottom end and starts feeding all the oil to the lifters. It's smart, and for an 80-inch motor obviously it works great, because there are a lot of motors out there running with the stock oil pump system and they work fine." But in any high-performance engine, he says, you're going to want positive oiling to the crankshaft at all engine speeds, and that's why the TP Pro Series oil pump was born.

Big Twins don't require a lot of oil pressure, but how much oil gets to the top end is critical. Some aftermarket companies think Twin Cams actually get too much oil to the top end, and restrict the volume to increase cooling. (Lawrence M. Works)

Pirone describes the first time he tested an Evolution engine's oil flow at low RPM. "Harley uses an opening in the end of the pinion shaft and oils the crank by feeding oil straight down the pinion shaft, up through the flywheel, and into the crankpin. So I drilled a hole in the pinion bushing and put on a fitting and a hose to measure the oil going to the crank. When we did our initial test on a stock-style pump we got all our stopwatches ready, and our beaker with the graduations on it, and said, okay, go, and at idle we pulled out the bolt and put it in the beaker — and we got nothing out of it, which I sort of knew would happen. Then we went to 1200, 1500, 1700 rpm, and we still had nothing coming out. I had no idea it was this bad. We actually tried several different pumps and they all did the same thing. At 1800 rpm we got about a teaspoon of oil. At 2200 rpm and up you get great flow. Below that, you have all that oil coming down from upstairs and it's splashing around in there anyway. For an 80-inch motor making 53 horsepower, that's plenty of oil. With 53 horsepower you don't make a lot of heat. For 130 horsepower, though, you're making some heat, and you need to get more oil in there to cool things off. That's where our pump comes into play."

The Pro Series oil pump differs from the stock Evo oil pump in the way it distributes oil throughout the engine. "The stock oil pump at, say, 1500 rpm, is making pretty good oil pressure, but there's nothing going to the crank yet, even though it's providing quite a bit of oil to the lifters. The lifters are a tight fit in the tappet blocks. It's done that way on purpose to maintain oil pressure. The hydraulic lifter itself also has some orifices in it that regulate how much oil will go through it. A hydraulic tappet is not so free-flowing that it'll flow all the oil you can give it. The lifters can't handle all the oil that the oil pump can deliver. If you take the cover off a stock oil pump you'll see there's a channel in the top area that's drilled straight down and loops back into the feed system," says Pirone. "What Harley did was create a channel through which the extra oil can back-feed through the cover of the oil pump and recirculate back to the feed gears — a loop if you will, right in the cover. We started regulating all that oil using three valves, and were able to feed oil to the crank at all times."

Pirone is skeptical of the claims made for high-pressure oils pumps designed to replace the stock Evo pump. He says Evos run just fine with stock oil pressure, and don't really need, or benefit from, higher pressure. "When you're on the highway and on the throttle you'll make 30 pounds of pressure. At idle you're going to make six. The oil-pressure sending unit used from 1973 to 1999 shuts that warning light off at between 4 and 6 pounds. So if you go below 4 pounds your oil light comes on, and when you go above 6 pounds it goes off." The Evolution Big Twin, he concludes, just doesn't need more than stock oil pressure to run right.

Pirone is also quick to point out that not even a high-performance oil pump like his own Pro Series will make a difference on every engine. "Let's say you have an Evo motor with 50,000 miles on it. The bushings are worn out, and the lifters are loose in the tappet blocks because they're aluminum and the lifters are steel, so the lifters wear out the blocks. So now you have this very loose motor, and what you really need is a complete rebuild. Well, you can't bolt our oil pump on there and expect the oil light to stop flickering. You need pressure to shut that light off. Our pump doesn't make any more pres-

Keeping the engine oil cool is an important part of any oil-system upgrade. Don't add a high-volume or high-pressure pump without also installing a high-flow oil filter.
(Jerry Smith)

sure than a stock pump, it just provides the same pressure, and also directs oil to the crankshaft. Anyone who says you can just put a pump on an engine and make more pressure — how do you do that? I don't know. You'd have to change the crankshaft to do it."

There are ways to help the stock oiling system work better, Pirone says, including an oil cooler, depending on where you mount it — airflow is critical. "Obviously an oil cooler is cooled by air, so if you're stuck on Main Street in Daytona that won't work. But once you're rolling down the highway an oil cooler works great. You can drop your oil temperature 20 degrees. But the thing is, you don't want to put it behind the front fender, which is what everybody does." Pirone says to mount the cooler as low as possible for the best airflow, unobstructed by the front fender, or mount it on a crashbar, or vertically on a frame downtube.

No discussion of oil is going to get very far before the topic of synthetic oil comes up. "Here at TP Engineering, the jury is still out on synthetic oil," says Pirone. "We're testing it right now. One

thing we did find with synthetic oils is the detergent capabilities are phenomenal. Let's say you have some debris in your engine, like deposits stuck in the corners of the motor, that regular petroleum-based oil hasn't cleaned out. If you start running synthetic oil, it can dislodge these little bits of debris, and now they're floating around on their way to the oil filter. On a stock Evo motor, the oil is filtered on the return side, so anything that's floating around on the feed side is going to have to make its way all the way through the motor before it can get filtered. The problem with that is it may lodge itself in a roller bearing somewhere and stop that bearing from spinning. If that happens you get a flat spot on that bearing and there goes your crankpin." This is the reason most riders switch to synthetic oil at the first oil change on a new engine, after flushing out the break-in petroleum oil.

Twin Cam Big Twins

The Twin Cam 88 is an update of the Evolution Big Twin and improves on its predecessor in many important ways, including its oiling system. But as

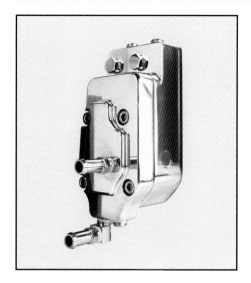

The Pro-Series billet oil pump from TP Engineering provides oil to the crankshaft at all RPM, unlike the stock Evo pump, which shuts off flow below 1900 rpm. It comes assembled or as a kit with a slotted breather gear and oil pump drive gears. (TP Engineering)

with the Evolution motor, pumping up a Twin Cam isn't as easy as just making everything bigger. A case in point is the oiling system. Feuling Motor Company discovered the Twin Cam actually works better with less oil getting to some parts of the motor than is the case in a stock engine.

"The oiling system in a Twin Cam is pretty much the same as in an Evolution," says Feuling's Allon McBee. "Depending on the model, it's a three- or four-quart system with an oil tank. The pressure side of the pump sucks oil out of the tank, pushes it through the filter, and then through different channels inside the motor to lubricate the crankshaft, pump up the lifters, go up through the pushrods and the rocker arms, and lubricate the tips of the valves. Then it drains back into the cam chest cavity. The only oil that enters the crankcase cavity is that which gets fed to the crankshaft. The Twin Cam system also uses what they call piston squirters, which cool the cylinders and the pistons by spraying oil on the bottom of the pistons."

Like the Evo, the Twin Cam is a dry-sump system. "What that means is you want as little oil in the engine as

possible, and you want the oil to move through the engine as quickly as possible. There are two separate cavities in there that need to be scavenged of oil. You also want to maintain the proper volume and pressure to the lifters, maintain proper lubrication in the top end, and not over-lubricate the engine," says McBee.

Over-lubrication doesn't sound like it would be a problem, since many aftermarket oil pumps trumpet their high-volume flow compared to the stock pump. But as McBee points out, more is not necessarily better: "We've found through testing that over-lubricating the engine — having a high volume of oil in the engine, especially in the top end — tends to heat the oil up, and it has trouble draining out. We flooded the top end with oil thinking we could use some of that oil to cool the cylinder head. What actually happened is it puddled so badly up around the valves it was heating them instead of allowing the oil to pass quickly over the components to cool them."

If it's hard to wrap your mind around the notion that less oil is better than more, it's not much easier to understand that Feuling's solution to the problem is a high-volume oil pump. But it becomes clear in light of the fact that Feuling has also designed a special set of lifters to be used in conjunction with the pump. "The lifter itself is actually the metering valve, or the jet, you might say, that determines the volume of oil that goes to the top end," says McBee. "Our lifters don't flow more oil than stock, they flow what we consider to be the proper amount, right around 16 to 18 percent less than stock. There are lifters on the market that flow more oil than ours, and there are lifters that flow less."

The slightly restrictive lifters work in concert with the high-volume Feuling oil pump to keep pressure high, while reducing the volume of oil that reaches the top end, preventing the puddling that can cause overheating. "Our oil pump has 40 percent more volume on the pressure side than

The HVHP (High-Pressure, High-Volume) oil pump from S&S was designed for the company's Super Sidewinder Plus engine, but also fits Harley Evo Big Twins from 1992-1999. The supply and return gears are wider than stock, but the pump itself is no thicker than a stock pump, and uses the stock oil pump drive shaft. (S&S)

stock," says McBee. "If you're running stock lifters, and you go to a high-volume pump like ours, then there's actually more oil that goes through the lifters because the pump is pushing a higher volume, which creates the higher pressure which allows that lifter to flow more oil. When you use our pump with stock lifters, it will over-lubricate the top end. It tends to make the drainback hole get way too full so the oil doesn't drain as well. That's why the combination of our lifters and our pump works the best. When you put our pump and lifters in, what you're seeing at the top end is maybe a 3 to 8 percent less than the stock system."

With a dry-sump design like the one on the Twin Cam, it's important to get oil out of the motor as quickly as possible, too, to reduce parasitic drag on rotating parts. This is one more reason it's important not to over-lubricate an engine. "Because the crankcase cavity is so small around the crankshaft itself, any oil that's left over after it has lubricated the parts becomes a problem for the engine because it's trying to turn the oil like a paddle-wheel down inside the crankcase. The crankshaft itself picks the oil up and does what we call 'roping,' which is the oil trying to rope itself around the crankshaft. That creates friction and that robs horsepower. Any time horsepower is robbed the rider wants to apply more throttle to get the power back up. That in turn creates heat. So if we scavenge all that oil out of there and get the oil off the crankshaft, the friction goes away, the motor frees up, and the temperature comes down."

In order to scavenge the bottom end effectively, the scavenge side of the Feuling oil pump is 60 percent larger than stock. Scavenging is vital to a high-performance engine, McBee says. "In high-performance, high-RPM engines, they hook a pump right to the sump and create a vacuum there to keep the oil off of rotating parts. Also, any oil that's getting aerated by being flung in the air gets pulled to the scavenge pump and gets sucked out. High-performance engines try to shoot for 3-5psi negative pressure in the crankcase."

Some riders don't like oil coolers because they don't complement the style of their bikes. With a little creativity, the cooler can become part of the style. This one is color-matched and uses stainless-braided lines. Cool look, cool engine — win-win. (Jerry Smith)

OIL COOLERS

Many of the things that Harley riders love about their bikes' engines — the long-stroke V-twin design, the narrow 45-degree cylinder angle, the huge air-cooled cylinders — turn out to be drawbacks when you go looking for more performance. The long stroke, for example, pretty much rules out getting your horsepower from RPM, since the engine's reciprocating components won't last long, if at all, when spun to the sort of engine speeds common in some metric cruisers. The narrow cylinder angle is inherently unbalanced, and creates problems that have to be solved by careful balancing of the engine internals, or by rubber-mounting or counterbalancing the engine itself. And air-cooling leaves the engine at the mercy of the unpredictable factors such as the ambient temperature, and whatever accessories might be blocking the flow of cooling air.

While you can sort of get around the stroke problem by increasing the bore, and you can balance rotating parts for

Here's a good reason why most high-performance Harleys can benefit from an oil cooler. Note how little of the cylinder fin area is exposed to cooling air coming in from the front of the bike. Now put the front wheel in the way, and there's even less airflow. (Jerry Smith)

high-RPM running, when you modify an engine to make more horsepower, you only make a bad situation worse with respect to engine cooling. More power equals more heat, and unless you add more cylinder fins or do something else to help your engine reject heat faster,

Jagg's Slimline oil cooler is designed for Harley-Davidsons and has six oil passages with inline turbulators that provide maximum cooling with no additional restrictions in flow. It can be mounted vertically, as shown here, or horizontally. (Jagg)

Mounting the cooler vertically on the frame tube gets it farther out into the air stream where the front wheel and fender aren't in the way. It also lets you use a longer cooler core with more fins and longer cooling tubes. (Jerry Smith)

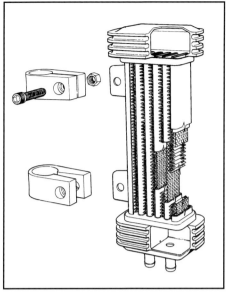

This cutaway of a Jagg cooler shows the cooling tubes, the turbulators inside them, and the cooling fins attached to the outside. This is the Deluxe model cooler with finned end caps that give you a bit more fin surface area. (Jagg)

you're going to run up against an impenetrable wall of friction. What many high-performance tuners do, in fact, is add more cooling fins, but not to the cylinders. Instead they bolt on an oil cooler.

In a liquid-cooled engine, coolant — a mixture of water and antifreeze — transfers the heat of combustion away from hot engine parts and allows it to pass to the outside air by routing it through tubes in the radiator. These tubes have small cooling fins on them, and these fins do exactly what the big ones on your cylinders do. An oil cooler works the same way, except that instead of using coolant to transfer heat away from the engine, it uses engine oil.

Cooler oil means a cooler-running engine, and a cooler-running engine loses less of its available power in frictional losses than one that's running too hot. In addition, cooler oil increases your engine's life. "There's a rule of thumb that says for every 20-degree reduction in oil temperature, you double the life of the oil," says Marvin Beals of oil-cooler manufacturer Jagg/Setrab. "You also double the oil's cooling and lubricating properties. That's going to have a related effect on every internal compo-

The Deluxe oil cooler from Jagg has the same features as the Slimline — six turbulators with minimum flow restrictions, and the ability to be mounted either vertically or horizontally — as well as end caps with polished fins for a stylish look that adds a touch more cooling fin area. (Jagg)

nent the oil comes in contact with."

An oil cooler doesn't just cool hot oil, it keeps it from getting so hot it can't cool down again. "You can't cool the oil as well once it gets hot," Beals says. "It's like a sliding scale. The hotter it gets the fewer BTUs it's rejecting as a result of air-cooling."

As simple as an oil cooler might seem from the outside, there's a lot more going on inside a well-built oil cooler than meets the eye. "There's nothing really high tech about an air-to-oil cooler — it's a heat-exchanger that you blow air across to cool the medium inside. But even though they're not high tech, the engineering behind ours is fairly high tech," says Beals. "We have an internal turbulator that gently stirs the oil as it travels through the tubes, exposing it to more internal surface area

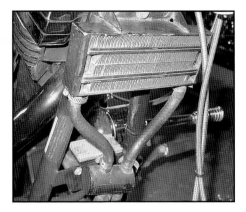

This oil cooler has a thermostat plumbed into the system. When the engine is started, cold oil bypasses the cooler for faster warm-up. When the oil heats up, the thermostat opens and directs it through the cooler. (Jerry Smith)

Lockhart's Model 600 oil cooler is designed for horizontal mounting and features an internal thermostat that routes oil back through the engine until oil temperature reaches 180 degrees, at which time it's directed through the cooler. (Lockhart)

of the tube. What that does is break down the boundary layer effect so you're not getting a hot path of oil through the middle of the tube while the air going around the tube is just cooling the oil on the outside."

Ordinarily a bigger cooler would work better than a smaller one, but Jagg gets around this problem with some more hard-to-spot engineering. "In our cooler we can get more surface area in a smaller package," Beals says. "Heat will dissipate faster from sharp edges than from large flat surfaces, so each one of our air fins has six mini-louvers on each side, so there are a lot of sharp edges for heat to radiate off. And when the air blows across them there's more opportunity for the air that's exchanging the heat to catch the sharp edges and carry the heat away."

The more tubes, the more surface area the oil is exposed to, and the better the cooler works. Some other designs try to get by with fewer tubes, and a turbulator system that holds the oil in the tube longer to more cooling air flows over it. But Beals says the restrictive turbulator has a drawback: "With a Harley, the volume of oil going through the engine is so low that any restriction is an opportunity to starve your motor of oil." Compared to the competing cooler, "we get our cooling by having more surface area, so even though our tubes are less restrictive, there are three more of them, and more opportunity for heat exchange because of the fins and louvers."

A popular oil cooler accessory is a thermostat that diverts the oil back into the engine until it reaches a certain temperature, at which time it's routed through the cooler. Aside from allowing the engine to warm up faster, in theory it helps boil off the water that collects in motor oil. But theory and reality don't always mesh.

"There's an old wives tale out there that says you have to heat oil to 212 degrees to burn out the water," Beals says. "It's my understanding that oil will begin to separate from water naturally. Even at ambient temps it wants to separate. In the hot portions of the motor, as the water separates it hits the hot piston wall, or the piston skirt, or cavities on the motor that are very hot, and eventually, when the motor gets warm enough, the water turns to steam and vents out." As for faster warm-ups, Beals concedes it might be true. "But how much faster is anybody's guess."

Some riders steer clear of oil coolers because they're afraid of overcooling their engine. Beals says that won't happen. "An air-cooled motor is more subject to the ambient temperature than a

The Model 420 oil cooler from Lockhart is designed to mount to the left frame downtube on late-model Sportsters. It comes in black or chrome and includes all the necessary hardware and brackets, as well as rubber reinforced hoses. (Lockhart)

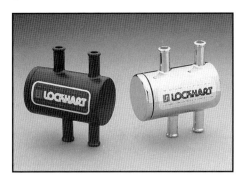

Lockhart's oil cooler thermostat is available separately. It allows you to maintain the oil system at the ideal running temperature of 160-180 degrees. It comes in either black or chrome. (Lockhart)

liquid-cooled motor, but an oil cooler is not going to overcool an air-cooled motor. Every air-cooled motor is a little bit different, but every one will have a minimum threshold temperature it will achieve regardless of the ambient conditions, and regardless of whether there's an oil cooler or not. It might be 155 degrees, or 165 degrees, but it will reach those temperatures."

Finally, it's important to realize that it's not just pumped-up, high-performance engines that can benefit from the installation of an oil cooler. Adding load to a stock motor subjects it to much the

same sort of heat stresses that a high-performance engine experiences. Beals explains, "You get a lot of extra heat when you add performance modifications, but you also get it when you add luggage or a trailer or a sidecar, because it's more weight you have to tow around with your motor."

Switching from a carburetor to fuel injection sometimes increases engine heat, too, not only because FI is typically set lean for emissions reasons, but because "fuel-injection doesn't give the engine that extra little wisp of cool fuel at the end of the acceleration cycle," says Beals. Then there's just the nature of the beast, especially the Twin Cam. "The Twin Cams run hot anyway because they're doing such a good job of squirting oil all over the inside of the motor — like on the bottom of the piston — to cool them down, and that heats the oil up," adds Beals.

SYNTHETIC OILS AND LUBRICANTS

To most riders, the only significant difference between a three-dollar quart of regular mineral-based motor oil and a twelve-dollar quart of synthetic oil is nine dollars. But the difference goes a lot deeper than that, and that nine dollars can buy you not only more performance but more protection for all your other expensive high-performance parts, too.

Mincral-based motor oil starts out as crude oil — that sludge that dead dinosaurs and plant life turned into after millions of years with nothing else to do. Crude oil contains impurities, some of which are removed, and others of which are actually good, and so are left in. Crude also contains useful things like gasoline and natural gas, which are separated out. What's left is the base oil that eventually becomes motor oil.

It doesn't make sense to spend thousands of dollars on a trick motor and then try to save a few bucks on oil. Synthetic oil provides a much higher level of protection for your investment than discount-store motor goo. (Jerry Smith)

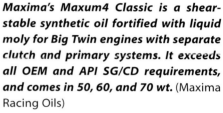

Maxima's Maxum4 Classic is a shear-stable synthetic oil fortified with liquid moly for Big Twin engines with separate clutch and primary systems. It exceeds all OEM and API SG/CD requirements, and comes in 50, 60, and 70 wt. (Maxima Racing Oils)

It's not just high-performance engines that need good oil. Heavy loads put a lot of stress on an engine, upping the heat output and working the oil harder than usual. In the case of this sidecar hauler, more frequent oil changes would be a fine idea, too. (Lawrence M. Works)

No dinosaurs are harmed in the making of synthetic oil. "With synthetic oil, you're starting with a synthesized olefin," says Jason Anagnostis, a research chemist with Bel-Ray. "The main benefit you get from synthetics is that all the molecules within that oil are very similar. This has benefits like higher lubricity, which means you're not getting as much internal friction of the fluid. That's why synthetics are always considered slipperier."

This difference in internal friction is the main difference between mineral-based oils and synthetics. Inside an engine, when two oil-coated parts rub against one another, it takes a certain amount of energy to pull the oil apart. Mineral-based oil is made up of a number of molecules of different sizes and shapes, and they resist being pulled apart. "Imagine you've just trimmed a bush," says Anagnostis, "and you have a pile of branches, and you try to pull one out from the middle of the pile. All the branches are sticking every which way, holding onto each other." But because of the greater homogeneity of the molecules in synthetic oils, they're

Bel-Ray's EXS synthetic has a flash point of over 460 degrees and bonds molecularly to engine surfaces for great start-up protection. It'll last longer than petroleum-based oils, so less frequent oil changes are possible. (Bel-Ray)

easier to pull apart. "It's more like pulling a stick out of the pile, or a piece of spaghetti out of a package," says Anagnostis, "With less friction you have less heat buildup, so the oil can spend more time pulling heat out of components and absorbing heat that's created and transferring heat out of the motor."

This synthetic primary case lube from Maxima is specially designed for Harley-Davidsons. Its advanced additives reduce clutch and fluid drag, and it has superior film strength for greater protection against shock loads. It's designed to use in all 1984-and-later models with wet diaphragm-spring clutches. (Maxima Racing Oils)

Synthetic oil has some other advantages not directly related to high performance but which can make life easier on you and your engine. It clings to internal engine parts better, so you have more protection during that second or two between the time you hit the starter

button and the oil pressure light goes off. And it's more resistant to solidifying at very low temperatures. Some of the impurities in mineral-based oils tend to form crystals at low temperatures.

There's a lot of talk about insanely long oil-change intervals with synthetic oil, but Anagnostis warns not to listen to all of them. "You can generally go longer because synthetic oil has a higher resistance to oxidation, and higher shear stability," he says. "The oil will stay at a certain quality level for longer. But it depends on how you're riding. For someone who's just cruising around, taking it easy, maybe doing a little green-light racing now and then, the oil will last a long time. But if you're beating the crap out of the bike and hauling around everywhere, the oil's not going to last as long."

He has similar cautions about viscosity. "You can go maybe a little bit

For primary lubrication Bel-Ray recommends its Gear Saver. Its ultra-high film strength eliminates metal-to-metal contact and its extreme-pressure additives absorb shock loads ordinary oils can't. (Bel-Ray)

Bel-Ray's Gear Saver Hypoid is designed for heavily loaded transmissions and contains extreme-pressure additives that prevent metal-to-metal contact, reduce heat and wear, and improve shifting. Less friction in the gearbox means more power to the ground. (Bel-Ray)

Red Line's ShockProof gear oil is recommended for heavily loaded transmissions. It contains a unique solid dispersion that cushions gear teeth to help prevent tooth breakage and allows the use of lower viscosities. Available in SuperLight, LightWeight, and Heavy grades. (Red Line)

Red Line says its 20W-50 synthetic works best in engines that run large clearances such as air-cooled engines, or in large-displacement, all-out racing engines that see occasional street use. It provides 25 percent more viscosity in bearings than petroleum 20W-50s. (Red Line)

Spectro's 20W-50 Golden American 4 is a premium petroleum-base engine lubricant with the advantage of the latest advances in synthetic lubricant technology. This part-synthetic blend incorporates the highest shear stable viscosity index improvers to withstand the shearing environment of gear-driven cams and hydraulic valve lifters. (Spectro Oils)

Spectro Golden American Synthetic Gear Oil is formulated from the most advanced synthetic base stocks and additive technology to offer super performance in all Harley-Davidson Big Twin transmissions, including reduced wear, smoother shifting, extended component life, and less noise. (Spectro Oils)

Spectro's Golden American Primary lube is a petroleum-based gear lubricant with advanced synthetic technology. It's the ideal choice for all Big Twin and Sportster chaincases. It's also made especially to provide smooth shifting in Sportster and all Big Twin transmissions. (Spectro Oils)

Racers can get away with using lighter-viscosity oil for short-term horsepower gains, but they get oil changes — and engine rebuilds — often. Stick with the manufacturer's viscosity recommendation for bikes ridden on the street. (Jerry Smith)

lighter, but viscosity recommendations come from the bearing manufacturers, because there's a minimum film that needs to be there. When they recommend a 20W-50, stay pretty close to that recommendation. Thinner oil uses less power, true, but you're also running right up against the oil itself not being able to withstand the load. There are plenty of race bikes and cars running 0W-30 oil — but not for a real long time, and those engines are rebuilt after every race. And if you go too low in viscosity, the oil doesn't have the same capacity to dissipate heat." Heat dissipation is especially important with air-cooled engines, which regularly see operating temperatures much higher than those of water-cooled engines and can be subjected to wild swings in temperature during the course of a single ride.

EXHAUST

EXHAUST SYSTEMS

There are plenty of reason aftermarket exhaust systems are so popular among Harley riders. The most obvious is looks. Because stock exhaust systems have to conform to various legal requirements, there's not a lot of leeway when it comes to styling. There are only so many ways to make a pipe look good and still keep the EPA and DOT happy. But because the aftermarket is under few such constraints, it's free to go wild — and so are you. Whatever shapes, size, style, and configuration of exhaust you're looking for, it's probably out there somewhere, from shorty duals for your Softail to slash-cut mufflers for your Road King to race-proven two-into-ones for your hot-rod Sportster.

This exhaust might not appeal visually to Harley traditionalists, but if you're looking for performance, you'd best forget about form and concentrate on function. A properly designed two-into-one can boost power and save weight compared to two separate mufflers. (Ron Goodger)

And if you don't want to replace your entire exhaust system, you can unbolt your stock mufflers and slide on a set of slip-ons — it's as easy as loosening a few bolts and tightening them back up again. With slip-ons, you can even change your pipes to suit your mood and the type of ride you're planning.

As soon as your fire up your bike with that new exhaust system in place, you'll notice the second reason for shelving your stock pipes — sound. Most aftermarket exhausts for Harleys take that distinctive loping V-twin

Some riders don't care if a bike goes fast as long as it sounds fast. There's no reason your bike can't do both, if you pick the right pipes for your setup. (Dain Gingerelli)

You might think a big, heavy touring bike would benefit from high-RPM power when it comes to passing, but with a bagger's weight, and its high load capacity, you're better off tuning for torque. Many exhausts that work well at high RPM don't work so well at low engine speeds. (Lawrence M. Works)

Two-into-one designs produce more peak power, but over a narrower spread than two-into-twos. For anything less than all-out performance, two-into-twos work better, especially on the street. (Jerry Smith)

cadence and magnify it, some a little, others a lot, but almost all for the better. As with styling, the sound you choose for your bike will probably depend on what you ride. Many bagger riders, for example, prefer a mellow rumble to keep them company as the miles roll along under the wheels, while those on Softails and Dynas might want something with a little more authority to announce their arrival.

Roll down the driveway, turn onto the street, and pin the throttle, and you'll discover the third advantage aftermarket exhausts have compared to stock — performance. After all, the exhaust aftermarket was born because stock pipes prevent the engine from breathing properly. Uncorking the exhaust side can open up a world of new-found power.

But don't make the mistake of equating noise with power. A properly designed performance system must do several things, such as improve scavenging so all the burnt gas is removed from the cylinder before the fresh fuel-air charge is drawn in, and create enough back-pressure to keep that fresh charge from being sucked out the exhaust port along with the burnt gas. This usually means a system with equal-length header pipes to make sure each cylinder is tuned as closely as possible to the other.

Without the basics, it doesn't matter how much noise an exhaust system makes — unless all you want is sound and no power, in which case the pipes of your dreams are no farther away than that hacksaw hanging on the garage wall.

Remember, too, that to get the most out of any high-performance exhaust system, you'll need to open up the intake side with a high-flow air cleaner, and you'll probably have to re-jet the carb or recalibrate the fuel-injection while you're at it. But the rewards will be worth the effort. Big Twins are notoriously restricted engines in stock form, and equally famous for respond-

Staggered duals, shotgun pipes, two-into-two — call them what you will, they remain the most popular style of pipes for Harleys. Built right, they produce the kind of power that's best on the street. (Jerry Smith)

Want to decrease your bike's power and increase your neighbors' anger at the same time? Here's the ticket — straight, unbaffled pipes. They're noisy, slow, and a poor choice for a high-performance bike. (Jerry Smith)

The triumph of form over function. If an exhaust like this starts to seem like even a remotely good idea for your high-performance street bike, get a buddy to whack you on the head with a hammer until you forget why he's doing it. (Ron Goodger)

Here's the exhaust system on a bike that's pretty obviously never ridden any farther than from the trailer to the show grounds — or if it is, it shouldn't be. Performance was not a consideration when these tubes were bent. (Ron Goodger)

ing to minor performance tuning with big performance gains. With an aftermarket exhaust system as the centerpiece of your tuning efforts, you can improve your bike's acceleration, throttle response, and even mileage in a few hours with nothing more than hand tools.

You'll notice the final advantage of aftermarket pipes over stock when you hoist that set of stock pipes you just took off up onto the top shelf in the garage. No, you don't need to go to the gym more often, it's just that stock pipes are heavier than performance pipes. Performance can be improved two ways, by adding horsepower or taking away weight, and aftermarket exhausts do both. The racer's rule of thumb is ten pounds equals one horsepower. Replace your stock pipes with a set that weighs 20 pounds less, and you're two horsepower ahead before you even turn the key on.

CHOOSING THE RIGHT EXHAUST SYSTEM

If there were a single exhaust system that worked best for all bikes, no one would be building anything else but that one system. But not all bikes are alike, which is why there are so many different types and styles and designs of exhaust systems out there. Choosing the right one to go with your high-performance engine takes a lot of work, a little bit of luck, and a plan. Here's what some of the major builders of exhaust systems have to say about choosing the right system.

Bub Enterprises

Denis Manning, owner of Bub Enterprises, likens a rider trying to decide which exhaust system to buy to a guy walking down the street past a row of strip clubs, only in this case the barkers stand outside and promise they have the best, the fastest, and the coolest pipes in town. "If you call anybody in the high-performance market they'll say they're the best and the other guys just don't know what they're doing," he says.

"We have people call and go through the whole list of things they've

The Rinehart exhaust system for FL models is a true dual system, with separate pipes for each cylinder, exiting opposite sides of the bike. They use a multi-step header design for more power throughout the RPM range. Oversized 2-1/4-inch heat shields fight off bluing. The end caps are black-anodized aluminum. (BUB Enterprises)

done to their motorcycle — the cam, the carb, the ignition, the springs and pushrods and valves — and then ask, 'Will your pipes work with that?' First of all, if we tested every variable out there, we wouldn't have built our first pipe yet, because there are so many variables," says Manning, "It's the same for the customer because he's presented with such a vast choice of products. It's sort of like a doctor, who has to figure out if one pill will counteract another. That's the way it is with pipes."

Manning's first word of caution to exhaust buyers is to approach the modification process slowly and methodically. "The method I use is to change one thing at a time, and then evaluate it." This is a hard-learned lesson from his days tuning race bikes, and especially building record-breaking motorcycle-powered Bonneville streamliners. "If you do two or three things at one time, you don't know which is helping you and which isn't," he says.

"I go back to when I was just an enthusiast and try to remember how I used to separate the wheat from the chaff. Some of that hasn't rubbed off," says Manning. For example, he maintains his respect for dynamometers. They can tell you if you're headed in the right direc-

tion, and in some cases represent the quickest way to test a single component. They'll also good at helping you tune an engine for peak horsepower and torque. But Manning also warns that a bike that works great on the dyno doesn't always work as well on the street.

"Sometimes a bike will really jump on the dyno," he says. "When you go from setting to setting, the bike literally lunges into the dyno, or the motor literally moves on the engine stand. You can see it, it's like a thoroughbred race horse straining at the starting gate. Others sort of just go through the motions, and even though the numbers are right, riding them is like kissing your sister. They take a lot longer to accelerate. That's why when we're building a pipe we spend as much time in the real world evaluating it as we do on the dyno."

Manning's real-world testing might seem quaint to some, but his results prove otherwise. "I'm lucky enough to live in the country, and I have a dyno hill. This is what I tell people to do to evaluate what they buy from me. Take rider skill completely out of the equation. Put the bike in high gear. Ride past a marker — in my case it's an oak tree. I pass that oak tree at 35 mph and I turn the throttle wide open and wait for things to happen. About an eighth of a mile later there's a fence and when I get there I look at the speedo. Before I get to the fence I can tell you if it's better or worse. There's stuff that really works

BUB offers Rinehart exhaust systems for Softail models in both flush and staggered designs. A multi-stepped header increases flow while specially designed baffles strike a balance between sound and backpressure. Big 2 1/2-inch heat shields resist bluing, and the end caps are polished black-anodized aluminum. (BUB Enterprises)

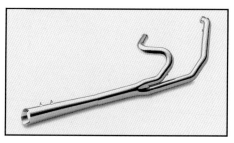

The Kerker 2:1 SuperMeg system from SuperTrapp fits FLH and FLT models from 1985 through 2002. It comes with triple-chrome plating, a full-coverage integrated three-piece heat shield, and a straight-through core design for crisp throttle response. (SuperTrapp)

Python³ pipes from Drag Specialties are designed to bring out the best in modified and stroker engines. The equal-length header pipes are 1-3/4 inches in diameter flowing into 2 1/2-inch muffler bodies. SnakeSkins heat shields are available as an option. (Drag Specialties)

The Samson Powerflow 2-into-1 uses a power chamber design to boost power throughout the rev range. The show-chromed pipes are heli-arc welded and come with heavy-duty steel brackets and hardware. The muffler end is available straight-cut or turn-out versions, and the straight-cut accepts optional billet tips. (Samson)

figures. "You're accelerating a mass, so it gives you this hypothetical horsepower," says Manning, "It doesn't tell you what the real torque and horsepower is. Don't get me wrong, it's scientific. But it's not the '501 dyno, ' — seat of the pants. And results from the 501 dyno are what we're really after. I don't care what the numbers are — I want to know what's it doing for me?" For Manning, the riding experience is more important, and in the end, more satisfying, than the dyno experience.

"In road racing, you can beat guys every time if you can beat them in the low RPM range coming out of a corner. The riding experience isn't top end, it's what it's like coming out of corners, what it's like accelerating from a standstill," says Manning. "That means all the RPM has to be good. You can give away 10 percent on the top and put it on the bottom and just kill other bikes with it. Torque is everything."

Manning says there are other drawbacks to doing only dyno testing. "I had a bike on my dyno and we got to the point where we just couldn't make any more horsepower no matter what we put on that bike. And we came to find out it was the vent on the gas cap. We were dynoing the vent." On the road, he says, he probably would have noticed the stumble caused by fuel starvation and diagnosed it as a clogged vent. But the static, sometimes artificial nature of dyno testing masked this real-world problem. "Also, nobody talks to me about tire slippage on a rear-wheel

on the dyno that if you give it that test it falls flat on its ass."

Manning explains why: "First, in some dynos you can factor things, you can change things around. Second, most of the dynos that people are using now are really accelerometers, they're not dynamometers." The Dynojet dyno, probably the most common type in use today, is such a unit. The bike's rear wheel is placed on a heavy (about 900 pounds) rotating drum. The bike is then run up through a gear. The amount of time it takes to spin the drum from a standstill to redline on the bike's tach is used to calculate power

Bassani's Road Rage two-into-one system fits all Evo models including Softails without floorboards, Sportsters, and Dynas. Each system features a stepped 1-3/4 – 1-7/8-inch pipe configuration, with equal-length head pipes merging into a reverse-cone megaphone. (North County Customs)

Python³ slip-ons come in tapered and slash-cut styles and bolt directly onto the stock header pipes. They come with the same baffle as the complete Python3 systems, and each muffler features an embossed Python3 logo. (Drag Specialties)

dyno. We found one of our dynos would only take 86 horsepower before the rear tire started to slip. The rear tire was the weak link in the chain," he adds.

There's a danger, too, in putting all your faith in the numbers you get from dyno testing, and not paying enough attention to the way the bike actually runs. "I hear over and over from people who say they have to have that last big number," says Manning, "But if you were to take that guy and his bike out on a race track, while he's waiting for the big number, you're already at the finish line. Ultimate performance isn't necessarily the big number on the dyno. And it isn't necessarily the top RPM."

Manning says if you're looking for the best pipe for your street Harley, the first thing you should do is look beyond the kinds of numbers you see in advertisements for exhaust systems and ask yourself several questions. "Does it really work for you, and do you have the horsepower where you want it? Does it work in the real, everyday motorcycling world? That's what I'm always after when I design a pipe."

Practical matters need to be taken into account, too. "The pipe has to go on the bike and it has to look good. It has to look like it belongs on the motorcycle, not like it was adapted from something else. There are a lot of people building pipes for motorcycles who have one chicken, and they try to turn it into an eagle, a hawk, a crow, and every other damn thing," says Manning. "Is this pipe really designed for this bike, or is it really designed for something else?" Finally, Manning adds, "It has to last on the motorcycle. It doesn't matter how good it is if it breaks and falls off."

There are some aspects of exhaust design that aren't apparent from the outside to anyone who doesn't design and build pipes for a living. Manning, however, knows what to look for based on his years of experience and countless hours of testing both in the dyno room

Python³ slip-on mufflers from Drag Specialties use high-velocity shielded muffler cores that offer protection from discoloration while producing better power than stock. The slash-cut end is concave, and the baffles are removable. They're available for 1995-2003 bagger models. (Drag Specialties)

Bassani Slant Cut slip-ons fit all 1995-2001 dresser models and can be ordered with up to 3-inch replaceable baffles. The diameter of the slip-ons is 4 inches, and their show quality chrome finish resists discoloration thanks to the unique baffling system. (North County Customs)

Designed for Road Kings, dressers, and Twin Cam models with engine modifications, Bassani's HO Series slip-on mufflers measure 32 inches long with a 4-inch diameter at the tip. Large-diameter replaceable baffles are designed to work best with high-performance engines. (North County Customs)

Bassani's reverse-cone megaphone slip-ons are made of 16-gauge steel and feature a spiral louvered resonator, show-quality chrome, and billet-aluminum, system-specific end caps. They're available for 1995 and later baggers, and are a direct replacement for factory pieces. They use the OEM mounting hardware. (North County Customs)

and out in the real world. "There are lots of different mathematical equations that tell you how to build a pipe. But none of them, not one of them that I'm aware of, takes into consideration the pipe making a bend. When you go around a bend you lose velocity. For example, when you have a river that goes around a bend a couple of things happen. First of all the velocity comes down. Second, you have different velocities in different parts of the bend. That's why it drops sand on the inside of the bend and hauls ass around the outside of the bend. Air behaves the same way. The straighter the pipe, the least amount of bends, the better."

The next factor is pipe diameter. Many of today's popular exhaust systems feature header pipes upwards of two inches in diameter, and mufflers as big around as telephone poles. While the fat-pipe look obviously succeeds from a styling standpoint, Manning is not so sure it's such a good idea from a performance standpoint. "Again, I'll equate it to a river," he says, "the bigger the river the slower the water, because it has friction, and more surface area. If you look at air or water moving through a pipe, the center of the pipe has a different velocity than the edge of the pipe, and when you turn it around a corner it exacerbates the problem." Bigger pipes aren't nec-

essarily a good thing, because a smaller pipe will give you higher velocities. "Higher velocity is the name of the game," he adds.

Going back to the rider walking down the street lined with exhaust system manufacturers touting the benefits of their systems over those of the other guys, Manning cautions against listening to anyone who talks the talk but hasn't walked the walk. For example, he says, any company whose pipes win at the drag races and dyno shootouts has probably done its homework, and is more than likely to pass that hard-won wisdom on to its customers.

"The guy that's out on the front row of the grid is there because of his accumulation of knowledge," Manning says. "When he's going to design something for the street and he's going to call it 'performance,' he's going to reach into his bag of tricks to do it." Manning's own bag of tricks is deep and full of all kinds of tricks that few others have learned. "Five of the 10 fastest motorcycles in history are mine. Two of them are Harleys. The bike Cal Rayborn rode in 1970, that's my bike, a

268-mph ironhead Sportster. "Am I going to throw all that away when I come up with a new pipe for a street Harley? No, I'm not."

Many riders choose an exhaust system based as much on its style and sound as its performance. Manning says you can take some of the guesswork out of finding a pipe that works as good as it looks. "You can get more peak horsepower and torque out of a two-into-one because it has a better scavenging ability — you have one cylinder creating that lower pressure for the next cylinder to fire into — but it's only in a limited RPM. Two-into-twos don't usually make as much horsepower on top — although there are exceptions — but they make a better curve. There's more horsepower and torque above a particular line than there is with a two-into-one." In short, a two-into-one will typically have a higher but narrower powerband, where a two-into-two's peak will be lower but wider. "If you go strictly by the dyno, and strictly high horsepower, the two-into-one is best. But if you want to go riding, take the two-into-two every time," says Manning. "That's why everybody is running around with two-into-twos."

"One exception to the rule that two-into-ones put out higher peak power than two-into-twos is the Rinehart two-into-two," Manning says. Bub Enterprises builds and markets the Rinehart line through Drag Specialties. "They have three steps in them, and because they're in exactly the right spot, they outperform a two-into-one in most cases, and they have all the benefits of a two-into-two."

Some riders turn to slip-on mufflers to save money, or because their stock mufflers are damaged and need to be replaced. How well they'll work in high-performance applications depends on several factors outside the control of the slip-on manufacturer, including the length and diameter of the header pipes they're being bolted up to. "There are some good slip-ons," Manning says, "and there are some that are just decoration. A lot of times you can put a slip-on on an extra long pipe like an FL, and it doesn't matter what magic you put on

the end, the pipe is too long. The pipe has already compromised everything, because the longer the pipe the lower the velocity. But it'll have a nice sound and a nice look, and be cheaper than the OEM part. There are slip-ons for other things that work quite well."

Vance & Hines

Vance & Hines came to the Harley exhaust aftermarket after establishing its reputation among racers and sport-bike riders. When the company turned its attention to V-twins, it used the same approach to research and development that made it one of the biggest names in racing to create its Harley pipes.

Jim Leonard, one of Vance & Hines' top R&D techs, says, "When you talk about exhaust systems with Harley guys, all your hear about is peak horsepower numbers. I think it's much more important to look at the torque curve on a Harley. You're talking about an engine that you're usually shifting on the street at 2,500 to 3,000 rpm. The area of the torque curve from 1,500 rpm to 3,000 is very important. That's where you're riding most of the time. When we design a new system we want something that's going to perform well in that low-RPM range and still make good numbers on top at wide-open

Vance & Hines Oval slip-on mufflers for FL models replace the stock mufflers and not only flow better, but also produce a mellower sound, thanks to a high-velocity chambered baffle design. They're claimed to be virtually blue-proof, too, and come in a show-quality chrome finish. (Vance & Hines)

throttle. We also want it to fit the bike, we want the heat shields to fit, we want it to last, and we want it to look good and have a nice sound level."

Designing an exhaust system for a Harley is a tougher job than some of Vance & Hines's sportbike customers might suspect. "There's a perception that Harley-Davidson is way behind in terms of engineering, like they were in

Vance & Hines Big Shots pipes come in long and staggered designs. The two-into-two systems feature a power chamber that acts like a crossover to increase horsepower and torque. Also included are full-coverage, full-length heat shields and beautifully finished billet end caps. (Drag Specialties)

Vance & Hines has been making serious go-fast pipes for imported sportbikes for years. When they got into the Harley market, they moved right to the head of the class. This Sportster system looks and sounds great, and really wakes up the motor. (Jerry Smith)

the 1970s," Leonard says. "I don't think it's that way any more. People don't realize how good these bikes really work. The cruiser category is growing tremendously, and there are reasons for it. They're fun to ride, they work well, they look and sound good. Harley does the best job of all."

Vance & Hines combines dyno testing, road-testing, and sound-testing to come up with pipes that work and sound good. Leonard says it's a very involved process, one that makes him glad Harley doesn't change models and come out with new ones as often as the Japanese manufacturers do. "When a new model comes out, first we'll get a motorcycle," he says. "Generally we work with the OEMs and they'll provide us with a bike. We'll remove the stock system and start mocking up a prototype. Then we'll go to the dyno and test it to see where we are and make a few changes." Vance & Hines uses standard SAE testing procedures so they know they're testing each system to identical standards. "Then we'll have meetings, look at the data, take suggestions from several different people, make another iteration of that prototype, and keep working on it until we're all happy with it in terms of both performance and looks," says Leonard, "With regard to the aesthetics, we have one guy who's the bottom line on that, and his name's on the side of the building."

Even so, sometimes styling decisions are made not in-house, but on the street, by the riders who buy exhaust systems. Leonard gives an example of one such occasion. "One of our earliest products was the Pro-Pipe, which is a two-into-one system. It was a great pipe but we found a lot of people just didn't like that look for a Harley." What they wanted, as it turned out, was drag pipes, or at least the look of drag pipes. "As anybody knows, drag pipes work good at wide-open throttle in a limited RPM," says Leonard. "On the street they don't really work that good. They kill the bottom half of the powerband. So we said okay, how can we make drag pipes that perform like a two-into-one but look like drag pipes?" The solution was the Power Chamber, "a crossover that links the two pipes together. It's hidden under the individual heat shields. It's difficult to manufacture, but it's doing quite well. Performance is almost as good as a Pro-Pipe."

Vance & Hines has learned a lot of other things about Harley riders, such as what they do to their bikes and how they do it, in order to get more performance. "The most popular combo for Harleys is to put on an aftermarket air filter and a good exhaust system," Leonard says. "If it's a carbureted bike, they'll get a jet kit of some sort, and if it's fuel-injected we recommend the

Vance & Hines builds a crossover called the Power Chamber into its two-into-two systems. It's hidden under the heat shields and lets the system approximate the performance of a two-into-one pipe while maintaining the look of drag pipes. (Vance & Hines)

Power Commander. Talking about the Power Commander scares some people, but it works so well if it's done correctly that everyone comes away happy." Vance & Hines recommends either a jet kit or a Power Commander with all its exhaust systems. "Otherwise you can get into some rideability issues, like a stumble at a particular throttle opening or RPM. You want to match the exhaust side with an air cleaner, too. That's where you'll really see the big gain. It comes at part throttle probably more dramatically than at wide-open throttle and it really makes riding the bike a much nicer experience," Leonard explains. Part-throttle, as Leonard and many others in the Harley aftermarket will readily point out, is where most riders do most of their riding, and where a Harley is the most fun to ride, too. "You didn't buy your $20,000 Harley to run it wide open up and down the street."

Sometimes a manufacturer has to draw the line between what it can do and what it will do. Leonard says loud pipes are a good example. "There are some people who want pipes as loud as they can get them. We have a known target that we shoot for that we feel is acceptable. We also offer quieter baffles for our most popular products. They take a small amount of top end power off, and a lot of times they boost the bottom end, so it's a trade-off." Which raises the questions of whether a pipe

Straightshots from Vance & Hines come in high/low or dual stagger models, and feature Vance & Hines' full-coverage heat shields that match the 1-3/4-inch header pipes and the 2-1/4-inch mufflers. Seven styles of Hot-Tips muffler ends are available. (Vance & Hines)

JIMS 116-inch Stroker Kit

There's no replacement for displacement, and when JIMS set out to build this pavement-rippling Twin Cam, they went about it with cubic inches and lots of 'em — 116 for those of you who are keeping score.

The 116-inch stroker kit in a Twin Cam 88 motor is good for a claimed 130 horsepower and 145 foot-pounds of torque, more than enough to get you down to the 7-Eleven and back home before your Slurpee melts. The heads on this bike were ported and polished and contain JIMS Black Tulip racing valves, JIMS springs with titanium collars, JIMS seats and guides, JIMS Hydrosolid tappets, and 1.7-ratio rocker arms. The kit pistons give a compression ratio of 10.88:1, and the carb is a 45-mm Mikuni flat-slide.

The bump in displacement means a trip to the machine shop to add some clearance to the crankcases to accommo-date the 4-inch-bore cylinders. A 1.63-inch-deep cut is required to let the taller liners sink in enough to still fit in a stock frame. Down in the wheelhouse, there's a JIMS stroker bottom end, consisting of H-beam rods and stroker flywheels.

The crankshaft's longer stroke has the pistons moving farther down than normal, and this means the stock cooling jets that shoot oil onto the underside of the hot piston can't do their jobs as well. So JIMS shortens them so they sit a half-inch lower.

The bigger engines get the harder they are to start, and that's why JIMS fitted a compression release to the cylinder heads. Thumbing the release lever while you crank the starter takes a lot of the strain off the starter motor, and lets the big motor crank over. As soon as it catches, let go of the release lever and the motor settles down to an idle.

It's a given that there's no replacement for displacement. What often goes unsaid is that there's also no replacement for that feeling you get when you give a 116-inch motor the gas. (Dain Gingerelli)

A bike doesn't have to advertise horsepower as long as it can deliver it when needed. A clean, simple look and a knockout punch set these bikes apart from the crowd. (Dain Gingerelli)

product, you don't want to mess with it because you're probably going to make it perform worse." As a final thought on the loudness question, he says this: "I think in coming years sound is going to be more and more of an issue. If Harley is making 285,000 bikes this year, that's that many more of them out there, so the noise issue is going to grow."

Vance & Hines is always looking to the future, watching for new models on the horizon, and considering how trends in the Harley aftermarket might affect its exhaust product line. One trend that Leonard sees, and which Vance & Hines is already making plans for, is the number of high mileage bikes on the road today, ready for rebuilds. "As guys start to rebuild their engines, they're probably going to look around and see all these big-engine combos out there," he says. "We're going to develop some products specifically targeting these bigger motors. As you go from 88 inches to 107, 114, even 125, the requirements are going to be different, so we're stating to look ahead." Even Harley-Davidson is upping the displacement ante these days. "Now were seeing the 113-inch Screamin' Eagle dresser. People are very happy with that bike," he says. "Harley is very focused on creating new and improved products, and I think you're going to see a lot more models based on that engine combination."

The race-inspired Pro Pipe uses a two-into-one design with a race-type collector. The Pro Pipe HS uses Vance & Hines' full-length heat shield for the headers and collector. Instructions and all brackets are included. (Vance & Hines)

has to be loud in order to make a lot of power. "It doesn't have to be. Our Pro-Pipe has a very nice sound level. It's deep and throaty and it makes really good power and it's very acceptable," answers Leonard. To those riders who yank the baffles out of their exhaust systems, Leonard says, "Most of the time if you do that you'll hurt the performance. If you buy a well-engineered

DRIVELINE

Harleys are virtually alone among modern bikes in using primary chains. Harley tuners have found ways to clean up the system, but not necessarily improve on it. (Ron Goodger)

Doug Morrow, son of Carl Morrow of Carl's Speed Shop, demonstrates one instance in which a beefed-up clutch is more than just an accessory to brag to your buddies about. Do this often enough and you'll become familiar with the clutch rebuilding procedure, too. (Jerry Smith)

CLUTCHES

You're forgiven if you sense something counterintuitive about a device like a clutch, whose function is after all to create friction, being designed to operate in an oil bath. But so-called wet clutches are common not only in Harley-Davidsons, but in just about every other motorcycle made. "The oil's function is to cool the clutch and keep the ambient temperature down," says Mike Taylor of Barnett Tool and Engineering, a company whose name has been synonymous with high-performance clutches for as long as many of today's Harley riders have had driver's licenses. "It also acts as a lubricant for the other primary components." In the process, it lubricates the clutch plates, too, and Taylor says that can be a problems sometimes. "More and more riders are going to synthetic oils, and they're even more slippery, just a little bit more detrimental to clutch action and clutch life. But most of these companies have added friction modifiers to the oil to keep the adverse effects to a minimum."

The clutch is able to function despite the oil coating both the friction and steel plates thanks to clamping pressure and oil grooves in the friction plates. These grooves give the oil somewhere to go when the plates start to squeeze together, in the same way as the grooves in a tire's tread channel water away from the contact patch. In a stock clutch, the clamping pressure is provided by a single diaphragm spring that looks like a big beveled washer.

Given that all of the engine's horsepower and torque has to pass through the clutch on the way to the rear wheel, a high-performance clutch is a must for a high-performance engine. That's when the positive attributes of a stock clutch can become liabilities. "Stock clutches are designed for smoothness, ease of operation, and light lever pressure, and are intended to handle maybe 60 horsepower at the most," Taylor says. "When you start boosting the horsepower, you start to overload the capacity and capabilities of that particular clutch design."

There are several ways to beef up a stock clutch to handle the demands imposed on it by a high-performance engine. "You want to use a little more aggressive friction compound, heavier springs, more surface area, and more plates. In some cases, like in our Scorpion clutch, we just redesign the whole clutch. We double the surface area, and go from the diaphragm spring to coil springs, which are a lot more tunable. It's easy to increase or decrease the amount of spring pressure as needed," Taylor explains.

The friction material that goes on a clutch plate contributes a lot to how much power the clutch can handle. "In the early days everybody used asbestos," Taylor says. "Now that's no

Any time you increase the horsepower and torque of an engine, you need to beef up the primary drive — especially the clutch. Replace the old primary chain while you're at it. (John Hyder)

This cutaway of a Bandit Super Clutch gives you an idea of what's involved in putting genuine high-performance power to the ground, like a steel basket, hefty center bearing, heavy hub, and plates with more than twice the surface area of a stock clutch. (Bandit Machine Works)

longer available. Today there are different materials, like Kevlar, carbon, ceramics, and a lot of organic materials." These materials are similar, in fact, to the material used in many types of disc brake pads, except for being designed to operate in oil. "Those particular materials aren't really friction materials," says Taylor, "they're a component of the compound to protect it from heat. The biggest enemy of clutch plates is heat." The base material that makes up the friction compound is made from a variety of resins, polymers, and silicas. Friction materials can be tailored for specific applications and friction characteristics by mixing the ingredients, in much the same way as the compound that goes into brake pads is mixed.

A Harley clutch consists of a stack of plates, alternating between friction plates and steel plates. One set of plates turns with the clutch basket, which is driven by the engine through the primary chains, and the other turns with the inner hub, which is attached to the transmission. When you're sitting at a stoplight with the clutch lever pulled in, the spring pressure on the plates is relaxed, and the two sets are free to rotate independently of one another. When the light turns green and you start to let out the clutch lever, friction

and spring pressure create drag between the driven plates and the drive plates, causing the bike to roll forward. By the time you've let the clutch out all the way, it's primarily spring pressure that's keeping the plates together.

But even the strongest spring can't make up for worn or incorrect friction materials. "There are characteristics in the friction material that'll cause it to hook up or not hook up," Taylor says. "If you have a bad friction material, you can put a ton of spring pressure on it and it might not work. If your steel plates are highly polished, or warped or bent, anything out of the ordinary, that will detract from the efficiency of the clutch."

The nature of clutches makes them consumable items to some degree, says Taylor. "It's not a part you put in that will last forever, even under the best of circumstances. One question everybody asks me is how long a clutch will last. There's no single answer. So much depends on what they're used for, and how they're used, and the skills of the rider. You hear about some guys getting 80,000 miles out of a set of plates and others getting 800 miles. These might both be Harleys, but one is a full-on weekend racer on a Sportster and the other is a touring guy. There are too many variables that come into play. It's like asking how long tires will last, or brake pads. It just depends on how they're used."

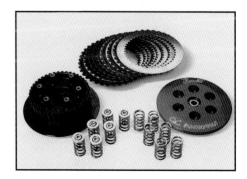

Barnett's Scorpion billet clutch for Sportsters and Big Twins has twice as much friction area as the stock clutch. Steel spacers on the clutch-pack end eliminate wear on the aluminum surfaces, and an extra spring set is included so you can tune the clutch for street riding or racing. (Barnett Performance Products)

Zipper's 120-inch Muscle Kit

If you're one of those riders who thinks you can't tune fuel-injection to work in a high-performance motor, here's proof that you're wrong — Zipper's Performance Products' 120-inch Muscle Kit. The kit starts with 4-1/8-inch-bore cylinders that require case machining for clearance. The cam chest has to be clearanced, too, to accommodate the high-lift cams that come in the kit.

The 4-1/8-inch bore and 4-1/2-inch stroke pencil out to a displacement of 120.3 cubic inches, and a 9.7:1 compression ratio. The kit comes with a larger Thunder Jet fuel-injection throttle body that measures 54 mm — 9 mm larger than stock. A high-flow air cleaner is part of the package, too, as is a programmed, plug-in engine control module. Compression releases come installed in the heads to make starting easier.

Zipper's says this kit works great with a 34-tooth motor sprocket, which changes the final drive ratio to 2.96:1 and lets the bike cruise along at 80 with just under 3,000 rpm showing on the tach. A claimed 124 horsepower and 140 foot-pounds of torque at the rear wheel are on tap, no further away than a twist of the right wrist.

Fuel-injection is no impediment to high performance. This Zipper's 120-incher uses a bored-out throttle body topped by a high-flow air cleaner to feed the beast. (Dain Gingerelli)

Here's what 124 horsepower and 140 ft-lbs of torque can do to a rear tire. You don't necessarily need to be stopped to make it happen, either. (Dain Gingerelli)

This Clutch Spring Conversion kit from Barnett lets you swap out the stock diaphragm spring for coil springs. The coils are more tunable than the diaphragm, and they provide improved clutch action for better shifting and smoother engagement. (Barnett Performance Products)

around here, and racers we've worked with for years who'll test our products. Sometimes we find things that work great on a race bike that don't work well at all on a streetbike."

Barnett makes its own diaphragm springs in replacement and heavy-duty grades, but in their Scorpion high-performance clutch kits they use coil springs for a little bit more flexibility in tuning. The Scorpion uses the stock Harley clutch basket, but replaces the inner hub with one of a smaller diameter so the clutch plates can be larger, resulting in anywhere from two to three times as much surface area. They usually include an extra plate. "Typically, by doing that you can get more performance with less spring pressure so you don't have to have arms like Popeye to pull in the clutch," says Taylor. "And one of the nice things about the coil springs is that if you're running a closed primary, you can change the springs without taking the primary cover off — you can do it through the derby cover. If you want to go to the races you can put in the heavy springs at the track then put the regular ones back in for the ride home."

BELT PRIMARY DRIVE

It's true confessions time. Belt-drive primaries look great, but don't contribute much if any to performance, except on all-out drag bikes, according

Barnett makes two basic high-performance plates. "One is Kevlar-based and one is carbon-based. Right now we're concentrating more on carbon than Kevlar. Carbon is used in brake applications, and one of its advantages is also a disadvantage to some extent. It works more efficiently when it gets hotter. It's used in extreme high-heat applications like racing brakes and Formula One clutches," says Taylor. "Motorcycles, particularly streetbikes, don't get hot enough to the point where you can run just pure carbon, so we use carbon in combination with others compounds

to make it so it will work well cooler, but also a little bit better when it's hot."

Like many companies that manufacture their own products, Barnett has special dynos and other equipment to test clutch friction materials and clutch designs. "Mostly what the dynos do is help you in comparison testing," Taylor says, "finding out how one material works compared to another. But one of the things we learned years ago is that you can do all this theoretical stuff on a machine, but the only way you can tell how it's really going to work is put it on a bike and try it. We have a lot of bikes

This belt-drive primary from Bandit Machine Works fits 1990 and later Softails. The belt is 85 mm (3.35 inches) wide. On high-performance motors producing more than 100 horsepower, an outboard bearing support is recommended. (Bandit Machine Works)

A guard or screen of some kind is a very good idea on an open primary. This is the minimum you'd want. Even better is a mesh screen over the top to keep debris from falling onto the rotating belt. (Jerry Smith)

Primary drive belts require far less attention than the stock chain-drive primary, and they never need lubrication or adjustment. The belt and its accompanying dry clutch are one reason why Harley riders don't wear bell-bottoms. (Ron Goodger)

Risky business. Not only can rocks, dirt, and small animals get lodged between the belt and the pulleys, you can lose a pant cuff or a chunk of your left ankle if you're careless about putting the sidestand down with the engine running. (Jerry Smith)

Belt primaries are tough and strong enough to work well on extremely powerful drag-race motors. Note the crankshaft position sensor forward of the clutch, and the clutch cover — no chewed-up ankles for this racer. (Jerry Smith)

to John Magee, owner of Bandit Clutches, which makes both clutches and belt-drive primary kits. "For streetbikes the big appeal of belt-drive primaries is appearance," he says. "In theory, the belt-drive has less turning resistance so it frees up horsepower to

the rear wheel. In practice we haven't proven that. They're supposed to be lighter, and once up on a time they were. Now, after you put on all the motor plates and outboard bearing supports, you usually wind up with a heavier motorcycle."

Okay, now that that's out of the way, it must also be acknowledged that lots of Harley riders are willing to give

up some performance in return for the relatively hassle-free nature of a belt primary drive. In fact, Magee says, that's how they became popular in the first place. "Way back in the panhead days, when choppers were first born, the chain drives were enclosed in tin primaries, and they leaked. Everywhere you parked you left a puddle because it was a constant-loss oil system. You

Belt Drives Ltd. makes a variety of belt-drive conversions like this bolt-on one for Big Twins. The clutch basket has 12 replaceable cylindrical dogs, and the polished pressure plate uses nine shoulder bolts and springs for a simple installation. The clutch plates are made of Kevlar. (Belt Drives Ltd.)

The all-billet Top Fuel Street Drive from Belt Drives Ltd. is the same one used on 600-horsepower Top Fuel drag bikes. The Kevlar clutch has varying spring pressure to work with any size motor on the market. The kit mounts the oil filter in the motor plate. (Belt Drives Ltd.)

could get away from all that by putting a belt-drive on pans, shovels, and knuckles. You could leave the tin primaries off, and you didn't have to deal with oil, and you didn't have to adjust it. The belt didn't wear out as fast as an improperly lubricated chain. It was a big improvement."

Then Harley-Davidson came along with an improvement of its own. "Starting in the 1960s, Harley started putting the primary inside a closed aluminum case and lubricating it with recirculating oil. You didn't have the wear problem, and it didn't require as much adjustment or leak as badly, so there was less of a need for belt-drive," says Magee.

Magee started out in making clutches, and turned to belt-drives when he found he couldn't get what he wanted from anyone else. "Back in the 1980s, I was drag-racing a shovelhead with a turbocharger on it," he says. "I could get a run and a half out of the best clutch I could buy, so I built my own clutch." He followed pretty much the same path into the primary-drive business. "We started using other people's pulleys and modifying them, and now

we're making our own pulleys just to make them the way we need them to be. The same thing is happening with the primary drive kits."

Today, belt-drive is still the way to go if you hate checking primary oil and adjusting chains, but it has its limitations when used inside a stock primary case. "On a streetbike, inside a closed primary, you can only run a 1 3/4-inch, or sometimes a 2-inch belt," Magee says, "and they're not strong enough to stand up to a big motor, say anything 120 inches or more. Above 120 horsepower, belts are not real long-lived inside a closed primary. They get too hot, and they break a lot."

Big-inch, high-horsepower motors need big belts — the bigger the better. "With a big motor you either run a chain-drive or you run a wide belt, 3-inch-plus belt," says Magee. And the bigger the belt, the more help it needs to keep from tying the engine and transmission in knots. "For high-horsepower motors, you really need an outboard bearing support that supports the engine and transmission pulleys. The transmission shaft is only 25 mm in

diameter and it will bend under high load. The ring gear can gouge into the motor plate when the transmission shaft flexes. A wide belt-drive aggravates that because it's pulling from farther way from the motor," explains Magee. "An outboard bearing support will stop that from happening. If you don't support the engine then the same thing happens to the engine sprocket shaft and you're trying to untrue the flywheels by pulling on them with the belt. Putting a bearing on the outside of the clutch and engine pulleys makes it so the load of the belt is sandwiched between the inner and outer bearings."

Converting the belt-drive involves removing the inner and outer primary case, and all the chain-drive components — the sprockets, adjusting shoe, chain, and clutch shell — and replacing them with a motor plate that bolts on in place of the inner primary, and then putting the clutch, rear pulley, and front pulley and belt on the engine and transmission shafts. "Usually a belt-drive comes with a clutch," Magee says. "Most of the open belt drives do not use the stock clutch. The only one that does is the Karata. Generally guys are putting aftermarket clutches in the belt drives like our Super Clutch or the Barnett Scorpion to get away from the stock Harley clutch parts."

Primary belts are tough, but they're not immortal. "Wide belts generally get replaced because of road-hazard damage rather than wearing out or breaking," Magee says, adding that's why it's important to put a mesh cover or guard of some kind on an open belt primary. "If a rock gets in the drive and gets punched between the belt and the pulley, what it does is poke a hole in the belt and make a mark on the pulley at the same time." Barring accidents like this, primary belts last a long time and never need adjustment. "If the engine and transmission are made to the specified centers for the belt and pulley combo," says Magee, "you never need to adjust the belt, it doesn't stretch."

It's not just rocks you have to watch out for, but with very wide belt primaries you need to be aware of the road itself. "They drag on the ground if you go around a hard left. It's like a 12-over front end, you don't play road-racer with it," says Magee.

TRANSMISSIONS

Stock Harley Big Twin transmissions are pretty tough, even when hooked up to a high-horsepower engine. So why would you want to replace a perfectly good stock transmission with an aftermarket one? You wouldn't, says Paul Platts of JIMS,

Love that rigid-mount Softail but hate the freeway vibration? A 6-speed transmission lets you cruise at lower RPM, out of the bone-shaking range. Some 6-speeds also have lower first gears for better acceleration off the line. (Dain Gingerelli)

unless your stock transmission was worn out or broken, at which time you'd want to upgrade to the hottest trend in gear-shifting since the foot-operated shift pedal. "Right now 6-speeds are hot," he says, "and there's a good reason for it. Once you ride with one there's no going back. Experience it on a solid-mount Softail and it changes your life."

Raise your hand if this sounds like you: "Anyone who rides a Harley knows that when you're in fifth gear on the freeway you always try to shift up." That's where a 6-speed comes in handy, Platts says. Sixth gear is .86:1, a true overdrive. "If you're cruising down the highway at 3500 rpm in fifth gear, when you go to sixth gear it drops about 475-500 rpm." says Platt. JIMS 6-speed

A Baker gear set in a Merch transmission case. Custom builders and motor manufacturers are the biggest customers for 5-speed transmissions. Most riders who replace their transmissions go with 6-speeds. (Buzz Buzzelli/*American Rider* magazine)

The Pro-Series 5-speed transmission from TP Engineering comes with a 356 T-6 aircraft-grade aluminum case that's polished to a high luster. Inside is an Andrews close-ratio gear set that closes the gap between first and second gears. They are available to replace pre-2000 FXST-style transmissions. (Drag Specialties)

It's hard to tell a good transmission from a not-so-good one, even if you're holding the gears in your hands. But if you really want to know what works, just look at what most builders are using. This JIMS 6-speed overdrive is one of the most popular. (Ron Goodger)

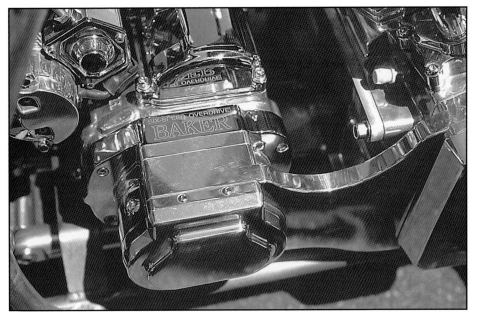

This Baker-designed 6-speed from Andrews fits all 5-speed Sportsters. First gear is slightly taller than stock, and sixth is a 14-percent overdrive. The kit comes with shift drums, a trap door, and a laser-etched "XL6" derby cover. (Andrews Products)

Six-speed overdrive transmissions like this one by Baker can smooth out engine vibration at freeway speeds by dropping engine RPM out of the buzzy range. Cruising mileage is improved, too, so you could argue that buying a 6-speed is helping to save the environment. (Ron Goodger)

Baker makes 6-speed transmissions for Twin Cams in plain, wrinkle-black, or chrome finishes. They use Baker's exclusive Andrews-made Performance Contact Ratio gear design with an extremely high single-tooth bending strength. (Baker Drivetrain)

JIMS 6-speed transmissions use gears that are standard width for strength, with a close-ratio 2.94:1 first gear, second through fifth the same as stock, and a sixth-gear .86:1 overdrive that drops engine speed 500 rpm. Twelve models fit most late-model Big Twins. Pro-cut gears are also available for quicker shifts during heavy acceleration. (JIMS)

toms when the added cost of a 6-speed is an issue. All JIMS transmissions, however, come with back-cut gears and lead-in ramping.

Imagine a pair of transmission gears, one with a number of pegs on it — these are called dogs — and the other with slots, called dog pockets. When the two slide toward each other, the dogs fall into the dog pockets and the gears are engaged, "The mating walls on stock gears might be a perfect right angle," Platts says, "whereas a back-cut gear can have a 4- or 6-degree cut into the face so when it's engaged, it's basically locked." Lead-in ramping assures smoother shifting. "As the dog spins on the face of the other gear, and just before it hits the pocket it's going to drop into, there's a ramp that drops it down, a very slight cut that leads down into the pocket," he adds.

In addition to complete transmissions ready to bolt in, JIMS and most other transmission manufacturers sell what are called builder's kits, or in the JIMS catalog, Super Kits. The Super Kit contains just the gears and shafts needed to upgrade or refurbish a transmission, so if your transmission case is in good shape, you don't have to replace it. Slid-

transmissions also come with a close-ratio first gear for better acceleration off the line. Quicker down low, lazier up top — that's the charm of 6-speeds.

JIMS also make a line of 5-speed transmissions, but most of them go into 4-speed frames as upgrades, or into cus-

The Baker XL6 kit fits Sportsters from 1991 on up and includes shafts and gears, minus the fifth (main drive) gear pair. The gear set comes assembled to the trapdoor. A shift drum, shift forks, and an engraved derby cover are included. (Baker Drivetrain)

ing a Super Kit into your own transmission case is a time-saver, too, since the job can be done with the engine in the frame. "Basically you remove the old trap door with all the gears and slide the new trap door with the gears in there, and you're down the road," Platts says.

Right-Side Drive

Though not strictly a high-performance modification like a blower or a set of exhaust pipes, a right-side-drive transmission can often be the easiest way to equip a bike with a really wide rear tire without messing up its handling.

The one factor that most limits rear-tire size on Big Twins is the primary drive. The wider the rear tire, the farther to the left from the bike's centerline the drive belt must be displaced in order to clear the tire. But the engine's primary drive, including the clutch, hangs off the left side of the bike, outside the drive belt. So the farther left you move the drive belt, the farther left

you need to move the primary case and everything in it.

It's not hard to see that the farther you move the drive belt to the left, the closer the primary comes to becoming a sidestand. As long as you're riding in a straight line, you can probably live with it — in fact many riders who have performed this particular modification claim not to notice any difference in handling on the highway. But the first time you need to turn left you're going to be reminded that your primary drive is stuck way out there by the sound of aluminum grinding on asphalt. Riders who are sensitive to their bikes' handling might also notice the "sidecar effect," similar to what sidecar riders experience when they get on the throttle or hit the brakes. Under extremes of acceleration or deceleration, the large, heavy sidecar lags behind, pulling the bike to the right under acceleration (assuming a right-side-mounted sidecar), and wants to keep on going under braking, pulling the unit to the left

(assuming no sidecar wheel brake). A substantially displaced primary drive can, to a lesser but still noticeable degree, have the same effort on a two-wheeler's handling.

The solution is to move the entire final drive — front and rear pulleys and drive belt — to the right side of the bike, leaving the primary drive in the stock position on the left side of the engine. The final drive still needs to be moved outboard of the bike's centerline in order to clear the tire, but there's no big, heavy primary case to deal with, since it stays put. Of course the stock transmission has to go, but it's replaced by a special right-side-drive transmission with the output shaft on the right instead of the left. You can get them with five or six speeds, in a variety of ratios, for hydraulic or cable actuation. Note, however, that this isn't a modification you make to a stock frame. By the time you're into a rear tire big enough to need a right-side-drive transmission, you're already into a custom frame and swingarm.

Chain Final Drive

When Harley-Davidson began going over to belt final drive in the early 1980s, there were plenty of skeptics. Belts are for holding up pants, they said, not for putting the brute power of a big-inch V-twin to the ground. As it turned out, the skeptics were wrong and Harley was right. Belt drive is clean, quiet, and reliable, and typically lasts longer than even the most fastidiously maintained chains ever did.

Chain drive still has it uses, though, from custom applications where extremely wide tires prohibit the use of a belt for space reasons, to racing, where chain drive allows quick gearing changes to match track conditions. Since it's probably been a long time, if ever, since most Harley riders have seen a chain outside their engine's primary case, it's worthwhile to take a closer look at chains, how they work, and how to keep them in top shape for maximum performance.

A chain and its two sprockets are in reality little more than a long, unbroken

Shifting the drive belt from the left side of a Big Twin to the right allows you to fit one of those enormous rear tires without spacing your primary drive so far to the left that you can use it for a sidestand. (Ron Goodger)

Right-hand drive with a chain instead of a belt lets you keep things a bit narrower, but adds the complication of adjustment and the mess of lubrication. Many well-known custom builders consider drive chains a step backward. (Ron Goodger)

Drive chains aren't gone from Harleys yet, and are unlikely to disappear as long as riders want the ability to change gearing quickly for racing. Chains also stand in for belts in wide-tire applications where the belt is too wide. (Jerry Smith)

Early Evo Sportsters came with chain final drive. If cared for properly, there's no reason to swap it out for a belt. If you decide to go racing, you can change gearing quickly, too. If it ain't broke... (Jerry Smith)

A drive chain and its sprockets are the only finely machined bearing surfaces on a bike that operate without the benefit of seals or a constant oil supply. It's the rider's job to keep them clean and lubricated. (Jerry Smith)

string of machined bearing surfaces. But unlike the rest of the bearing surfaces in a motorcycle, which are sealed away from contaminants and fed a constant supply of oil, the chain and sprockets whirl around out in the open air, exposed to dirt, water, and who knows what else. They get their lubrication from a notoriously unreliable source — the rider — and then promptly fling it off, coating the back half of the bike with sticky, gritty goo.

The history of drive chains can be divided into two parts, before and after O-rings. Keeping non-O-ring chains lubricated didn't just seem like a losing battle — in most cases it really was. Not only will you have a hard time finding a good non-O-ring chain these days, but there's no reason to use one anyway, so we'll skip over the ancient history and get right to the good stuff: O-ring chains.

There are three important bearing surfaces in a drive chain. The first is the roller — that round part that fits on the sprocket between the sprocket's teeth. The roller's surface needs to be lubricated primarily to prevent rust and corrosion, since it doesn't really turn much in the space between the teeth, but rather settles into it and then rises out as the sprocket turns. The roller itself rides on a bushing, and the tiny space between the inner diameter of the roller and the outer diameter of the bushing needs

Cool idea, using the rear brake rotor as a sprocket, right? Maybe not. Think about where the hot chain lube drips when you park the bike. That's right, on the brake rotor. Odds are this bike goes through lots of chains because the rider doesn't lube them enough. (Ron Goodger)

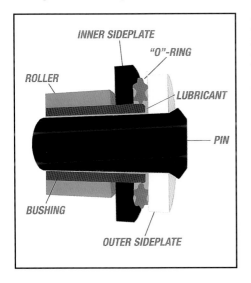

There are three important bearing areas inside a drive chain. They all need to be lubricated to prevent friction and wear. The most heavily loaded is the space between the bushing and the pin. Note how the O-ring seals lubricant into this space. (RK Chain/FTM Enterprises)

lubrication, too. Finally, the bushing rides on a pin, which holds the side plates of the chain together.

Before O-ring chains came along, you had to practically baste the chain in boiling oil to get the lubricant to penetrate all the way down to the space between the bushing and the pin, which is, of course, both the most critical lubrication point and the hardest to reach. No matter how good a job you did, though, as soon as the chain heated up, the hot lube ran out, leaving the chain dry where you needed lubrication most, and leaving most of the lubricant where you didn't want it, namely all over the back of the bike.

Then somebody came up with the idea of sealing a tiny dab of grease into the bushing-pin space with a rubber O-ring. The result was an instant increase in chain longevity, and a decrease in the amount of lubricant needed to keep the

chain healthy and happy. That's not to say O-ring chains don't need to be lubricated at all — they still need a thin coating of lube on the rollers and in the roller-bushing space. But these relatively low-load areas can get by with a lot less lubricant, which means the bike stays cleaner. And the sealed-in grease supply for each pin means less power is lost to friction, and more transferred to the rear wheel.

If any of the chain's bearing surfaces — and that includes the sprockets — are allowed to operate for any length of time without sufficient lubrication, they'll wear each other down, creating excess clearance between the various parts and effectively increasing the length of the chain. In practice, this lengthening manifests itself as a loose chain that has too much slack in it when the bike is at rest, and which causes jerkiness under acceleration as the engine first takes up the slack, then the

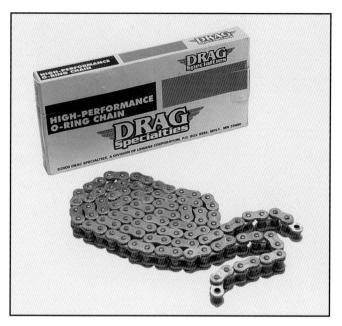

Drag Specialties offers a drive chain in black or chrome with an average tensile strength of 9,100 pounds. It also has four-point pin riveting, solid bushings and rollers, and tough O-rings that seal in factory K3 lubricant and keep out grit. (Drag Specialties)

RK uses an "XW-ring" design on its GXW-series chains. The XW-ring is made of nitrile butadiene and has three contact lips and two convex inner/outer stabilizers, resulting in three separate lubrication pools. This design lets the chain last up to 50 percent longer than conventional O-ring designs. (RK Chain/FTM Enterprises)

chain tightens and pulls on the wheel, and then slackens again. A worn chain is especially obvious on Harley V-twins, with their widely spaced power impulses, and can contribute to the premature wear and early demise of other drivetrain components as the constant jerking motion puts extra stress on them.

The easiest way to lube a chain is with an aerosol chain lube. The typical chain lube consists of an oil or other lubricant — wax, for example, or a thin grease — mixed with a solvent. When it comes out of the can the thin liquid easily penetrates the tiny spaces between the rollers, bushings, and pins, and coats the bearing surfaces with oil. Then the solvent evaporates, leaving the thicker lubricant behind. If you're the kind of rider who lives and dies by the twitch of the dyno's needle, you can get a tiny horsepower advantage by using thin oil or even WD-40 to lubricate your chain instead of thicker, more clingy chain lube. Just be prepared to lube your chain a lot more often.

Because you need to lube the entire run of the chain, it's easiest to get the bike up on a lift or track stand so you can spin the wheel while applying lube to the chain. While you're at it, apply a small amount of lube to the chain's side plates to keep them from rusting, and be sure to squirt some onto the O-rings themselves to keep them from drying out and cracking.

And give the chain lube a head start on its way to the deepest recesses of your chain by riding the bike long enough to get the chain warm before you lubricate it. That way the lube will soak in farther and faster than if you put it on a cold chain.

Just as lubrication is vital to chain's performance, so is cleaning. The sticky lubricant that protects your chain from friction wear also collects dirt and grit. This gritty paste will wear out your chain and sprockets as surely as no lube at all, so it's necessary to clean it all off now and then and start over again. If the chain has a master link and is easily removable, take it off and clean the chain in a pan of non-flammable solvent. Although some O-ring chains come with removable, clip-type master links, those designed for high-performance engines usually come with rivet-type links that are permanently staked on when you install the chain. If that's the case, put the bike up on a stand to get the rear wheel off the ground and clean it with a soft-bristled brush. Be extra careful when cleaning the surfaces of the O-rings not to nick or cut them.

Don't forget to clean the sprocket teeth while you're cleaning the chain, and check them for wear. The teeth should be symmetrical, and none should be bent or broken off. If a sprocket shows any signs of advanced wear or damage, replace it, and the

chain, which might well have been damaged by running over bad teeth. Similarly, a worn-out chain can accelerate the wear of sprocket teeth. Wrapping a new chain around worn-out sprockets is a waste of money, since the sprockets will quickly wear out the chain. Bottom line, it's a good idea to always replace a chain and its sprockets as a set, even if some of the parts look good.

All good things come to an end, even high-performance drive chains. There are several ways to tell when a chain is worn out. The most obvious is when the chain has used up all of the available adjustment. Chain manufacturers have various wear standards, some based on the percentage of elongation compared to a new chain, others on the distance you can pull a link off the back of the rear sprocket. Both of these methods are indicative not of stretching, as many riders believe — the metal in a chain does not stretch — but of an accumulation of clearance in the friction surfaces of the chain itself. The more miles on a chain, the more wear on the rollers, bushings, and pins, and the more clearance there is between them.

When you go looking for a new chain, pay close attention not only to getting the right size, but the right strength, as well. Some chain manufacturers rate their chains by the largest displacement engine they're made to

Gearing for Speed and Acceleration

If you ride two-up a lot you've probably thought about modifying your engine for more power. But a change of gearing, say a rear pulley that's two teeth larger, might give you what you're looking for (better acceleration) at a much lower price. On the other hand, you can extend your range on the open road by changing the gearing so your engine turns fewer RPM at highway speeds. (Jerry Smith)

Racers often change their bike's final drive gearing to improve acceleration, or top speed, or to get a few more laps out of a tank of gas before pitting to refuel. These goals are not incompatible with street riding, and can be accomplished by the average street rider the same way that racers go about it. But before we get into why and how you can change gearing, let's get our terminology straight.

When you hear racers talk about "gearing up" a bike, they're really talking about changing the ratio of the number of teeth on the transmission and rear wheel pulleys to allow the bike to go faster for a given RPM in top gear. If, for instance, the front pulley has 32 teeth and the rear 65, the bike's gearing is 65 divided by 32, or 2.03. The lower the numerical ratio, the higher the gearing is said to be. Thus, if you replace the 65-tooth rear pulley with a 61-tooth pulley, the ratio becomes 1.90 (61 divided by 32). The lower numerical ratio results in a theoretically higher top speed in top gear at the same rpm, and is therefore called a "higher" gearing.

There's a trade-off for higher top speed, though, and that's more leisurely acceleration. Gearing a bike "down," which is to say raising the numerical ratio, will let a bike accelerate harder, but its engine will hit maximum RPM in top gear at a lower speed. Our bike with 32/65 (2.03) gearing will accelerate harder with a 70-tooth pulley on the rear (2.18), or fractionally harder with a 31-tooth on the front (2.09), but in both cases its theoretical top speed will be lower, assuming the engine redlines at the same RPM in both cases (although slightly lower gearing often lets the engine rev a little higher in top gear).

With a little judicious numbers-juggling, you can gear your bike for better acceleration by gearing it lower (resulting in a higher numerical ratio) or improve its touring range and mileage by gearing it higher (a lower numerical ratio). This is to some extent what 6-speed transmissions were made to do, although they cost a lot more doing it. 6-speeds add an extra gear on top of the stock fifth gear to bring the engine down out of the vibration range at highway speeds. Of course, if you accomplish this with gearing you're affecting your bike's performance through all the gears, not just top gear, while a 6-speed transmission offers different gear ratios to make up for the loss of acceleration in the lower gears. But if you're willing to put up with the compromise, gearing is a lot cheaper.

be used with, while others rate them by tensile strength. This is no time to try to save a buck. What do you want connecting your 120-inch S&S and your 280-series Avon, a cheap chain or the very best you can get?

Adjust a new chain to the motorcycle manufacturer's specifications. As a rule, too loose is better than too tight, which puts a strain not only on the chain but on the transmission and rear wheel bearings. Too loose can be overdone, too, such as when the chain begins taking bites out of the swingarm.

Check the adjustment 50 miles after installing a new chain, and again at 250 miles, and then go back to the recommended intervals. If you ride hard, carry heavy loads, or ride where it's dusty or wet, check the chain — and lube and clean it — more often.

SUSPENSION AND BRAKES

FRONT SUSPENSION

There are two types of front forks commonly in use today, one that's been used on Harley-Davidsons for a long time, and another that's fairly new on Harleys. The first type is the damper-rod fork, so-called because its damping characteristics are determined in large part by the size, number, and location of holes in a rod inside the fork.

When the fork compresses, the oil is forced through holes in the damping rod. When the fork rebounds, the oil is forced through another set of holes in another part of the rod. Because you want the wheel to get up and over the bump as quickly as possible, the compression holes are larger than the rebound holes so they flow more oil more quickly, and offer less resistance to wheel movement. On the rebound stroke the natural tendency of the fork spring to extend the fork quickly is damped by the smaller rebound orifices the oil flows through.

In practice, however, fixed orifices such as these only work efficiently at certain wheel speeds. Wheel speed in this case means the speed at which the wheel moves up and down, not vehicle speed. At very low wheel speeds, the fork oil flows freely though the orifices, offering no resistance to suspension movement. The most common manifestation of this is front-end dive when you grab the front brake at low speed. The oil isn't moving fast enough to create resistance, so the fork compresses quickly. You get the same effect when you hit a low, round-edged bump at low speed.

Very high wheel speeds can have the opposite effect. When the suspension is suddenly compressed, such as when you hit a high, sharp-edged bump, the oil just can't flow through the compression orifices fast enough, and for a fraction of a second, the front suspension is essentially rigid. This is called hydraulic lock, and it's usually accompanied by a teeth-jarring jolt through the handlebar.

In recent years, suspension engineers, including those at Harley-Davidson, have turned to cartridge forks to solve the problems inherent in damper-

There's more to riding than straight-line performance. Handling and braking come in handy on those curvy bits that connect the straight parts. (Dain Gingerelli)

Suspension Overview

Getting power to the ground, and keeping it there, is just one of the jobs your bike's suspension has to do. Poorly tuned suspension can make even the most powerful bike so uncomfortable you won't want to ride it. (Dain Gingerelli)

In a perfect world, with smooth roads and gently sweeping corners, you wouldn't need suspension at all. But here in the actual world, smooth roads are as rare as tax refunds. Even well-maintained highways can be minefields of bumps, potholes, and debris. Once, when I lived I southern California, on a single ride on a heavily traveled freeway, I had to dodge a car muffler, an eight-foot aluminum ladder, a box spring, and a dead sheep. When a motorcycle's wheels hit any of these obstructions, they have no choice but to roll up and over them. The faster you're going, the more quickly they have to do it.

Bicycles provide a dandy demonstration of why motorcycles have suspension. Ride a bike over a small, rounded bump, a speed bump in a supermarket parking lot, for example, and the wheel rides up and over, taking the entire bike with it. You get a tiny jolt through the handlebar and seat, but no biggie. Now take another run at the bump, this time pedaling for all you're worth (if you're feeling brave try riding into a curb) and you'll see soon enough the advantages of a system that lets the wheels ride up and over a bump without disturbing the chassis.

The earliest solution to the problem was to isolate the wheels from the chassis with springs. But while the springs compressed when the wheel hit a bump, they rebounded just as fast. Replacing the short, sharp shock with a long oscillating weave was a fair trade-off at horse-drawn speeds — remember Marshall Dillon and Miss Kitty bouncing along a Dodge City back road in Matt's buggy? But when self-powered vehicles got faster, a method was needed to control the spring's motion. Thus shock absorbers were born.

For the purposes of this discussion, a motorcycle's front fork and its rear shocks are more or less the same. Both typically consist of a spring (sometimes in the form of compressed air) and a damping unit. The spring's primary tasks are to hold the motorcycle up to re-extend the suspension after the wheel rides over the bump. The damper's job is to make sure none of this happens too fast.

At heart, most damping units work the same way, whether they're in a rear shock or a front fork. The damper's movement causes oil to be forced through orifices in a piston or a rod. The oil resists this movement, thereby slowing the motion and preventing the kind of trampoline effect you get with springs alone. The faster you try to force the oil through the orifices, the more resistance it offers.

This technology has worked pretty well for decades, and still works well today. But it can work even better.

rod designs. In a typical cartridge fork the fixed orifices are replaced by pistons, one for compression damping and another separate one for rebound. Each piston has a stack of flexible shims that look like thin washers controlling the flow of oil through holes in the piston body. The size, quantity, and thickness of the shims determine damping characteristics. When the fork compresses, oil forces its way through the orifices in the piston by deflecting the shims — same on the rebound stroke. But unlike the fixed orifices in a damper rod, the holes in the piston are completely closed off by the shims until acted on by oil, and so provide damping even at the slowest wheel speeds. At very high wheel speeds, when a damper-rod fork would go into hydraulic lock, the shims deflect fully. The holes in the pistons are so big that hydraulic lock isn't an issue, even at very high wheel speeds.

Because there are two separate pistons, the fork's compression and rebound damping can be adjusted independently, a feature that endears cartridge forks to racers and serious sportbike riders. Each piston's shim stack can be adjusted, too, to get exactly the kind of performance required. It's not an easy job, since the fork has to be taken completely apart each time, and it's not really something you want to try on your own without a lot of sophisticated equipment like a shock dyno and years of experience running it.

Improving Fork Damping

The most effective way to change a damper-rod fork's damping characteristics is to take the damper rod out and modify the orifices. But most often this just moves the range of efficient damping up or down without improving the fork's performance at the extremes of wheel speed. You can play with the viscosity of the fork oil (thicker oil makes for heavier damping, thinner oil for lighter damping) but whatever change you make this way affects compression and rebound damping more or less equally.

What you really want to be able to do is separately tune the compression and rebound damping characteristics

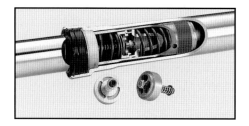

Gold Valve cartridge fork emulators make damper-rod forks perform like well-tuned cartridge forks. The tunable valves sit on top of the damper rods and are held in place by the fork springs. They are easy to install and adjust. (Race-Tech)

like you can in a cartridge fork. The easiest and most effective way to do that is with a device called the Emulator. Made by Race-Tech, the Emulator replaces the fixed-orifice compression-damping circuit with an adjustable cartridge-type valve.

To install the Emulator you first remove the stock damper rod and drill out the compression orifices, then drill several new ones. The idea is to neuter the stock compression-damping circuit and let the Emulator take over the job. The Emulator sits on top of the damper rod and looks like the piston from a cartridge fork, except that instead of a stack of flexible shims the Emulator uses a single washer held down by an adjustable preload spring. It functions the same way as a cartridge piston, restricting the flow of oil at low wheel speeds and "blowing off" at high wheel speeds. Front-end dive under braking is reduced, and hydraulic lock is virtually eliminated.

Because Race-Tech feels that compression damping has more of an effect on suspension performance, they leave rebound damping to be controlled by the stock rebound orifices in the damper rod. You can easily adjust rebound damping with fork springs and for oil if you think it's necessary, but according to Race-Tech, in most cases the stock rebound damping is fine.

The key to the Emulator's effectiveness is the elimination of fixed orifices from the damping system, and it's a method that allows Race-Tech to improve cartridge forks, too. A cartridge fork's pistons are designed to produce damping through a combination of restrictive piston orifices and the shims over the orifices. Their Gold Valve replacement pistons for cartridge forks have larger piston orifices than stock, putting the responsibility for damping wholly on the shims.

Fork Springs

Like a lot of the stock suspension components on a Harley, the fork springs represent a compromise in terms of both cost and performance. On smooth roads you can get away with soft springs that do little to resist the wheel's upward motion in response to bumps. On rough roads, however, you need a stiff spring to prevent the wheel from hitting a really big bump and moving upward so fast it bottoms out the fork. The problem is finding one spring that handles both situations.

The solution is to wind a spring so it has both soft and hard sections. The soft section comes into play over small bumps, giving you a smooth ride. When the wheel hits a bump big enough to fully compress the soft section — a condition called coil-binding — the stiffer section takes over, offering more resistance to the fork bottoming out. Such a spring is called a dual-rate spring (or triple-rate, depending on the number of different sections).

Dual-rate springs work very well in most street applications, but they aren't

This dual-rate fork spring kit from Works Performance features a soft initial rate that crosses over to a stiffer final rate. Three crossover sets are available to suit different riding styles and rider weights. (Works Performance)

Race-Tech makes a complete front end suspension kit that includes high-performance springs, Gold Valve cartridge fork emulators, and the hardware to lower the front end 1 or 2 inches. Different spring rates are available to account for rider weight. (Race-Tech)

perfect. You might have noticed the transition of a dual-rate spring from soft to hard if you've ever hit a bump while you're on the brakes. In such situations the forward weight transfer from braking has already used up the soft part of the fork spring, and when you hit the bump — wham — you're into the hard part with a jarring thud.

A true progressive spring is even better than a dual-rate. With progressive springs there's no transition, no thud — just smooth, progressive resistance throughout the fork's travel. To understand why, start with the simplest kind of spring, called a straight-rate. It takes 10 pounds to compress a 10-pound straight-rate spring one inch, 20 pounds to compress it two inches, and so on. A dual-rate spring might require 10 pounds per inch for several inches and then, as the soft section coil-binds, abruptly switch to 20 pounds per inch. A true progressive 10-pound spring takes 10 pounds to compress it one inch, and — depending on how it's wound — 11 pounds to compress it two inches, 12 to compress it three, and on that way until it coil-binds, with no harsh transition from the soft rate to the hard rate.

Fork Oil

Fork oil does two main things. First, whether in a damper-rod fork or a cartridge fork, the oil's viscosity has an effect on damping — the thicker the oil,

Tool Time

The type and quality of tools used on a bike show up in the end result. Use only the best for your high-performance project. Second-rate tools belong in your kitchen drawer. (John Hyder)

It should go without saying that you need the right tools to work on a Harley-Davidson — but it needs to be said anyway, because even though your rollaway might be brimming with the best that Craftsman, Snap-on, and Mac have to offer, you'll need a few more tools to do a lot of jobs on a Harley, and the just about only place to buy them is from your Harley-Davidson dealer.

Take a look in the service department at your local Harley shop and you'll probably see a dozen or more special tools hanging on the wall. You can bet these weren't ordered just to impress guys who like to watch their bikes being worked on. In many cases, these tools are absolutely necessary to avoid ruining a part, or to remove or install it quickly, or to align, adjust, and otherwise deal with it in a way that ensures it won't eventually be the cause of a shouting match between the customer and the service manager.

The price of these tools won't be such a burden if you budget for them as you're planning your high-performance project. And besides, odds are if you're bitten by the high-performance bug once, you'll be bitten again. That means if you needed a tool once, you'll need it again someday.

Maxima fork oil contains specially additives to control foaming, oxidation, rust, and corrosion. It conditions fork seals, and reduces friction for smoother suspension movement over a wide temperature range. It is available in 10, 15, and 20 wt. Maxima also makes lighter weights for racing. (Maxima Racing Oils)

Bel-Ray High-Performance fork oil is designed for use in all high-performance suspension systems, including damper-rod, cartridge, bladder, conventional and upside-down designs. It comes in 5, 7, 10, 15, 20, and 30 wt. (Bel-Ray)

the more damping it provides. As the oil breaks down from long use, it becomes less viscous, and your damping starts to go away. If you're dissatisfied with your front fork's performance, the first thing to ask yourself is how long it's been since the last time you changed the fork oil. Sometimes that's all it takes to fix the problem.

Fork oil also provides lubrication for the sliding parts inside the fork itself. As those parts wear, particles of metal break loose and settle into the fork oil. Dirty, gritty oil can accelerate wear, increasing the critical slider-to-tube fit to the point where handling, braking and even straight-line stability are adversely affected. You wouldn't

leave the same oil in your engine for 20,000 miles, and yet that's how long some riders go between fork-oil changes.

Two things happen to fork oil, even fresh fork oil, when the suspension is worked hard. First, its viscosity decreases as its temperature rises. This probably won't be an issue with a street-ridden Harley, but if you road-race a Sportster, for example, it will be. Since damping is dependent to a degree on the viscosity of the damper oil, a fork oil should maintain its viscosity, or most of it, at high temperature.

The second thing that happens is that the rapid movement of oil through damping orifices causes it to foam up and mix with air inside the fork. This frothy mix shoots through the damper orifices with little resistance, and damping fades. Fork oil contains anti-foaming agents to keep this from happening.

One more thing fork oil has that ordinary oil doesn't is an ingredient that makes the fork seals swell slightly. This gives the seals a tighter grip on the tubes, preventing leakage. Bottom line on fork oil is to change it regularly to make sure it's doing all the jobs it's designed to do as well as it can.

Fork Assemblies

A lot of companies sell complete fork assemblies for Harleys, but not all of those forks have performance to match their looks. Many of them use stock Harley damper-rod internals and springs, and deliver a ride no better than stock. For the kind of money you'll spend on a complete fork assembly, you should get the latest technology, including cartridge damping and progressive springs. For all-around better handling, you should also make sure the fork you buy has larger-diameter tubes than stock. The bigger the tubes the more

rigid the fork assembly is, reducing the flexing caused by braking and cornering.

Steve Storz, owner of Storz Performance, manufactures and sells the legendary Ceriani forks in both the conventional configuration and the newer inverted type, which first became popular on imported sportbikes and are now not only an effective performance option for Harleys but also, because of their brawny look, a styling must-have for many riders, too.

Steve Storz is testing a fork on the suspension dyno. This is just one of the pieces of insanely expensive equipment it takes to design and build quality suspension components. The grin is reserved for those who think they can hack-saw their way to better performance. (Storz Performance)

"The first benefit you're going to see is much better steering response," Storz says. "Either one of these fork designs is much stronger and more rigid than stock by virtue of the fact that the tubes are bigger." Both styles of Cerianis have larger-than-stock fork tubes, 45 mm for the conventional fork versus 41 mm stock, and 55 mm for the inverted model versus 39 mm or 41 mm, depending on the model of Harley. "Then there's damping. Both use cartridge-

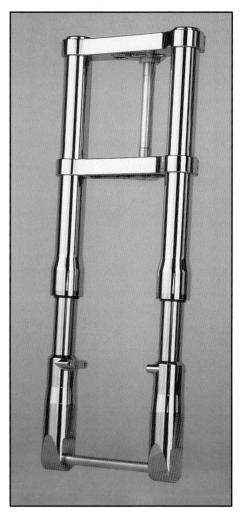

This Storz/Ceriani inverted fork features 55-mm outer tubes and 45-mm lower tubes in a short or long length. A built-in adjustable lowering kit allows a 1-inch ride height adjustment by adding or removing a spacer, without removal of the fork legs. Travel is 4 inches in the lowered position, 5 inches in the extended position, and spring preload is also internally adjustable. (Storz Performance, courtesy Drag Specialties)

The springer-type fork was the hot setup in grampa's day, and though it still works tolerably well today, its strong point is looking good. Modern forks work much better, offering more rigidity and better damping, and they require less maintenance. Sorry, gramps. (Jerry Smith)

Big style points for the classic chopper look, but the long fork tubes will flex during cornering, making fast riding more excitement than you bargained for. Shorter tubes are the way to go for good handling, as is a more sophisticated internal damping mechanism. (Ron Goodger)

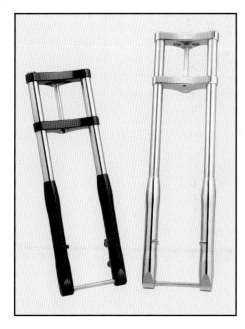

Designed for use on custom bike applications as well as standard frames, Storz Fat 49-mm forks have the largest diameter conventional fork tubes on the market. The increase in tube diameter improves steering input and reduces the tendency of the fork tubes to flex and twist, traditionally a problem with extended forks made in the smaller stock diameter sizes. (Storz Performance)

Money Matters

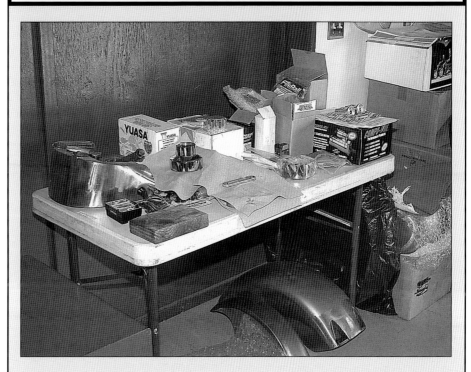

It might not look like much, but wait until that credit card bill comes. Settling on a budget for the job in advance can help you avoid spending more than you want to. (John Hyder)

Building a high-performance Harley is seldom a cheap proposition, and budgeting is just as important a part of a high-performance project as choosing the right components. By sitting down before you begin and making a list of the parts you want, you can avoid running out of money halfway through the job. You can also make sure you don't start off down a road that you can't afford to see all the way to the end by committing to a list of high-dollar parts that'll bankrupt you long before you reach your performance goal.

Smart builders start out by picking a number that represents the total amount of money they want to spend on a project. Then they choose the parts and performance level that's achievable within that budget. They might have to lower their original expectations a little, or settle for some components that maybe aren't as tasty and exotic as others, but their chances of completing the job without cashing in the kids' college fund — or not completing it at all — are much better than those of builders who just start writing checks for anything that catches their eye.

style damping, a much more sophisticated system than damper rods," he adds.

Inverted forks are gaining in popularity, and not just for styling reasons. "I think what drives it is people like the way they look, but then they get it and say 'Hey, this really works!'" Storz says. "Every fork tries to flex below the lower triple clamp under braking or when you hit a bump. It's like a big lever arm trying to bend the fork tube assembly back toward the motor. The bigger diameter you have at that point right below the lower clamp, the greater rigidity you have. The system's not trying to bind itself up and load the tube in such a way that it makes it hard to move up and down."

The inverted design also allows more overlap between the slider and the tube. In a conventional fork, the aluminum slider fits over the tube, the bottom of which extends into the slider. The more overlap between the two, the more rigid the fork is. But when the

fork compresses, the slider can't move any higher than the bottom of the lower fork clamp. With an inverted fork, the roles of tube and slider are reversed, sort of, because the tube can extend up into the slider higher than the bottom fork clamp. Under the severe fork-compressing stresses of hard braking, for

example, the added overlap gives the fork more rigidity.

Storz uses progressive fork springs in all his Ceriani forks, and takes the extra step of shot-peening and polishing the spring to reduce internal friction. "One of the enemies of suspension is friction of any kind," he says. "The smoother outer surface of the spring creates less friction with the inner surface of the fork."

REAR SUSPENSION

Rear shocks differ from front forks in terms of their mechanical details, but work on the same principles. The typical shock uses a piston on the end of the shaft that protrudes into the body of the shock, which contains oil. The piston can have fixed orifices in it, and a one-way valve that opens on the compression strokes and closes on the rebound stroke. Or it can use a flexible shim stack similar to the damping pistons in a cartridge fork. Either way, the goal is the same as that of a fork — light compression damping and heavier rebound damping.

The shock body can't be filled completely with oil because when the shock

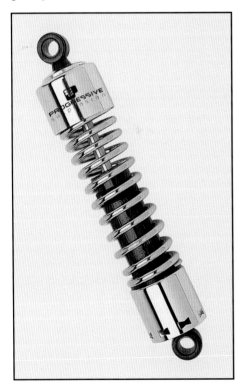

The 412 Series from Progressive Suspension is a gas-charged, double-walled, steel-bodied shock with five-position preload adjustment. Multi-stage velocity-sensitive damping gives it a good ride. It's available in many lengths, with standard or heavy-duty springs. (Progressive Suspension)

compresses the oil needs somewhere to go. Early shocks simply filled the shock to a certain level then capped it. But the air trapped inside the shock mixed with the oil under hard use, creating a foam that reduced damping. Later shocks used pressurized inert nitrogen instead of air to prevent foaming, or separated the oil and the nitrogen mechanically with a flexible bladder or a movable piston.

One major difference between a shock and a fork is that while the fork's spring is inside the tube, a shock's is outside. Sometimes air is used to supplement the spring, and in some case, the spring is dispensed with altogether in favor of total reliance on air. Touring bikes whose saddlebags complicate access to the shock sometimes resort to air-springing because adjusting spring preload with the ramped collar used on most shocks would be difficult to the point where no one would bother, whereas adding air via a remotely mounted air valve is a cinch.

Shock Absorbers

Rear-wheel control is essential to performance, regardless of whether you define performance and road-holding or load-handling, and replacing the stock rear shock absorbers is one of the easiest ways to improve both. But shocks suffer from the same price-point effect as many other stock components. Larry Langley of Progressive Suspension, one of the largest aftermarket suspension manufacturers, says most motorcycle manufacturers use "the cheapest mass-produced piece of crap they can put on the bike and get away with. They specialize in motorcycles, and some of the parts on them are marginal at best. We specialize in suspension."

Langley is equally candid when it comes to what to look for in an aftermarket shock. "If you're looking for better handling, you need to go to a reputable company like Progressive, or Works Performance, or Race-Tech. We all offer better damping and springs, damping especially. Almost all aftermarket shocks offer better damping than stock."

The aftermarket offers more variety, too. "Even our basic shock, the 412

series, has much better damping than stock," Langley says. "With our 418 series you get into aluminum bodies, and you can adjust the rebound damp-

Here's an example of your basic rear shock absorber, heavy on the basic. Built to a price, with a minimum of adjustability — just spring preload, in this case. After several thousand miles all it's good for is keeping the fender off the tire. The aftermarket can do much better. (Jerry Smith)

Up a big step from the bottom-of-the-line rear shock, this Sportster Sport rear shock is gas-charged, and has adjustable compression and rebound damping, as well as spring preload adjustment for the dual-rate spring. It works much better than the stock shock that comes on other Sportsters. (Jerry Smith)

Progressive Suspension's 440 Series shock features the Inertia Active System that's able to distinguish chassis movement from wheel movement. It comes with a threaded preload adjuster that can be operated by hand, and is available in chrome or black. (Progressive Suspension)

These shocks from Works Performance feature adjustable-rate suspension, which allows you to increase or decrease the load-carrying capacity up to 50 percent without changing the spring preload. Dresser models come in 400-pound and 500-pound models to accommodate rider and passenger weight. (Drag Specialties)

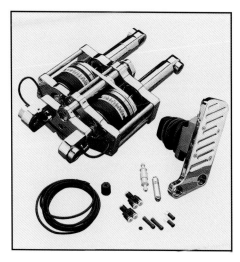

The Pro-Air suspension system from Pro-One fits Softails from 1986 on up and allows you to change the ride height up to 3 inches at the touch of a button via the onboard 150-psi air compressor. Each kit comes complete with necessary mounting hardware, a chrome rocker box mount with a compression gauge, switches, and instructions. (Pro-One)

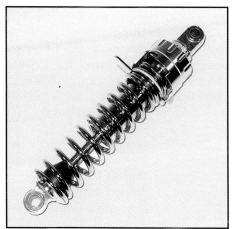

Street Trackers from Works Performance use the ARS (Adjustable Rate Suspension) system that lets you increase the load-carrying capacity of the shock up to 50 percent without changing the preload of the springs. Fully polished aluminum parts are optional. (Works Performance)

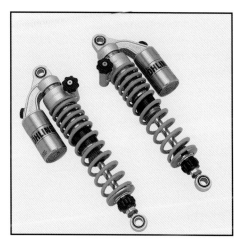

Ohlins' type 36 PRCLB rear shocks have steel bodies and aluminum reservoirs, and they come with chrome-silicone springs. They also have external gas-charged piggyback reservoirs, adjustable rebound and compression damping, and spring preload. (Drag Specialties)

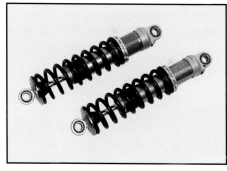

The 36E shock from Ohlins is an emulsion-type shock, with oil and gas mixed in the body. The body is made of precision-drawn steel and the spring is chrome-silicone. The internal piston diameter is 36 mm. (Drag Specialties)

ing. Our 440 series has inertial damping, a more sophisticated damping system. It can sense the difference between wheel travel and chassis travel. When the rear wheel hits a bump it changes damping instantly from what we call hard or heavy damping to softer damping and lets the rear wheel move over that bump rather than transmit the jolt to the frame."

Progressive Suspension's testing and development process mirrors that of other big-name suspension manufacturers. They start with an in-house formula developed over the years that factors the weight and type of the motorcycle, its lever ratio (which we'll discuss shortly), and several other measurements. That usually gets them pretty close to what they want, but just to be on the safe side, they double-check their

Pro-One Pro Quad

Most high-performance customs take more or less the same road as all the others, with maybe a detour here or a side trip there. As a result many turn out enough alike that's it's hard to tell one from the others. That's not the case by a long shot with Pro-One's Pro Quad, however, a bike that not only has all the right stuff, but some very unusual stuff to boot.

You don't have to choose between show and go, as the Pro Quad proves. It can bend through corners all day, and light up Main Street at night. (Dain Gingerelli)

If you ever find yourself jaded by a 113-inch S&S engine like the one that lives in the Pro Quad's stretched Pro-One frame, it's time to see your family doctor, or maybe start composing your obituary. The motor is fed by an S&S Super G carb, and the chassis rolls on Pro-One wheels and brakes. But what really lifts the Pro Quad head and shoulders above other customs is its four-bar rear suspension.

The four-bar design might be new to bikes, but it's been a common feature

on race cars and hot rods for years. The Pro Quad's take on this technology starts with four billet-aluminum control arms, each with a Heim joint at either end. Up front the arms are connected to the frame, and out back they link up to billet uprights that carry the rear axle. The bottom arms are actually triangular for strength and rigidity.

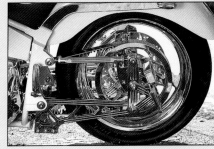

The Pro Quad's 4-bar rear suspension is designed to cancel out a lot of the up-and-down motion caused by turning the throttle on and off. (Dain Gingerelli)

In theory, the control arms are put under compression during acceleration and tension during braking. This eliminates to a large extent the up-and-down motion you get in a swingarm design when the bike squats or rises in response to turning the throttle on and off. It also moves the theoretical pivot point of the swingarm farther forward, making in effect a very long swingarm that's better able to transmit the engine's power to the ground.

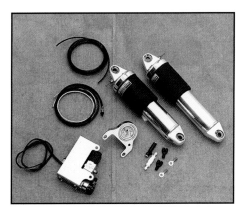

This air suspension system for FL models from Legend comes with an onboard compressor and solenoid that allows east on-the-go suspension adjustments. The shocks use Kevlar spring technology and have gas cell reservoirs. (Drag Specialties)

maybe 100-pound springs, so the shocks are going to be way too stiff."

Another critical factor is lever ratio. "The lever ratio is the distance the shock travels versus the rear-wheel travel," Langley says. "On a bike with a 2 to 1 lever ratio, the shock moves half the distance of the rear wheel. This is important, because the slower the shock moves the better you can control the damping. On a Sportster the ratio is about 1.1 to 1. On a Dyna, it's 1.44 to 1, and because the lever ratio is higher, you have to run heavier springs and damping to match."

Another common problem arises when riders lower their Harleys an inch or more for a dragster look, unaware of what they're doing to ride quality, handling, and safety. Langley says the average stock rear shock has about 4 inches of travel. "If you lower the bike an inch, you've given up 25 percent of your travel. Now the shocks have to be a little stiffer to compensate. That shorter travel has to do the work formerly done by longer travel." And of course the lower the bike, the less cornering clearance it has. With so many aftermarket exhaust systems already compromising cornering clearance, you could find yourself dragging hard parts at very shallow lean angles.

You can also run into problems with the clearance between the rear tire and the fender. A shock that's 2 inches

results with a $100,000 shock dyno. Finally, because lab results don't always survive exposure to the real world, the dyno is double-checked by seat-of-the-pants road-testing.

While it's hard to go wrong with a reputable aftermarket shock, Langley warns that there's more to it than just getting a set the same length as the stock shock, something he sees all too often.

"Two shocks might look identical, but they're aren't necessarily equal. You have to match them to the application. Let's say a guy walks into a dealer and asks for a pair of 11-inch shocks for his Sportster. The dealer looks on the wall and sees a pair of 11-inch Progressives for a Dyna. But the Dyna shock has maybe 350-pound springs and damping to match, and the Sportster needs shorter than stock, but has the same amount of travel, can allow the tire to hit the fender over big bumps, locking the rear wheel. Progressive's approach is to lower the bike by taking it out of the shock's travel, not just its overall length. "For example, take a 13-inch XL shock with a compressed length of 10 inches," says Langley, "If we make an 11-inch shock for that application, the compressed length is still 10 inches, because no matter how much you lower it the tire is still the same distance from the fender."

When you get in touch with an aftermarket shock manufacturer, have some information ready, including the year and model of your motorcycle, how you most often ride — solo, two-up, or with luggage, and whether you're an aggressive rider — and your own weight and that of your passenger. If you ride solo, you'll probably want a lighter set of springs than if you often carry a passenger. Changing shock springs isn't hard if you have the special tool, but few shops have one, so it's best to get the right spring installed on the shock by the manufacturer.

Swingarms and Wide-Tire Kits

It's arguable whether the trend toward ultra-fat rear tires is a styling exercise that got out of hand, or a serendipitous development in an age of reliable 120-cubic-inch engines that can smoke a stock rear tire like a cheap cigar. Either way, if you're going to fit a significantly larger-than-stock rear tire, you're in for a major undertaking, one not without compromises.

The limiting factor in such a job is the location of the final drive belt, whose location is in turn dictated by the transmission's output sprocket and its distance from the bike's centerline. You don't have to fit a tire very much wider than stock to run into interference problems between the belt and the tire. You're not going to shoehorn one almost twice as wide as stock under the fender without some serious work.

Most wide-tire kits come with spacers that bolt between the primary drive case and the crankcase and transmission, moving the whole shebang far

Softail Subtleties

Harley's Softail models do a great job of capturing the look of a rigid or hard-tail chassis by placing the shocks under the bike, out of sight, and fashioning a triangular swingarm that appears at first glance to be a solid extension of the frame. While it's okay to be fooled by this, don't get tricked into thinking the Softail follows the same rules as other bikes when it comes to shocks, especially if you're planning on changing the ride height.

When you sit on a Softail and compress the rear suspension, you're actually extending the rear shocks. The longer the shock is, the lower the bike will sit. To raise the bike, fit shorter shocks. Many aftermarket Softail shocks have adjusters to let you change lengthen or shorten the shocks to set the right height, but the job is more complicated than doing the same to a conventionally mounted shock, since you have to either lift the bike or crawl under it to get at the adjusters.

The job is just hard enough that few riders bother. This is why remote ride-height

Harley Softails use a rear suspension setup that positions the shocks under the bike, out of sight. Adjusting them for ride height is counterintuitive compared to conventional rear-shock systems. (Buzz Buzzelli/*American Rider* magazine)

adjustment for Softail shocks is a handy feature. Typically it's done by using air-shocks with a remote air valve. The adjustment is made with a small pocket air pump, or on some high-end shocks with a small 12-volt DC air compressor mounted on the bike in an out-of-the-way spot.

enough to the left so the belt can still clear the wider tire. Extended transmission shafts are usually included, too. The next result is a bike that's slightly unbalanced, with a weight bias to the left, but many riders are willing to put up with that (if they notice it at all) in exchange for the huge rear tire. Although handling isn't improved, at least it's not completely ruined, and all is forgiven when you drop the hammer on that killer motor and every last horsepower makes it to the ground.

If you want to get the power to the ground, you need a big tire — but maybe not this big, unless you have a wildly pumped motor. This 250-series Metzeler requires extensive mods to the chassis, a classic case of the tail wagging the dog. (Buzz Buzzelli/American Rider magazine)

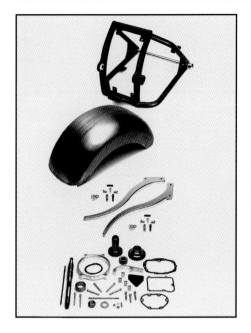

Performance Machine's Phatail kit for Softails comes with a wide swingarm and rear axle, a steel fender and billet aluminum fender struts, a primary spacer kit, extended transmission shafts, a starter shaft extension, and all the gaskets you need to do the job. (Performance Machine)

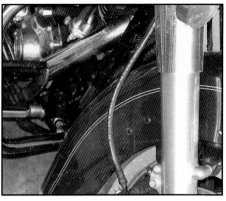

When you squeeze the front brake lever, some of that effort goes into swelling this long rubber hose, and in the case of this Electra Glide, another one on the other side. The longer the hose, the more vague the feel at the lever. Braided stainless-steel lines are the fix. (Jerry Smith)

The braided stainless-steel brake line on this custom front brake not only looks better than rubber, it works better, too. It resists swelling, and the Teflon hose offers less resistance to the flow of brake fluid, so more of your effort goes toward stopping the bike. (Jerry Smith)

There's another, better way to install a wide tire and swingarm without affecting handling as much, and that's to replace the stock transmission with one with the output sprocket on the right side. Right-side-drive transmissions are covered in Chapter 6.

BRAKES

Braided Stainless-Steel Brake Lines

The typical Harley hydraulic brake line is composed of a length of metal hose, usually near the master, connected at some point to a flexible rubber hose that goes on to attach to the caliper. If a motorcycle's front wheel didn't turn from side to side, and if neither the front nor the rear moved up and down, you could get by with all-metal brake lines. But because the wheels (and the brake calipers attached to them) do move, at least part of the brake line has to be flexible. That flexibility also keeps your brakes from working as well as they could.

When you pull on the front brake lever or step on the rear pedal, part of the pressure you're exerting on the brake system via the master cylinder causes the flexible rubber hose to swell, increasing its diameter slightly, and giving the brake a mushy feel. The fix is to replace the spongy rubber hose with a material that's still flexible but doesn't swell nearly as much.

That material is Teflon, which not only resists swelling better than rubber, but also offers less internal resistance to the flow of brake fluid. The Teflon line is covered with a layer of braided stainless-steel that helps it resist swelling even more. Although it looks thinner than the stock rubber hose, the Teflon line's inner diameter is pretty much the same.

Braided stainless-steel brake lines aren't the cure-all for wimpy brakes, but they make some brake systems feel more powerful. You don't need to yank the lever as hard because more of the pressure in the brake line is working directly on the caliper pistons instead of swelling the rubber hose. The resulting improvement in feel will be welcome in wet weather or on surfaces where traction is iffy. In these circumstances a firm brake that lets you know what's happening at the contact patch can mean the difference between going down and riding on.

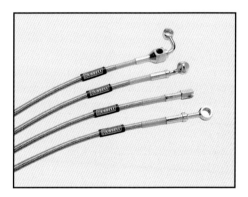

Russell brake lines come as factory-assembled kits to replace stock lines, or you can buy universal lines and the appropriate fittings to custom-build your own. Russell also carries a huge selection of fittings and adapters. (Russell Performance Products)

Unlike some other high-performance bolt-ons, braided steel brake lines have no downside. They're a cheap way to improve any brake system, and anyone who can bleed a brake system can install them. Direct bolt-on replacements for stock Harley-Davidson brake hoses are readily available, and for applications where the lines might rub against painted surfaces like a fender, they're available with a clear plastic coating that protects paint.

For custom applications, you can buy the component parts of stainless steel brake lines and assemble your own. If you're not entirely sure you're up to the job, farm it out to the local dealer or have an experienced buddy walk you through it. This isn't something you want to do half-assed if you value your whole ass.

Brake Fluid

Harley-Davidson has never been a company to follow the crowd, and that might partially explain why, in 1977, H-D made an across-the-board switch from the polyglycol brake fluids — used by practically every other motorcycle and car manufacturer on the planet — to silicone brake fluid. The reasons for the switch go deeper than contrariness, though. At the time, silicone had a very high boiling point compared to commonly available polyglycols, and it still does today. Silicone doesn't attack and corrode paint the way polyglycols do, so a spill while you're adding brake fluid doesn't necessarily mean your next stop is the paint shop. And unlike polyglycols, which absorb moisture out of the air, past seals, and even through

Bel-Ray Silicone DOT 5 brake fluid will not affect painted or plastic surfaces, or absorb water. It has an extremely high boiling point of 500 degrees for optimum performance under the harshest conditions. (Bel-Ray)

the walls of rubber brake hoses, silicone doesn't attract moisture — or even mix with water.

While silicone has proven its worth in street applications, it isn't perfect, especially for extreme high-performance applications, a fact Harley tacitly admitted when in the 2000 model year it changed the brake fluid specification of Buells from silicone back to polyglycol. To understand why, we need to take a look at why each type of fluid is good, and why it's not so good. We'll start with polyglycols.

There are three polyglycols in common use today — DOT 3, DOT 4, and DOT 5.1 — each classified by the U.S Department of Transportation according to viscosity and temperature range. One of the peculiarities of polyglycol fluid is that it's hygroscopic, which means it pulls moisture out of the air and, as already mentioned, past seals and through rubber hoses. It can even draw moisture out of the tiny air space in the top of a bottle of fresh, unopened brake fluid, which is why some manufacturers go to the trouble of filling that air space with inert nitrogen before sealing the cap.

Brake fluid is incompressible, and when it's fresh and clean it transmits all of the power you apply to the lever or pedal to the brakes, less a bit used up in making the rubber brake hoses swell. As the heat of braking generated at the caliper heats first the pads, then the caliper pistons, then the brake fluid, the fluid approaches its boiling point. Boiling fluid is no longer a fluid, it's a gas, and gas is compressible, so when you pull the brake lever all you're doing is compressing a gas. Very little of the pressure you apply to the brakes actually gets there. What you experience is a mushy feel at the lever, in addition to a rising sense of panic as you brake harder and harder to no obvious effect.

The boiling point of a brake fluid when it's fresh and uncontaminated by moisture is called its "dry" boiling point. But since polyglycol fluids start absorbing moisture out of the air as soon as you open the bottle, the dry boiling point is more academic than anything else. So the DOT also specifies

Russell will not only sell you brake lines, they'll sell you the fluid to put into them. It meets DOT 5 specs, and will not boil at temperatures up to 500 degrees. A single 12-ounce bottle should take care of both brakes. (Russell Performance Products)

a "wet" boiling point, determined when the fluid is 3.5 percent water. Water boils at a mere 212 degrees, and at that temperature the water in the fluid turns into tiny pockets of compressible steam. The effect is the same as you get when fresh brake fluid reaches its boiling point, except it happens at a far lower temperature.

Now we come to silicone brake fluid, which is designated DOT 5. A short digression is in order here to clear up a common misconception. When most people see all the DOT numbers in order — 3, 4, 5, and 5.1 — they naturally assume that each number is an improvement on its predecessor, 4 being better than 3, and so on. In the case of 3 and 4, it's true — but 5.1 is not only not an improvement on 5, but as we just learned, it's not even the same kind of fluid at all. Anti-lock brake systems — which have been common on cars for years and are showing up on more Japanese and European motorcycles every year — require a thinner polyglycol fluid to work with the rapid on-off cycling of anti-lock brakes. DOT 4 is too thick to do the job, and silicone already had dibs on DOT 5, so the Fed-

Maxima makes DOT 3, 4, and 5 brake fluid. Their DOT 5 fluid has a dry boiling point of 550 degrees, and won't harm paint or plastic. Maxima DOT 4 can be used in DOT 3 or DOT 4 systems. Racing DOT 3 has a dry boiling point of 550 degrees. (Maxima Racing Oils)

eral Bureau of Needless Confusion came up with DOT 5.1.

Silicone brake fluid doesn't absorb water, but that doesn't mean water can't get into a silicone brake system. Humidity, riding in the rain, and washing your bike with a high-pressure hose can all contribute to the contamination of the brake system. But because water and silicone don't mix, and silicone is lighter, the water settles to the lowest point in the brake system, which is right next to the caliper pistons, which are right next to the brake pads, which are the first things to get hot when you use the brakes. At 212 degrees the water boils, and it's goodbye brakes, just like with polyglycols.

Even though it's susceptible to the same contamination problems as polyglycol, silicone's non-hygroscopic nature makes it a good choice for streetbikes whose brakes are seldom pushed to the limit for extended periods. It was originally developed for the military for use in vehicles that sat around for a long time with little or no maintenance and then had to be brought into service quickly. Harley-Davidson personnel

will usually cite its paint-friendly nature as the main reason for its use today, but there's no denying its suitability for use in bikes that are ridden infrequently and therefore serviced at less frequent intervals than bikes that pile on the miles and get serviced once or twice a year.

Still, for high-performance applications where you need strong, firm brakes, time after time, polyglycols work best — hence the shift by late-model Buells back to polyglycol. Silicone has an inherently mushy feel that's anathema to sport riders and racers, and its high boiling point is no longer as uncommon as it was in 1977. Note, however that racing polyglycol fluids are not the best choice for streetbikes. Racers want a fluid with an extremely high dry boiling point, because they'll use their brakes harder in practice than most other riders will ever use theirs riding at their fastest on the street. Racers don't give a hoot about the wet boiling point, because they change their brake fluid every race, sometimes between practice sessions.

Since it never stays in the system long enough to get contaminated to any significant degree, the wet boiling point of racing polyglycols never really matters. Good thing, too, because some racing fluids have lower wet boiling points that plain old non-racing brake fluid. In addition, many racing brake fluids are extremely hygroscopic, and will degrade a lot more quickly than ordinary brake fluid. Combine rapid contamination, a racing polyglycol with a dismally low wet boiling point, and an infrequently maintained streetbike, and you have a recipe for disaster.

Many aftermarket companies that make high-performance brakes for Harleys specify silicone fluid. There are a couple of good reasons for this. First, it's just easier that way, since most Harley shops have been using nothing but silicone for years and probably don't have a single bottle of polyglycol in the building. If you ever take your bike in for service, you won't have to sit around waiting while the service manager sends the shop grunt out to an auto parts store for the right polyglycol fluid.

Second, most aftermarket brake

systems are so much better than stock brakes that silicone's disadvantages compared to polyglycol won't matter. With the right master cylinders and brake pads, and a set of braided-steel lines, your brakes will be so much stronger and firmer you probably wouldn't notice the slight difference you'd get from using polyglycol.

But if you're a particularly aggressive street rider, or your ambitions extend to the race track, you might want to look into replacing the stock brakes with aftermarket components that are compatible with polyglycol brake fluids. You'll get better feel and firmer braking, even though you might have to change the fluid more often.

Finally, in case you're thinking of, say, draining the silicone fluid out of your Electra Glide and replacing it with polyglycol to get better feel at the brake lever, here's a word of advice — don't. Silicone and polyglycols fluids do not mix together. You should never put one in a system designed for the other unless

Spectro's Golden American DOT 5 Brake Fluid is a silicone brake fluid that does not absorb water and prohibits brake system corrosion. Its physical properties do not deteriorate with time, and it ensures long-term braking performance under extremely high and low temperatures. It's made for use in all Harley disc brake systems requiring DOT 5 silicone brake fluid. (Spectro Oils)

you replace all the seals and hoses with new ones compatible with the new fluid, and clean every last component thoroughly. Not that there's a compelling reason to do that in the first place, because if whatever you don't like about your brakes can't be cured with fresh stock brake fluid, your best bet is to start replacing the brake system a piece at a time until you get the braking performance you want.

Brake Pads

The easiest and cheapest — and oftentimes the most effective — way to upgrade your bike's braking is with a set of aftermarket brake pads. The pads that come stock in Harley-Davidsons are fine all-around pads. They work well cold, and in the wet, and they last a long time, and they're kind to rotors. But let's face it, they're built to a price. You might not think twice about spending, say, $50 on a set of high-performance pads instead of $30 on a stock set (both figures are wild-ass guesses, but you get the idea). It's a $20 difference, not much in the general

Bendix ceramic brake pads are designed for non-competition street riding, and are asbestos- and lead-free. They're easy on stock brake rotors, and provide excellent braking in both wet and dry conditions. (Bendix/FTM Enterprises)

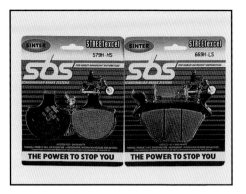

SBS sintered pads have the highest coefficient of friction available in an SBS pad. The HH-rated compound has high heat resistance and quick cool-down, and offers excellent stopping power in both wet and dry conditions. (Drag Specialties)

scheme of things, and bearing in mind that you're depending on them to bring a $25,000 motorcycle — and your priceless self — to a safe stop, certainly not a deal-breaker

Now pretend you're Harley-Davidson, and you're buying brake pads for each of the 200,000 or so bikes you intend to build next year. That $20 difference times a minimum of two calipers per bike times 200,000 units is a whopping eight million bucks. What to do — spend an extra eight million to equip each bike with high-performance brake pads, or go with good standard pads and use the eight mil for other things? It's a no-brainer.

Up until the mid-1980s, brake pads were made from a variety of materials, many of which contained asbestos. When the health hazards associated with inhaling asbestos particles became known, it was phased out and replaced by other materials like Kevlar composites and aramid fibers. These are called organic pads. Sometimes tiny bits of copper or brass are added to improve friction and pad life, resulting in what are called semi-metallic compounds. Both organics and semi-metallic pads are at the low end of the modern braking performance scale. Their chief virtue, and the one that's kept them from disappearing altogether, is they're cheap to make. Companies that sell a lot of brake components sometimes ship them with organics or semi-

SBS ceramic brake pads are designed for all-around street and touring use. They're easy on OE rotors and give long life and good stopping in both wet and dry conditions. (Drag Specialties)

SBS Carbontech brake pads are a direct replacement for Performance Machine pads, and fit many other stock Harley calipers, too. They're designed to be used with cast-iron or stainless-steel rotors, and give great feel and control at the lever. (Drag Specialties)

metallics because they're cheap to buy in bulk and they fatten up the bottom line. But more and more the high-performance brake pad of choice is made of sintered metal.

Just about every street-legal motorcycle sold since the mid-1980s has come equipped with sintered metal pads. For street riding, sintered metal is hard to beat. It has excellent cold-stopping capabilities, which means that when the old duffer in the Buick turns in front of you two blocks from your house when your brakes are cold, you'll still have plenty of braking power right now. Organics and semi-metallics typically

DP pads are the original sintered-metal pad. They have a quick break-in and give you hard, sure stops, hot or cold, every time. A ceramic material on the backing plate insulates the caliper and fluid from the heat of braking. (Drag Specialties)

These sintered-metal brake pads have just come out of the compacting process, where the loose powder that the compound is made from is packed into shape. The compacts are then placed on the metal backing plates, and the raw pads stacked about 20 layers high, ready for the furnace. (Don Emde)

work better the hotter they are, and don't work very well at all when they're cold. Sintered metal pads run quiet, seldom squealing the way organics and semi-metallics can. They offer consistent braking performance over a wide temperature range, and provide predictable stopping at temperatures that would have lesser pads smoking. They work very well in wet weather, too, because on a microscopic level the metal itself is porous, which helps the pad break through the layer of water that collects on the surface of the rotor.

Sintered metal starts life as a compound of powdered metal, almost a thick dust. Which materials go into the compound, and how much of each, determines how the end product works. For instance, a brake pad can be designed to give a strong initial "bite" when the brakes are applied by adding substances called friction modifiers. Graphite or lead can be added to reduce rotor wear and brake squeal, and copper and brass absorb heat and help bind the pad material together. The pad's final performance characteristics can be affected by the temperature and pres-

If you think your brake pads get really hot sometimes, it's nothing compared to how hot they were before you got them. Here in the furnace, under tremendous heat and pressure, they're fused into solid pieces, and the backing plate is bonded to the pad compound. (Don Emde)

sure at which the pad is cured, the duration of the curing process, even the ambient temperature and humidity of the manufacturing facility.

Because of all these variables, pad compounding is more of an art than a science. Small changes in any step along the way can turn what was supposed to be a long-lasting, hard-stopping brake pad into an interesting and expensive paperweight for the engineer's desk. Even when everything goes according to plan, and the pad performs flawlessly under simulated road conditions on a brake dyno in a climate-controlled testing lab, there's no guarantee it will work worth a damn out in the real world where it's hot and cold and wet and dirty and nasty.

DP Brakes is the premier manufacturer of aftermarket sintered-metal brake pads. Larry Mills, vice-president of DP, says even though they use the same proportions of material for every batch of a given pad compound, they still test every batch to make sure the mix is right. After mixing the compound is pressed in a mold called a compact, then the compact is put on the backing plate. "At that stage the pad is very brittle, like chalk," says Mills. "You can break it in half with your fingers." Then the pads are stacked, about 20 high, in a furnace that subjects them to both heat and pressure.

By the time the pads come out of the furnace, the powder is fused into a solid material, and the pad and the backing plate are fused to each other. The pads are then put in a grinder and ground to spec. Next a minimal coating of ceramic is applied under heat to the backing plate to act as a heat barrier. This insulating layer helps keep the heat of braking from heating the brake fluid to boiling, causing brake fade. "You don't need it in all applications," Mills says, "but we do it anyway."

While most brake pads are sintered metal, not all of them are alike. The braking industry classifies brake pads by their friction rating, using the letters A though H. The higher the letter, the higher the friction rating, so a pad rated E is higher than one rated C. According to Mills, the industry standard for original equipment

After the furnace stage, the pads are laid out in a single layer and ground down to the required thickness. (Don Emde)

The last step involves spraying a thin coating of a ceramic heat-barrier on the back side of the backing plates. The ceramic coating helps insulate the brake fluid from the heat generated by braking. (Don Emde)

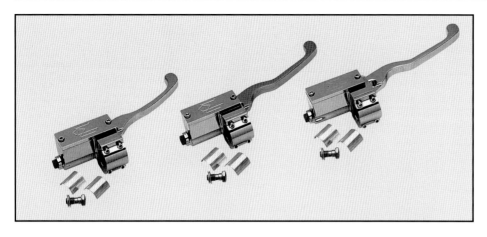

Joker master cylinders come with or without handlebar switch boxes in a 9/16-inch or 11/16-inch bore size. Brake master cylinders come with brake light switches. Rebuild kits are available for all master cylinders. (Drag Specialties)

Performance Machine chrome billet master cylinders fit 1-inch bars and come with 5/8-inch bores that move less fluid but create higher line pressure for less effort at the lever. Matching clutch lever assemblies are available. (Drag Specialties)

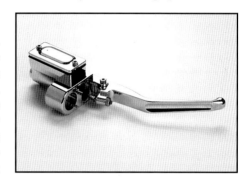

This front brake master cylinder from GMA Engineering is CNC-machined and chrome-plated, and fits all models of Harleys. Note the adjustment screw on the lever. With it you can adjust the lever to accommodate your hand size. Stock Harley levers don't give you this adjustment. Get a clue, Milwaukee. (GMA Engineering)

pads is GG. The first G indicates the pad's hot friction rating, and the second one its cold rating. A pad rated FG, for example, works a little better when cold than when hot. When the letters are the same, as in GG, its works the same in hot and cold conditions.

The highest friction rating is not always a good thing in a brake pad, Mills says. "We recommend GG for the rear brake because you don't want too strong a brake on the rear." That's because the weight transfer caused by heavy front braking takes weight off the rear tire momentarily, and you're more likely to lock the rear wheel with a strong brake than with one equipped with pads with a slightly lower friction rating. When it comes to front brakes, though, you want all the power you can get, and that's where DP pulls out the stops. "The industry high is HH," Mills says, "but we invented a step higher, which we call HH+. We recommend going with the HH+ on the front and our standard on the rear. There's nothing wrong with using our standard on the front, but the HH+ is going to give you better feel and stopping power."

And now a quick word about racing brake pads, a word, by the way, that you can apply in general to a lot of parts intended for racing. Some brake pad manufacturers, recognizing the allure of racing parts, put the label "For Racing Only" on pads they admit are suitable for street use. While they might work well enough for street riding, often their

best performance will still be found only at temperatures higher than the average streetbike's brakes will achieve under most riding conditions — and they might not even work as well as stock pads at any temperature below that. There are so many very good street pads on the market that there's really no reason to use a racing pad anywhere but the race track.

Brake Master Cylinders

There are lots of replacement brake parts for Harley-Davidsons, but many riders seem more interested in how shiny they are than in how much they improve braking. But looking good is not a brake system's primary reason for being.

"Brakes are all about heat dissipation," says Performance Machine's David Zemla. "Any decent front brake system will lock up your wheel at the end of the block. But high-performance braking isn't about braking the first time, it's about braking the tenth time. Braking is the translating of motion into heat. The energy has to go somewhere. A good brake system will dissipate that heat. Brake fluid will boil at a certain point, and brake pads will gas out at a certain point, so heat is the enemy of high-performance braking."

Zemla says a lot of riders look at the brakes as primarily the caliper. "In reality it's far more involved. It's a system, beginning with a master cylinder. Your braking system is never going to be

effective if you can't reach it. Our levers are adjustable for reach. The OEM lever is not adjustable — it is where it is, and you better hope your hand fits."

One of the most important characteristics of an aftermarket brake master cylinder is the diameter of the piston that exerts pressure on the brake fluid. "We want our master cylinders to be progressive in travel, which is to say a little bit of application gets you a little bit of braking," says Zemla. Performance Machine accomplishes this by juggling the piston diameter and the brake lever dimensions. "The brake lever is literally just a lever. It pivots at one point and forces the piston to move at another. The farther those two are

GMA Engineering sells complete bolt-on front brake and caliper kits. This one uses a 13-inch ductile iron rotor and a six-piston, differential-bore caliper. It's available for single- or dual-disc applications and can use the stock Harley brake lines. It fits all models from 1984-1999. (GMA Engineering)

The latest stock brake caliper has four pistons, all of them live. The larger caliper allows the use of brake pads with more surface area, and stops much better than the old single-piston design. (Jerry Smith)

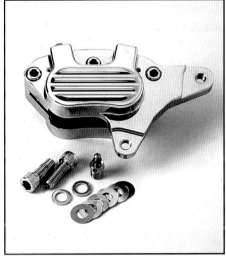

GMA Engineering's 400F series front brake calipers fit single-disc models from 1984-1999. The four-piston unit uses the stock Harley-Davidson brake lines. The 400F is also available for dual-disc bikes, and in a two-piston design for both single- and dual-disc bikes. (GMA Engineering)

apart the more movement it takes to apply the brakes," explains Zemla. "In the same way, a smaller master cylinder piston will generate more line pressure but require more travel, in some cases too much. A master cylinder on a twin-disc system has to move enough fluid to

This is the single-piston brake caliper that came stock on Evo Harleys. Even a pair of them on the front requires a hefty yank at the lever to get decent stopping power. (Jerry Smith)

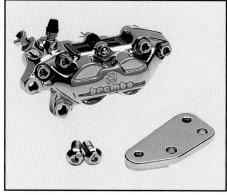

These four-piston, differential-bore, cast-aluminum calipers by Brembo are made in Italy and come polished or chrome-plated. The piston bores have a dual O-ring design to keep dirt out. Kits come with pads, brackets, and hardware, and work with OE rotors. (Drag Specialties)

Brembo's big-brake upgrades for 1987-2002 Sportsters include four-piston differential-bore calipers, high-performance brake pads, mounting brackets, and aircraft-quality hardware. The systems can include 11.8-inch or 12.6-inch cross-drilled, stainless-steel, floating Brembo discs mounted to chromed billet-aluminum carriers. (QTM Inc.)

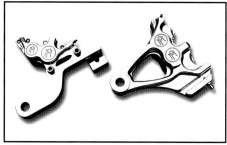

Performance Machine has a large selection of brake calipers in two-, four-, an six-piston configurations, in standard and differential-bore designs. They're available polished, chromed, or black anodized. (Performance Machine)

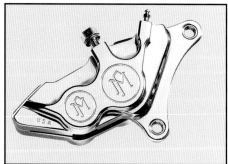

Performance Machine makes direct bolt-on calipers to replace the OE calipers on a variety of Harleys. They use differential-bore pistons for longer pad life and are designed to be used with the 11.5-inch rotors on stock bikes. (Drag Specialties)

Brembo makes rear disc kits for Sportsters, too, including the same four-piston differential-bore caliper, high-performance brake pads, mounting brackets, and aircraft-quality hardware. Floating disc rotors are standard in the kit. (QTM Inc.)

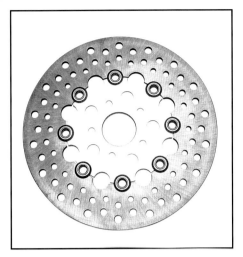

Russell's floating rotor is a two-piece design that lets the rotor expand independently of the chrome-plated carrier. It mounts using the stock hardware. There's a size to fit just about every Sportster, Dyna, FX, FL, and Softail. (Russell Performance Products)

This inside-out "brake pulley" from GMA Engineering features a four-piston brake caliper and a floating, chrome-plated, ductile-iron rotor attached to a 70-tooth rear pulley. The assembly is a straight bolt-on, and saves some weight compared to a separate rotor and pulley. It's available with a wire wheel hub, too. (GMA Engineering)

fill two calipers before it moves the pads far enough to contact the brake rotors. So such a system requires a larger piston than a single-disc system."

Every manufacturer plays around with "the triangle" — the relationship between the lever's pivot point, its point of contact with the master cylinder piston, and its overall length — and the piston sizes to get the optimum setup for a given motorcycle. Don't let yourself be dazzled by shiny chrome and curvy levers at the expense of good braking. Do some research, measure your own brake components, and make sure what you buy complements the rest of the brake system.

Brake Calipers

Harleys made prior to 2000 have single-piston brake calipers front and rear. The caliper body is free to "float," so when the piston pushes the brake pad against the brake rotor, the pressure pulls the caliper's "dead" pad into the rotor from the other side. From 2000 on, Harleys came stock with calipers with four pistons, two on each side.

The four-piston calipers are a big improvement over the single-piston design, but Performance Machine goes it one step better with a differential-

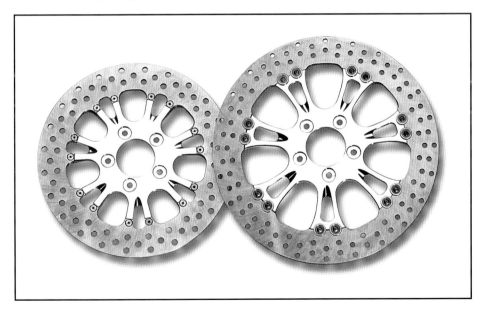

Performance Machine brake rotors are CNC-machined and then finish-ground. Stainless discs are made of uncoated 420 stainless steel. All two-piece, full-floating, and Image series carriers are billet aluminum and are available in custom finishes. (Performance Machine)

What's With the Holes in a Brake Rotor?

In the old days, solid rotors and organic brake pads pretty much refused to speak to each other in any meaningful way when either was wet. You'd grab a big handful of brake and nothing would happen. You'd squeeze harder and harder, while nothing continued to happen at an alarming rate, and then suddenly the pad would break through the layer of water on the rotor and everything would happen, all at once.

When drilled rotors began appearing in large numbers, a lot of riders thought the holes were there to channel water away from the pads in rainy conditions. But the performance of some brake systems with drilled rotors wasn't much better. In fact, some tests using high-speed photography showed that the holes in a brake rotor collected water in wet conditions, and that the spinning motion of the rotor trapped the water against the outer edge of the hole. It wasn't until sintered-metal brake pads came along that wet-weather braking took a great leap forward.

Still, the holes in brake rotors perform several important functions, especially in high-performance applications. They allow the super-heated boundary-layer gases that build up between the pad and rotor to escape, and they sweep dirt and debris that can reduce braking away from the pad surface. The number of holes or the pattern isn't important, except cosmetically.

Drilled rotors first appeared on race bikes to save weight. The holes have other advantages, too, and are now the norm on streetbikes as well as racebikes. (Jerry Smith)

which is the front of the caliper. The pad becomes more parallel to the disc, and evens out the heat build-up within the caliper so it's not localized at the entry point. You get more efficient, more effective braking."

Performance Machine also makes calipers with six pistons, three on each side. Zemla says they're typically used on Harleys with a single front disc brake, which need all the extra braking they can get. "You don't have any more pressure on the disc but you have more friction." It's about as good a brake as you can get short of fitting a new front end with dual discs.

Brake Rotors

Stock Harley-Davidson brake rotors are made of a single piece of stainless steel, bolted solidly to the wheel. They're easy to manufacture, but they're heavy, and they've been known to warp under the stress of repeated hard braking. Once the disc warps, and its braking surface is no longer parallel to the brake pad's surface, braking performance is severely decreased. The better the rotor can dissipate heat the less likely it is to warp.

"Rotors play a gigantic role in heat dissipation," Zemla says. "All of our 11.5-inch rotors are two-piece, bolt-together rotors. The outer band is stainless steel and the inner is aluminum. The aluminum center dissipates the heat very effectively." In addition to 11.5-inch rotors (the stock Harley size) Performance Machine makes 13-inch full-floating rotors, with the rotor attached to the carrier but not bolted solidly to it. This allows the rotor to expand independently of the carrier. "It'll deal with more heat before it warps," Zemla says. "If it were solid it would have to distort to deal with the heat." Because there isn't as much metal-to-metal contact between the rotor and the carrier as there is in a bolt-together rotor, there's not as much heat transfer from the rotor to the carrier. But because the rotor itself is larger, it acts as a heat-sink. "Guys that know how to ride and like to push their bikes a bit go to them on the single-disc Harleys," he adds.

bore caliper. "The entry point of the disc into caliper is where a lot of heat builds up," says David Zemla. "We reduce the amount of pressure at that point by using a smaller piston there and a larger piston at the disc exit,

TIRES AND WHEELS

TIRES

Tire engineers often lead stressful lives. The market is in constant flux, thanks to bigger and faster motorcycles coming out every year, as well as the demands of riders constantly howling for the often mutually exclusive virtues of more traction and better mileage in the same tire. Add to that the fact that the science of making motorcycle tires is more of an art than anything rooted in cause-and-effect. Take rubber compounds as an example. Although engineers know what they're looking for when they mix the ingredients that go into a compound, they're never quite sure what they're going to get until they try it out. There's a lot of trial-and-error involved in making a tire, which leads to more work going into those round, black, deceptively simply things on your wheels than is evident by just looking at them.

So it's doubly frustrating to tire engineers that many riders choose which tires to buy based not as much on the details of carcass construction and rubber compound as the tread pattern, and that behind closed doors in the marketing department, people in business clothes are sitting around the table coming up with terms like "aggressive" to describe what are essentially grooves cut into the tire's surface, reducing the

end result of long hours of research in the lab and in the field to an advertising catchphrase. It's enough to make trained, professional engineers chew their pocket protectors in half.

If you aspire to building a high-performance bike, however, you need to know there's more to tires than meets the eye. At one end of the bike a tire is responsible for transferring the power generated by your engine to the ground. At the other end, another tire gets the task of steering and most of the braking. And both tires affect handling and ride comfort. Knowing what's going on under that aggressive tread is critical to choosing the right high-performance tire for your Harley.

There's more science in a tire than most riders think, or even imagine. Wheels are more than just shiny round things, too. Matching the right tire to the right wheel is an important job. (Jerry Smith)

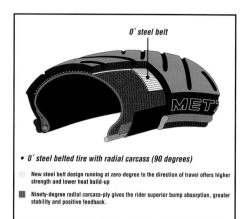

0° steel belt

- *0° steel belted tire with radial carcass (90 degrees)*

New steel belt design running at zero-degree to the direction of travel offers higher strength and lower heat build-up.

Ninety-degree radial carcass-ply gives the rider superior bump absorption, greater stability and positive feedback.

Avon's H-rated AM21 Roadrunner comes in stock Harley-Davidson sizes as well as a number of other sizes for custom applications. The tread pattern provides good water drainage, and the tire's contour is designed for progressive lean-in when cornering. (Avon Tyres)

Bias-Ply and Radial Tires

Life is full of compromises, and you'll find a lot of them staring you right in the face when you go shopping for high-performance tires. Even though most tires look alike, most are built to excel at a specific task, and it's a rare tire that's a standout at more than one.

The biggest differences between tires isn't visible, but buried deep inside the tire itself. The foundation of a tire is called the carcass, and it consists of overlapping layers of cords, made of nylon, rayon, or some other synthetic material, laid across the tire at an angle to the tire's direction of rotation. Each layer is called a ply, and each ply is angled in a direction opposite that of the plies above and below it. If you could look through the layers of plies, you'd see they cross each other in an X-shaped pattern.

Bike tires as wide as the ones on your car? Get used to it. This 230-series AM21 from Avon measures more than nine inches across when mounted. A heavily modified swingarm and driveline is necessary to use one, which might be why you usually only see them on customs. (Avon Tyres)

In bias-ply tires, the X-shape of the overlapping plies is pronounced. In radial tires, the plies run from bead to bead at or near a 90-degree angle to the direction of rotation. This is a critical difference, because the angle at which the plies lay with respect to each other determines to a large degree the nature and performance of the tire.

When a tire rotates, the part of it that comes in contact with the road — called, conveniently, the contact patch — deforms and flattens as the weight of the motorcycle presses down on it. After the contact patch rolls away from the road, it returns to its original rounded shape, a process that continues to take place once each rotation for as long as you ride. The constant flexing from flat to round generates heat inside the tire as the plies compress and rebound, rubbing against each other in a scissoring motion that generates heat inside the carcass.

This cutaway of a radial tire shows the plies in the carcass running directly from bead to bead at an angle perpendicular to the tire's rotation. The belt on top of the plies resists tire growth at speed, gives the tire a little more puncture resistance, and reduces heat build-up at high speed. (Metzeler)

Heat is the number one enemy of a tire. Bias-ply tires combat it with a number of strategies, including making the carcass stiffer and the tread and sidewalls thinner to reduce heat build-up. The trade-off is a harsher ride, lower tread life, and reduced load capacity.

High-speed riding generates more heat in a tire than normal riding because the contact patch flexes more often and has less time to cool off before it's asked to do it again. But load can generate excess heat, too, because the more weight a tire is carrying, the more its contact patch deforms, even at highway speeds. Touring-bike tires compensate for load by using thicker tread and a large air chamber that helps regulate internal heat. Such a tire is usually too big to shed heat fast enough to cope with the kinds of speeds and cornering loads that sportier tires are designed to, but touring riders don't mind that as long as they get a plush ride and long tread life, which is a touring tire's primary mission.

Radial tires generate less internal heat than bias-plies because the cords' angle reduces the amount of scissoring inside the carcass as the tire flexes. This allows the radial to use a thinner layer of tread composed of stickier rubber than a bias-ply, and still deliver comparable traction and tread life. The radial design, however, results in a weak sidewall that flexes easily, so radial tires have intentionally short, stiff sidewalls to compensate — some even have internal sidewall stiffeners. The short sidewalls are a tip-off that you're looking at a radial tire and not a bias-ply.

It's not always that easy to tell the difference at a glance, though. At first seen only on high-end sportbikes, radials are now common in the touring market. But most touring radials have the same tall sidewalls you'll find on bias-ply tires. This is because the term "radial" as understood by tire companies is a vague one at best. While in theory the plies of a true radial are laid at a 90-degree angle from bead to bead, in practice some tires whose plies are angled at as little as 75 degrees are considered radials. No one's trying to cheat you, though. The more the plies approach 90 degrees, the more radial-like the tire's performance tends to be, and that's a good thing.

Tire Compound

Just as there's no such thing as a free lunch, there's pretty much no such thing as a tire that both sticks like glue and wears like iron. Mike Manning of Dunlop Tires says, "With tires there are several characteristics, like dry grip, wet grip, stability, and mileage. A lot of those things are a trade-off. Touring guys are willing to give up a little traction to get the mileage. Sportier guys want grip over mileage. Sportier Harleys take our K591 tire. That tire was the AMA Superbike championship tire. It's literally a race tire modified for street use. They don't get great mileage but they have great wet and dry grip. Whereas the touring bikes, the Harleys come stock with the D402. The 'performance' there is mostly in load-carrying."

The speed, and to some extent the load, a tire is built to handle determines how much tread it will have. Running a tire at constant high speeds generates a lot of heat inside the tire, which accelerates tread wear, since the hotter a tire

runs the faster the tread rubber wears. So tires made for high-speed riding usually have a thinner layer of tread rubber than tires made for slower riding. The thinner layer of tread does a better job of shedding heat, but since there's less of it to begin with, it wears out more quickly. Make the already thin tread layer out of the sticky rubber compound that sporting riders prefer for good cornering grip, and it's easy to see the fun, while it lasts, will be short-lived.

On the flip-side you have touring bikes. The high loads touring tires are subjected to call for a thick layer of tread, both to act as a heat-sink for the heat generated by the flexing of the tire, and to give the kind of mileage touring riders demand. The latter consideration more than anything else mandates a harder tread compound that doesn't wear as fast as that of a sporty tire, but also offers less cornering grip.

There are, of course, many tires that strike a balance between grip and mileage. For any but the most narrow-focused kind of riding — like road-racing, or riding the Iron Butt Rally — they'll get both jobs done. But if you

The H-rated VT-01 from Bridgestone-Firestone is designed as a replacement tire for Harley-Davidsons. It comes in four sizes, 130/90-16, 100/90-19, 80/90-21, and 130/90-16. It uses a tread compound that balances traction and longevity, and has a unidirectional tread pattern for good grip in the wet or dry. (Bridgestone-Firestone)

Dunlop's D401 Elite is the only tire approved by Harley for both its sport (except those fitted with the Dunlop K591 stock) and cruiser models. This blackwall-only model comes in 100/90-19 front and 130/90-16 rear. Its advanced tread pattern and compound give outstanding grip in wet or dry weather. (Dunlop)

The grooves in a tire are called sipes, and their function is to channel water away from the tire's contact patch. The sipes in this tire lead toward the shoulder of the tread, moving water out of the way of the center of the tire. (Jerry Smith)

The center sipe on this front tire is pretty much gone. While it'll stick fine on dry pavement, the first rainstorm it has to deal with could make for an exciting ride, and not exciting in a good way. Tires this badly worn should be replaced. (Jerry Smith)

Because of the higher load on the rear wheel, and because it's the driven wheel, rear tires tend to wear much faster on Harleys than front tires. Worn sipes here not only impair the tire's ability to channel water, but the thinner tread is more susceptible to punctures. (Jerry Smith)

look past the advertising hype you'll often find a particular tire is better at one than the other.

Tread Pattern

The grooves in a tire, properly called sipes, serve one purpose, and that's to channel water and other fluids away from the tire's contact patch. If you rode on perfectly dry roads all the time, you could get by with the same kind of slicks that road-racers and drag-racers use. But here in the real world, where it rains, and water puddles on the road, slicks would be worse than useless, they'd be dangerous. Hit a layer of water on the road on a slick tire at speed, and if you're going fast enough, and it doesn't have to be all that fast, the tire will rise up onto the surface of the water — a phenomenon called hydroplaning. Water offers a lot less traction than asphalt, and if you can't guess what happens when you hydroplane at speed, be sure to ask the nice paramedic on the way to the hospital.

Some tires have more sipes in them than others, depending on the tire's intended use. Touring tires tend to have a lot of sipes, because they're used on bikes that get ridden in all kinds of weather. Sport tires don't get ridden in pouring rain very often, at least not on purpose, so they get by with fewer sipes, partly on the theory that you'll take it easy on the way home.

The number and placement of sipes can affect a tire's performance, too. A lot of sipes in the tread surface result in lot of unconnected blocks of rubber, which will flex more under cornering and acceleration loads than the larger blocks of a tire with fewer sipes. For sport tires, the fewer sipes the better, because the more rubber on the road, the more traction.

Bigger and Better Than Stock

Tires upgrades are common on Harley, but for different reasons depending on the type of Harley you're talking about. For example, Softail riders like the look of a wide tire, never mind the added load-carrying capacity. Then there are touring Harleys, which are fairly heavy — the average Electra

Dunlop's K591 is approved for Harley-Davidson's sport models and carries a V speed rating. It's available in 100/90-19 front and three sizes of 16- and 17-inch rears, all with black sidewalls. The K591 features a directional tread pattern with improved tread compounds to deliver optimum grip in wet or dry weather. (Dunlop)

Metzeler's entry in the monster-tire market is the ME 880 XXL. Forget wedging one of these into a stock swingarm. They're strictly for custom frames, and require offsetting the primary. Lots of rubber on the ground means all that power gets there, though. (Metzeler)

Glide weighs in at half a ton with a rider and gear — and yet come stock with 130-series rear tires, narrower than the 160-series front tire on a Honda GL1500. Concerns about load capacity and its effect on tire life, as well as the cost and downtime of constantly replacing the rear tire, which typically wears out two to three times as fast as the front, prompt some bagger riders to look into shoehorning a wider rear tire under the fender.

But you really can't go much bigger than a 140-series rear tire on most Big Twins without running into clearance problems. With the stock tire, the distance between the tire and the drive belt is pretty tight. A wider tire makes it even tighter, and makes precise rear-wheel alignment critical. There might also be problems with the belt guard and the rear fender. Manufacturing tolerances allow some leeway, too, so some tires are physically wider than others, despite being the same designated size.

Metzeler's ME 880 Whitewalls come in OE-replacement sizes and use a silica tread compound for improved wet grip. Fronts have a rounded tread profile for neutral steering, and rears have a flatter contact patch for better mileage. They're also available in blackwall. (Metzeler)

Tire Pressure

Experienced high-performance tuners know even the most mundane things can add to, or detract from, performance. The right tire pressure is critical to handling and braking, and despite how quick and easy is it to check on most bikes, it's one of the most often neglected adjustments.

The amount of air in a tire has a direct effect on how well it works. If a tire has too much air in it, the contact patch becomes too narrow, concentrating the bike's weight on a smaller portion of the tread, increasing wear. This can also affect handling by changing the tire's profile and altering its cornering behavior.

If the tire is under-inflated, the contact patch flexes more than it's designed to, generating more internal heat than normal and accelerating wear, as well as affecting cornering performance. An under-inflated tire takes more power to rotate, too, consuming more of your engine's power.

A decent pencil gauge only costs a couple of bucks and fits in your jacket pocket. Write your bike's recommended tire pressure on a piece of paper, and tape it to the pencil gauge. Check your tires at least once a week, when they're cold. If you see the pressure dropping over time, check the tread for nails or cuts. And get new valves stems every time you buy new tires — it's cheap insurance.

The bigger motorcycle tires get, the more important it is to maintain the right air pressure in them. Big meats like this one hold a lot of air, and transmit a lot of horsepower to the ground. (Jerry Smith)

One brand might sneak in, while another brand might not.

Bigger isn't always better, either. Factors other than size enter into the equation. "A lot of people will say they want to upgrade the tire on a Harley, so they put a 140 on it," says Mike Manning of Dunlop Tires. "On our tires, which use the alpha-numeric designation, MT90-16 is the stock rear Harley tire. The MT equals 130. But what a lot of people don't realize is the reason it's MT and not 130 is it's actually a higher load rating tire. An MT90-16 can carry a higher load than a 140-16, even though it's a little narrower, because it's a heavier tire. People are actually downgrading their bikes when they put on what they think is a wider tire."

Before you get your heart set on a wide tire for your bagger (or indeed for any other Big Twin, Sportster, or Buell) dial up the tire manufacturer's website, or call their tech hotline, and ask if what you're thinking of doing will work. In most cases, you'll only be able to make a small improvement without resorting to spacing the primary drive in order to move the drive belt to the left.

Upgrading to Radials

Having just read of the benefits of radials on motorcycles — cooler running, increased tread life, better handling in corners — you might be tempted to spoon a set of the latest radials on your bike. This is another situation in which you should defer to the experience of the tire manufacturer. On

Reading the Sidewall

A tire's sidewall reveals just about everything you need to know about its size, construction, speed and load rating, and direction of rotation. Here's the scoop, by the numbers. (Some markings are optional depending on the brand and model of tire.)

1. Brand name (and cute elephant trademark).
2. The type of tread pattern.
3. The name of the product line.

4-5. The tire's size. A motorcycle tire's size is typically expressed in one of two ways. The metric designation (shown here, and common on most replacement tires for Harleys) tells you the inflated width of a mounted tire in millimeters (measured at the sidewall's widest point), its aspect ratio (the height expressed as a percentage of the width), and the diameter of the rim it's designed for. For example, a 120/80-18 tire is 120 mm wide, 80 percent as tall as it is wide (96 mm), and fits an 18-inch rim. In the other system, alpha-numeric, the 120/80 becomes MT85, denoting a motorcycle tire (M), a width of 120 mm (P), and an aspect ratio of 85. And although no longer common, you'll sometimes see tires marked in the old inch system, too.

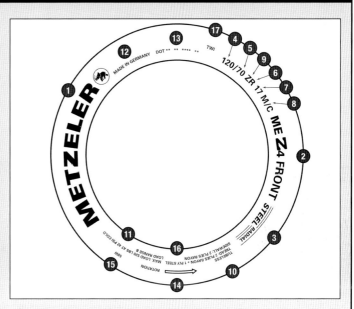

Want to know all about your tire? Everything you need to know about it written on the sidewall, and it's easy to read once you break the code. (Metzeler)

SIZE

Size may be indicated in Inches, Metric, or by Letters (Alpha). The chart shows the approximate comparison of the different size indications.

INCH:	2.75/ 3.00	3.25	3.50	3.75/ 4.00	4.25/ 4.50	5.00/ 5.10	5.50	6.00
METRIC:	80	90	100	110	120	130	140	150
ALPHA:	MH	MJ	MM	MN/MP	MR	MT	MU	MV

Size matters, especially when it comes to tires. Different companies use different size designations, and it's important to get the right size for your bike. (Metzeler)

6. The construction code, which tells you if the tire is a radial (R), a bias-belted (B), or a plain bias ply, in which case there won't be a letter here.
7. The rim size in inches.
8. This designates this is a motorcycle tire.
9. This is the tire's speed rating, indicating the highest sustained speed at which a tire can safely be run.

SPEED RATING CODES

	P	R	S	T	H	V/(VB)	Z/(ZR)	W
MPH	93	106	112	118	130	>130	>149	168
KPH	150	170	180	190	210	>210	>240	270

How fast do you want to go? Not faster than your tire is built for, that's for sure. Pay careful attention to the speed rating on any tire you buy. (Metzeler)

10. This indicates the tire is a tubeless tire.
11. This is the tire's maximum load capacity in pounds at the pressure listed.
12. This indicates where the tire was made.
13. This indicates the tire conforms to U. S. Department of Transportation (DOT) regulations. In the string of numbers that follow, the last four tell you when the tire was made. For example, "1501" means it was built in the 15th week of 2001.
14. This indicates the direction of rotation for this tire. This is important because when the layer of tread rubber is applied to the carcass during manufacturing, the ends of the slab are laid over each other. This splice isn't a straight butt of two flat ends, it's a beveled splice, with one end overlapping the other for extra surface area and strength. Properly mounted, the forces of braking (on the front wheel) or acceleration (on the rear) act on the trailing edge of the splice, pulling at it in the direction of its taper. If you mount a tire backwards, the forces will push the tapered end instead of pulling it, essentially trying to peel the splice open.
15. This indicates the load index.
16. This is the number and material of the plies.
17. This shows the position of the tread wear indicator on the tread. Adjacent to this mark, on the tread, you'll find a raised bar inside one of the sipes. If the tire wears to the point where the tread is even with the top of the bar, replace the tire.

Tube-Type and Tubeless Tires

If your bike came with tube-type tires — and every Harley that came stock with spoked wheels did — don't replace them with tubeless tires and leave out the tube. Similarly, original-equipment tubeless tires should not be replaced with tube-type tires. It's possible, however, to run a tube inside a tubeless tire, providing the tire manufacturer says it's okay. You wouldn't really want to do this except in an emergency, however, because unless a tubeless tire is specifically designed to be run full-time with a tube, the tire's speed rating is considered to be reduced by a full step. That's because friction between the tube and the inside of the tire will generate excess heat.

Wheels that require tube-style tires look great, but if you're traveling and you get a flat, your trip might well be over. Tubeless tires are easy to plug on the road, letting you ride on to a place where you can make permanent repairs. (Jerry Smith)

One Step at a Time

When you go to the races and take in the action, it's easy to come away with the impression that racers spend all their time rushing around, doing things at top speed. While that might be true of the time they spend on the track, behind the scenes, back at the race shop, things move along at a much slower pace. That's because race-tuning a motorcycle is a methodical operation, or at least it is for the top teams. And even though you'll probably never have to learn to run a dyno or a flow bench in order to make your streetbike faster, there is one thing that racers do that can make your high-performance project go more smoothly — never change more than one thing at a time.

Ideally, every component you bolt onto your bike will have a beneficial effect. Some won't, however, and you'll have to identify which ones they are before you can begin to find out why. That's hard to do, though, if you make several changes at once. Let's say you

bolt on a new carb and air cleaner, and a set of pipes, and throw in a hot cam while you're at it. Suddenly you're down on power, or there's a flat spot in the low RPM range that wasn't there before. But what caused it? A reversion problem in the exhaust system? A restriction in the air cleaner? The wrong jets in the carb? Instead of having just one place to look, now you have three.

As tempting as it might be to put on all your go-fast goodies at once and go for a ride, be patient. Try one component at a time, and make notes on how it affects performance. Is it a step in the right direction, or a step backwards, or no step at all? That way, when you put on the next part, you can tell how it works with the first one, and maybe save yourself the trouble of trying to run two components that don't work well together. By taking your time you'll not only build a bike with more performance, you'll learn more about high-performance tuning along the way, making your next project even easier.

Wild and crazy might do the trick on the track, but back in the pits slow and methodical winds the race. Tuning is a step-by-step procedure. Take too many steps at once and you'll stumble. (Jerry Smith)

a Sportster with stock suspension and spoked wheels, for example, a set of super-sticky radials might provide more grip than the chassis can cope with, and turn a decent-handling bike into a scary wobbler in the corners. In a case like this it could be better to go with a set of high-performance bias-ply tires whose performance is more suited to the Sportster's relatively unsophisticated chassis and suspension.

WHEELS

Solid Wheels

Early one-piece racing wheels were cast from magnesium, and were very light, breathtakingly expensive, and too fragile to use on the street. Cast aluminum wheels weighed a little more than magnesium, were a lot cheaper, and stood up to the rigors of real-world riding much better. Possibly because "als" doesn't sound as cool, today solid wheels are often still called "mags," even though almost all are made of aluminum.

Performance Machine, one of the biggest manufacturers of wheels, makes its one-piece aluminum wheels using a process called rotary forging. The forge

Some cast wheels aren't really cast, but machined from aluminum billet. They have all the same virtues as cast wheels, but can be styled much more elaborately because of the versatility of the manufacturing process. You can get matching front and rear wheels, too. (Jerry Smith)

GMA Engineering's W-7 wheel is a seven-spoke cast wheel that comes in sizes ranging from 18 x 8.5 to 21 x 2.15 inches. It comes with installed wheel bearings and a valve stem. The design matches GMA's Brake Pulley system and floating rotors. (GMA Engineering)

Stock cast wheels are a better deal than most riders think. First, they're strong, and it takes a pretty big wallop to bend or break them. Second, they're easy to keep clean compared to spoked wheels. Third, they're rated for tubeless tires, so you can run high-performance rubber. (Jerry Smith)

Wild West Motor Company

Next time you find yourself sitting at the kitchen table browsing through a stack of aftermarket catalogs and thinking, "I could build an entire motorcycle out of all these parts!" just remember you're not the first one to have that idea. As the Harley aftermarket grew over the years, it eventually became possible to put together a complete V-twin motorcycle that didn't have a single original Harley-Davidson part in it. The Vigilante from Wild West Motor Company has a few odd H-D bits scattered here and there, but for the most part its spec sheet is a tribute to the depth and quality of the aftermarket.

The centerpiece of the vigilante is a fully polished 107-inch S&S engine with an S&S 600 cam, a Super G carb, Crane roller rocker arms, forged pistons with a 9.6:1 compression ratio, and a Crane Hi-4 ignition. A Baker right-side-drive transmission makes room for the driveline powering the fat 240-series Metzeler rear tire, and the Vigilante announces its arrival through a Vance & Hines two-into-one exhaust system. A Rivera Pro nine-plate wet clutch handles the transfer of power, and a chrome CompuFire 1.5Kw starter gets everything going.

Performance Machine got the nod for the hand and foot controls, as well as the brakes and wheels. Given the Vigilante's resemblance to a Harley Softail you might expect to find a pair of rear shocks nestled under its frame. In fact, the Vigilante uses a single Progressive Suspension shock positioned upright just aft of the gearbox. Up front is a Mean Street 54-mm inverted fork.

The Vigilante's inverted Mean Street front end takes the bumps out of the dusty trail. You can bet ol' Cookie's chuck wagon didn't have forks like these. (Dain Gingerelli)

The Old West was never this wild. As long as a cattle drive, as low as a rattlesnake's belly, the Vigilante owes its existence to the V-twin aftermarket's relentless production of parts for Harleys. (Dain Gingerelli)

The Phat wheel from Performance Machine is an 18 x 8.5 incher that's more than twice the width of a stock Harley wheel. It was created specifically to use with the new generation of wide rear tires, and requires either a custom frame or Performance Machine's Phatail kit for Softails. (Performance Machine)

turns as the forging process takes place, aligning the grain of the aluminum so it comes out stronger. But what happens after the forging process is just as important. "Although there are no standards in the U.S., we test to German or Japanese standards — whichever is the toughest — for wheel strength and impact survivability," says Performance Machine's David Zemla. "One of the key tests we do is impact. It's the equivalent of hitting a curb at speed on a fully loaded motorcycle. We hit what we think is the weakest point on the rim, which is the middle of the space between

Insert your own "force" joke here. The Vader wheel, though, is serious stuff, with 10 sculpted spokes that merge with the rim in a subtle arc. Matching brake rotors, drive pulleys, and sprocket are available. (Performance Machine)

two spokes, and it has to hold air for a certain amount of time. The Japanese have a very tough standard when it comes to that. We do a half a dozen different tests to each wheel design and size. One example of each design and size has to pass all of these tests."

In addition to being lighter than stock, one-piece wheels let you run tubeless tires. Almost all spoked wheels need tubes inside their tires so the air won't leak out past the spoke nipples. As the tire flexes, the tube rubs against it, generating heat. A tubeless tire mounted on a solid, leak-proof wheel docsn't need a tube, and therefore generates that much less heat. Just about all high-performance tires are tubeless, and although many can be used with a tube on spoked wheels, you're not getting the most out of the tire that way. Even if you replace your stock spoked wheels with solid wheels of the same size, you're not only getting the benefit of lighter wheels, but the ability to run tubeless tires, too.

Spoked Wheels

The term "high-performance spoked wheel" is almost an oxymoron, according to Nancy Smith of Hallcraft's, one of the leading manufacturers of spoked wheels. "We don't call them

Performance Machine's Hooligan wheel is a 10-spoke design that combines arty, sculpted spokes with a sort of retro-machine touch embodied by the faux rivet heads. PM calls these rivet heads "detail dots," and suggests you paint them to match the bike. Matching pulleys, rotors, and sprockets are available. (Performance Machine)

A well-built spoked wheel is both light and strong, and many riders prefer the look over that of one-piece wheels. You'll need to run tubes in your tires, though, even if the tires are rated tubeless. (Lawrence M. Works)

Hallcraft's makes 80-spoke wheels in 16-inch and 21-inch sizes, using a straight lacing pattern. Though not the strongest setup — Hallcraft's recommends 100-spoke wheels in straight-laced designs — they're strong enough for applications where heavy load isn't often present. (Hallcraft's)

Want a wide rear tire but like the look of spokers? This 200-spoke rear wheel from Hallcraft's uses standard 6-gauge spokes and is designed solely for wide-tire applications. All sizes use a steel rim except the 18 x 9.5 inch, which uses an aluminum rim. (Hallcraft's)

high-performance," she says, "they're custom wheels. Spoked wheels are never meant for racing. They're not meant for that kind of abuse." But that doesn't mean they won't work on most stock-engined and big-inch streetbikes, with a few caveats.

Weld's Daytona wheel is a three-spoke design that's available in 19- and 21-inch front sizes, and rear widths ranging from 3 to 9.5 inches in 16- and 18-inch diameters. You can get the Daytona chrome-plated or with a polished finish. Matching pulleys are also available. (Weld Wheel)

Smith says there are three things to keep in mind when you look for a spoked wheel. First, "A cross-laced wheel is always going to be stronger than a straight-laced wheel. You can tell a straight-laced wheel from a cross-laced by looking at one spoke. If it doesn't cross over another spoke from the rim to the hub, it's a straight-laced wheel. If the spoke crosses another spoke, it's a cross-laced wheel. "If someone wants a straight-laced wheel we generally recommend they get a 100-spoke wheel," she adds. The higher

number of spokes makes up some for the reduced strength.

Second, Smith says, "The more spokes the better." This is especially true for wide wheels with fat rear tires. "We don't do any super-wide, fat-tire wheels in a 40 spoke. We do them in 80 and 100 spoke."

And finally, she says, "Spoked wheels have their limits. We'll get a wheel back with broken spokes, and it's always on the rear, never on the front. People don't understand why. They think if they don't have broken spokes on the front but they do on the back, then it's a defect. But the rear is where all the weight is."

With all that weight concentrated on the rear wheel, you need to be careful how you ride. Avoid big bumps like railroad tracks when the rear wheel is heavily loaded. Smith has seen all kinds of wheels come back for repair and has gotten very good at determining which ones broke from abuse. "We sell wheels to all the big custom builders who put them on bikes with big engines, and nine times out of ten we don't have any problems. If we get a wheel with broken

The more horsepower you're putting to the ground, the stronger and more rigid your rear wheel needs to be. Hard acceleration and cornering can loosen spokes over time, so check them regularly, or have it done when you get a new tire.
(Jerry Smith)

spokes back within a year, we'll fix it, no problem. But if it comes back a second time, then it's time to talk about what kind of rider you are, and what you're doing with the bike."

Another thing that contributes to broken rear spokes, Smith says, is "people who go real fast and then brake real hard. They can do burnouts and it's not going to hurt the wheel because they're spinning the tire, not stressing the hub." Many Harley riders overuse the rear brake, which only aggravates the problem.

Hallcraft's wheels use steel rims for strength rather than aluminum. "With aluminum, the spokes can pull through. We also use a heavier gauge spoke than stock, 6-gauge versus 8-gauge for stock," says Smith. They're also a rarity among spoked wheels in that they're guaranteed tubeless. Hallcraft's uses a special two-part epoxy around the spoke nipples once the wheel is assembled and trued.

Hallcraft's also uses an exclusive internal balancing system so you don't need to clamp wheel weights to the spokes. Smith explains, "It's a dynamic balancing system that works on inertia. It uses rubber tube with mercury in it to perfectly balance the wheel from 15 mph on. It increases tire life 40 to 50 percent. We're the only ones who do that."

Sinister wheels from Pro-One are made of forged billet aluminum and CNC-machined. Removable blades are secured with aircraft-quality hardware and can be ordered in colors to match, blend with, or contrast to the rim color. Each wheel comes with a hub, spacers, and bearings and can be ordered in a variety of sizes from 16 to 21 inches.
(Pro-One)

RESOURCES

ACCEL Motorcycle Products
10601 Memphis Ave., Suite 12
Cleveland, OH 44144
216-688-8300
www.mrgasket.com

Aerodyne (Aerocharger turbos)
8 Apollo Drive
Batavia, NY 14020
585-345-0055
www.aerocharger.com

Andrews Products
431 Kingston Court
Mt. Prospect, IL 60056
847-759-0190
www.andrews-products.com

Avon Tyres
407 Howell Way
Edmonds, WA 98020
800-624-7470
www.avonmotorcycle.com

Axtell Sales
1434 SE Maury
Des Moines, IA 50317
515-243-2518
www.axtellsales.com

Baker Drive Train
9804 E. Saginaw
Haslett, MI 48840
877-640-2004
www.bakerbuilt.com

Bandit Machine Works
222 Millwood Rd.
Lancaster, PA 17602
717-464-2800
www.banditmachineworks.com

Barnett Tool & Engineering
2238 Palma Drive
Ventura, CA 93003
805-642-9435
www.barnettclutches.com

Bel-Ray
P.O. Box 526
Farmingdale, NJ 07727 U.S.A.
732-938-2421
www.belray.com

Belt Drives Ltd.
1959 N. Main
Orange, CA 92865
714-685-3333
www.beltdrives.com

Branch Flowmetrics
5556 Corporate Drive
Cypress Cypress, CA 90630
714-827-5340
www.branchflowmetrics.com

Bridgestone/Firestone
1 Bridgestone Park
Nashville, TN 37214
800-543-7522
www.bridgestone-firestone.com

Bub Enterprises
180 Spring Hill Drive
Grass Valley, CA 95945
530-477-7490
www.bubent.com

Carl's Speed Shop
390 North Beach Street
Daytona Beach, FL 32114
386-258-3777
www.carlsspeedshop.com

Castrol Consumer North
America Inc.
1500 Valley Road
Wayne, NJ 07470
800-462-0835
www.castrol.com

Crane Cams Motorcycle Products
530 Fentress Blvd.
Daytona Beach, FL 32114
386-252-1151
www.cranecams.com

Custom Chrome
16100 Jacqueline Court
Morgan Hill, CA 95037
800-359-5700
www.customchrome.com

DaVinci Performance Products
1838 Rolling Hills Road
Conroe, TX 77303
936-264-1759
www.davincicarb.com

Denso Sales
3900 Via Oro Ave.
Long Beach, CA 90810
310-834-6352
www.densoaftermarket.com

Doherty Machine
1030 Sandretto Drive
Prescott, AZ 86305
928-541-7744
www.dohertymachine.com

DP Brakes
4401 Walden Ave.
Lancaster, NY 14086
716-681-8806
www.dp-brakes.com

Drag Specialties
9839 W. 69th St.
Eden Prairie, MN 55344
800-222-3400
www.dragspecialties.com

Dunlop Tire Corp.
P.O. Box 1109
Buffalo, NY 14240
www.dunlopmotorcycle.com

Dyna Performance Electronics
164 S. Valencia Street
Glendora, CA 91741
626-963-1669
www.dynaonline.com

Dynojet
2191 Mendenhall Drive
North Las Vegas, NV 89031
800-992-4993
www.dynojet.com

Edelbrock Corporation
2700 California Street
Torrance, CA 90503
310-781-2222
www.edelbrock.com

Engine Electronics (Compu-Fire)
196 University Parkway
Pomona, CA 91768
909-598-5485
www.compufire.com

Feuling Motor Company
1561 Pioneer Way
El Cajon, CA 92020
877-338-5464
www.feuling.com

FTM Enterprises
1960 Peacock Blvd.
Oceanside, CA 92056
760-732-3161
www.ftmbiz.com

GMA Engineering
13525 A Street
Omaha, NE 68144
402-330-5105
www.gmabrakes.com

Goodridge USA
20309 Gramercy Place
Torrance, CA 90501
310-533-1924
www.goodridge-uk.com

Hallcraft's Industries
1702 FM 1201 Moss Lake Road
P.O. Box 1036
Gainesville, TX 76241
940-668-0771
www.hallcrafts.com

J&P Cycles
13225 Circle Drive
Anamosa, IA 52205,
319-462-4817
www.jpcycles.com.

Jagg/Setrab Oil Coolers
24 S. Clayton St.
Centerburg, OH 43011
740-625-6228
www.jagg.com

JE Pistons
15312 Connector Lane
Huntington Beach, CA 92469
www.jepistons.com
714-894-6650

JIMS
555 Dawson Drive
Camarillo, CA 93012
805-482-6913
www.jimsusa.com

K&N
1455 Citrus Ave.
Riverside, CA 92502
800-858-3333
www.knpowersports.com

Kerker (see SuperTrapp)

Lockhart Phillips USA
151 Calle Iglesia
San Clemente, CA 92672
800-221-7291
www.lockhartphillipsusa.com

Magna Charger
4059 Highway 99 West
Orland, CA 95963
530-865-7010
www.magnacharger.com

Manley Performance
1960 Swarthmore Ave.
Lakewood, NJ 08701
732-905-3366
www.manleyperformance.com

Maxima Racing Oils
9266 Abraham Way
Santee, CA 92071
619-449-5000
www.maximausa.com

Merch Performance
10944 Gravois Industrial Court
St. Louis, MO 63128
888-637-2448.
www.merchperformance.com

Metzeler Motorcycle Tire
300 N. Pottsdown Pike, Suite 280
Exton, PA 19341
610-524-2190
www.metzelermoto.com

Mid-USA Cycle Parts
4937 Fyler Ave.
St. Louis, MO 63139
800-527-0501
www.mid-usa.com

Midwest Motorcycle Supply
111 Manufacturers Drive
Arnold, MO 63010
800-325-3914
www.midwest-mc.com

Mikuni American Corporation
8910 Mikuni Avenue
Northridge, CA 91324-3496
818-885-1242
www.mikuni.com

North County Customs
1631 North Placentia Avenue, Unit E
Anaheim, CA 92806
866-439-4287
www.northcountycustoms.com

Patrick Racing
12161 Mariners Way
Garden Grove, CA 92843
714-554-7223
www.patrick-racing.com

Performance Machine
6892 Marlin Circle
La Palma, CA 90623
714-523-3000
www.performancemachine.com.

Primo Belt Drives (Rivera Engineering)
12532 Lambert Road
Whittier, CA 90606
562-907-2600
www.riveraengineering.com

Pro Charger
P.O. Box 3102
Kansas City, KS 66103
913-338-2886
www.procharger.com

Progressive Suspension
11129 G Ave.
Hesperia, CA 92345
760-948-4012
www.progressivesuspension.com

Pro-One
2700 Melbourne Avenue
Pomona, CA 91767
800-884-4173
www.pro-one.com

QTM Brembo
2386 North Batavia Street
Orange, CA 92865
714-637-1151
www.qtmi.com

Race Tech Inc.
1501 Pomona Rd.
Corona, CA 92880
909-279-6655
www.race-tech.com

Red Line Synthetic Oil Corp.
6100 Egret Court
Benicia, CA 94510
(707)-745-6100
www.redlineoil.com

Russell Performance Products
2301 Dominguez Way
Torrance, CA 90501
310-781-2222
www.russellperformance.com

Samson Motorcycle Products
3818 E. Coronado St.
Anaheim, CA 92807
800-373-4217
www.samsonusa.com

Spectro Oils
993 Federal Road
Brookfield, CT 06804
203-775-1291
www.spectro-oils.com

SplitFire
800-323-5440
www.splitfire.com

S&S Cycle
14025 County Highway G
Viola, WI 54664
608-627-2080
www.sscycle.com.

STD Development
P.O. Box 3583
Chatsworth, CA 91311
818-998-8226
www.stddevelopment.com

Storz Performance
239 S. Olive
Ventura, CA 93001
805-641-9540
www.storzperf.com

SuperTrapp Industries
4540 W. 160th St.
Cleveland, OH 44135
216-265-8400
www.supertrapp.com

T.P. Engineering
5 Francis J. Clarke Circle
Bethel, CT 06801
203-744-4960
www.tpeng.com

Torco International Corp.
10652 Bloomfield Ave.
Santa Fe Springs, CA 90670
800-649-5722
www.torcoracingoils.com

Vance & Hines
13861 Rosecrans Ave.
Santa Fe Springs, CA 90670
800-592-2529
www.vanceandhines.com

Weld Wheel Industries
933 Mulberry Street
Kansas City, MO 64101
888-517-1594
www.weldracing.com

Wiseco
7201 Industrial Park Boulevard
Mentor, OH 44060
440-951-6600
www.wiseco.com

Works Performance
21045 Osborne St.
Canoga Park, CA 91304
818-701-1010
www.worksperformance.com

uasa Battery Inc.
P.O. Box 14715
Reading, PA
19612
610-208-1925
www.yuasabatteries.com

Zipper's Performance
6655-A Amberton Drive
Elkridge, MD 21075
410-579-2828
www.zippersperformance.com